From the Foreword by
Colonel Walter J. Boyne, USAF (Ret.)

"In this fascinating historical survey of land warfare from 1860 to 1991, Colonel J. D. Morelock reviews fourteen important land battles that changed the nature of both warfare and politics. Writing in clear, concise prose, and avoiding the usual military jargon and overuse of acronyms, Morelock has created a consistent, well-organized narrative that keeps each battle fresh yet firmly within the context of its time.

"The author calls upon a lifetime of research and his own extensive personal military experience to examine the battles in the fullest detail . . . including the principal personalities and a step-by-step account of the fighting. Each battle is well illustrated by maps developed by the author especially for this book.

"A former battery commander in Vietnam, Morelock is an army historian as well as an award-winning author. Packed with solid information, his book is a wonderful read for both military expert and interested amateur, and is sure to become required reading for the U.S. Army Command and General Staff College."

The Army Times Publishing Company is pleased to join with The Berkley Publishing Group in presenting this series of books on military history. We have proudly served the military community for over fifty years by means of our independent weekly newspapers, *Army Times, Navy Times,* and *Air Force Times.*

The other four books in the series are *Generals in Muddy Boots: A Concise Encyclopedia of Combat Commanders* by Dan Cragg; *The Army Times, Navy Times, Air Force Times Encyclopedia of Modern U.S. Military Weapons* by Timothy M. Laur and Steven L. Llanso; *Clash of Chariots: The Great Tank Battles* by Tom Donnelly and Sean Naylor; and *The Navy Times Book of Submarines* by Brayton Harris.

THE ARMY TIMES BOOK
OF GREAT LAND BATTLES

From the Civil War to the Gulf War

Colonel J. D. Morelock, USA

EDITED BY Colonel Walter J. Boyne, USAF (Ret.)

B

BERKLEY BOOKS, NEW YORK

This book is an original publication of The Berkley Publishing Group.

THE ARMY TIMES BOOK OF GREAT LAND BATTLES:
FROM THE CIVIL WAR TO THE GULF WAR

A Berkley Book / published by arrangement with
The Army Times Publishing Company

PRINTING HISTORY
Berkley hardcover edition / October 1994
Berkley trade paperback edition / April 1999

The Penguin Putnam Inc. World Wide Web site address is
http://www.penguinputnam.com

ISBN: 0-425-16531-0

BERKLEY®
Berkley Books are published by
The Berkley Publishing Group, a member of Penguin Putnam Inc.,
375 Hudson Street, New York, New York 10014.
BERKLEY and the "B" design are trademarks
belonging to Berkley Publishing Corporation.

PRINTED IN THE UNITED STATES OF AMERICA

10   9   8   7   6   5   4   3   2   1

CONTENTS

LIST OF MAPS

FOREWORD

In this fascinating historical survey of land warfare from 1860 to
1991, Colonel J. D. Morelock reviews fourteen important battles that
changed the nature of both warfare and politics. Writing in clear,
concise prose, and avoiding the usual military jargon and overuse of
acronyms, Morelock has created a consistent, well-organized narrative that keeps each battle fresh yet firmly within the context of its
time.

The author calls upon a lifetime of research and his own extensive
personal military experience to examine the battles in the fullest
detail. He takes a wide view of each contest, analyzing the opposing
forces, explaining the strategy and tactics, and comparing the weapons. Each of these elements is illuminated by vignettes that capture
the immediacy of war for its participants, and for the reader. A
thoughtful reader will be struck by how similar the soldiers are over
the years, both officers and enlisted men. It becomes immediately
evident that a successful commander at Gettysburg would probably
have done well in the Meuse-Argonne, at Bastogne, or in the Persian
Gulf War.

Morelock divides each chapter into two sections. In the first section he begins with a vignette focusing on a specific, real-life partic-

ipant in the battle, recognizing that no matter how monumental an engagement may be, it is always conducted at the personal, sharp-end-of-the-stick level. No matter the changes in technology, whether the weapon is a musket or an Abrams tank, the basic needs and hopes of the person using the weapon do not change.

The author next conducts an extensive historical overview of the events leading to the war and to the specific battle. This is followed by an analysis of the opposing armies, including their organization, leadership, and strengths and weaknesses.

Many readers will be fascinated by the in-depth discussions of weaponry, in which the most important equipment of each battle is highlighted. Colonel Morelock carefully details each weapon's place in the development of warfare, as well as its employment by the troops.

Finally, Morelock examines the war aims and strategies of the belligerents, explaining how these were fulfilled or aborted in the previous campaigns leading up to the battle under discussion.

In the second part of each chapter he offers a strong narrative presentation of the battle itself, including the principal personalities and a step-by-step account of the fighting. Each battle is well illustrated by maps developed by the author especially for the book.

A former battery commander in Vietnam, Morelock is an army historian as well as an award-winning author. Packed with solid information, his book is a wonderful read for both military expert and interested amateur, and is sure to become, like two of his previous works, required reading for the U.S. Army Command and General Staff College.

—Colonel Walter J. Boyne, USAF (Ret.)

INTRODUCTION

From the first of the "modern" wars, the American Civil War, to the most recent major example of modern warfare, the Gulf War, the history of the world for the last 130-odd years has been disappointingly violent, marred by a surprisingly large number of battles, conflicts, interventions, and "police actions." The likelihood of future violent conflicts seems all too probable. With such a wide range to choose from, selecting the "greatest" land battles is no simple task. Unlike professional football, which so freely borrows the vocabulary of combat to describe its maneuvers, battles cannot be neatly ranked according to their relative degree of greatness. Because of this, the process of identifying the "great" ones is necessarily subjective. The land battles described herein represent the author's personal choice among the engagements that have occurred during the era of "modern" war. While most readers will probably agree with the majority of his selections, not every reader will concur with them all. Inevitably, someone's favorite battles or conflicts will not be included. The author hopes that readers who find their own selections left out will, nevertheless, peruse the ones included with an open mind.

The nine chapters and fourteen battles that constitute this book broadly survey some of the most important land battles of the past thirteen decades. Ranging from sharp, bloody fights of a few tens of thousands of participants (like the tragic Chickamauga engagement during the American Civil War) to epic encounters involving millions of men (such as the battle of Stalingrad in World War II), these great land battles circle the globe from North America to the Far East. Each battle herein recounted has its own unique claim to "greatness," and each is examined within the context of the war in which it was fought and with reference to its impact on the course of that war. The fourteen great land battles and campaigns presented in this book were waged during nine major wars involving nearly two dozen nations.

Chapter One examines two pivotal land battles that took place during the American Civil War. The greatest single battle ever fought on the North American continent, the battle of **Gettysburg** (July 1–3, 1863), saw 150,000 Americans from North and South clash for three days to decide the fate of our nation. After 3:00 P.M. on July 3, 1863, the Confederacy was no longer capable of winning the war outright in the east. One of every three soldiers involved became a casualty in the fight that saved the Union.

The Confederacy's greatest western triumph of the Civil War was also that conflict's bloodiest two-day contest, and occurred in the dense woods along the banks of the sluggish **Chickamauga** Creek (September 19–20, 1863). Had Braxton Bragg, the Confederate commander, aggressively followed up his stunning victory here at the gates of Chattanooga, the course of the Civil War in the west could very well have been decisively changed.

Chapter Two focuses on the most crucial battle of the short, brutal war that firmly established Prussia as a great power—reborn at the end of the war as a united Germany. The battle of **Sedan** (September 1, 1870) ended French dreams of a return to Napoleonic greatness while it simultaneously marked the beginning of Germany's reign as the premier power in Europe. In so doing, it sowed the seeds of hate, envy, and revenge that led to World War I.

Chapter Three examines the principal land battle of the Russo-Japanese War of 1904–05, the battle and siege of **Port Arthur** (May 1904–January 1905). Although the battle of Mukden, which occurred two months later, involved more troops on each side, the capture of Port Arthur had already decided the issue. Just as Sedan firmly fixed Germany as the new power in Europe, so the Russian disaster at Port Arthur raised Japan to the position of major power in the Orient. Coupled with the decisive, overwhelming naval victory over the Russian fleet at Tsushima, this battle shattered the myth of inherent European superiority over Asian peoples and gave hope to colonized nations from Africa to the Philippines. The fact that European imperialism was merely being replaced by Japanese imperialism seemed not to have been immediately grasped.

Chapter Four presents three of the greatest battles of the Great War, 1914–18. Its most significant action on the Eastern Front was the battle of **Tannenberg** (August 26–31, 1914). An overwhelming German victory—virtually a second Cannae—this early-war success over a poorly prepared Russian army secured Germany and Austria's eastern borders, permitting them to wage the terrible slaughter in the west.

Characteristic of the great carnage on the stalemated Western Front was the nightmarish meat grinder at **Verdun** (February–December, 1916). Intending to bleed the French army white, the German leaders of this offensive against the famous French fortress city succeeded equally well in destroying their own army. A futile, horrific battle, Verdun stands as a terrible monument to an era of warfare in which the technology of killing far outstripped the abilities of generals and their staffs to provide some long-term justification for their bloody decisions.

America's role in the final Allied offensive of the Great War is epitomized in the **Meuse-Argonne** campaign (September 26–November 11, 1918), the largest employment of American forces since the Civil War. This great land battle found American officers commanding division-, corps-, and army-size formations where, just a few months before, it was rare even for a regiment to drill together. Pershing's insistence that American forces stay together, under American command, and fight as a national entity allowed the United States to emerge from the Great War as an authentic world power.

Chapter Five details three significant battles in the ultimate tragedy of the twentieth century—World War II. The most decisive battle
of the vast Eastern Front and one of the great battles of history was
waged between the German and Soviet armies in the rubble of **Stalingrad** (August 23, 1942–February 2, 1943). Prior to Stalingrad, the
German army in the east seemed invincible; after Stalingrad, the war
in the east was lost. A million Soviets and a third of a million Germans died in the frozen misery of the city on the Volga.

Perhaps the greatest American victory of all time occurred in the
Battle of the Bulge (December 16, 1944–February 1945). Hitler
risked everything on a final, all-out offensive, but American soldiers,
led by Eisenhower in what was his finest hour as supreme commander, gained control of the battle and turned back the German
attack. Nearly one of every ten American casualties in World War II
received his wounds in the Ardennes that bitter winter.

In the Pacific Theater of World War II, the greatest air-sea-land
battle ever fought was the battle of **Okinawa** (April 1–June 30, 1945).
In this bitter, grinding war of tunnels, pillboxes, and appalling casualty lists, neither the American commander, Lieutenant General
Simon B. Buckner, nor his Japanese counterpart, Lieutenant General Ushijima Mitsuru, survived. Although the end of the battle
brought an inevitable American victory, the horrible toll exacted by
the tenacious Japanese defenders was a major factor in convincing
the U.S. president to authorize the use of the atomic bomb.

Chapter Six relates the great campaign of 1950 to rescue a country—the battle to save South Korea—following the crucial land fighting of the first six months of the war from the **Naktong to the Yalu**
(June–November 1950). Pushed into the tiny Pusan perimeter by
superior North Korean forces, American, South Korean, and United
Nations forces struck back, regained the initiative through Mac-
Arthur's bold masterstroke at Inchon, then forced the fleeing enemy
north to the border of China. Only the intervention of hundreds of
thousands of Chinese troops saved North Korea from total annihi-
lation. Chinese swarming across the Manchurian border eventually
forced U.S. and UN troops back across the 38th parallel before the

front was stabilized, but not until the UN forces had saved South Korea.

Chapter Seven recounts the most significant land battle in Southeast Asia during the First Indochina War (1946–1954). The siege and battle that raged in the tiny village of **Dien Bien Phu** (March 13–May 7, 1954), lying in a remote valley between Vietnam and Laos, ended the French empire in Southeast Asia and led to the establishment of the independent nations of North and South Vietnam. The death and destruction visited on French and colonial forces in this guerrilla war in the mountains and jungles of Indochina helped turn French public opinion against the war. Within a few years after the French defeat by the Viet Minh, it was the United States' turn to learn these harsh lessons.

Chapter Eight details the major battles of the Arab-Israeli War of 1973—the Yom Kippur War. The battles of the **Sinai and the Golan Heights** (October 6–25, 1973) saved Israel from a surprisingly strong and coordinated attack by Arab armies, principally from Egypt and Syria. Launched during the holiday period of Yom Kippur, the Jewish day of atonement, the Arab attack was initially characterized by a superbly orchestrated assault crossing of the Suez Canal by Egyptian forces and a near breakthrough on the strategically important Golan Heights by Syria. Mobilizing faster than anyone on the Arab side thought possible, Israel survived the multipronged surprise attack, then quickly launched devastating counterattacks on both threatened fronts. Although Israel won the war in decisive fashion, the early Arab successes caused some of the most intense fighting the Middle East had yet witnessed.

Chapter Nine turns to the United States' most recent major military endeavor, the Gulf War (1991). This war marked the end of one era of warfare and ushered in what appears to be another. **Hail Mary! The 100-Hour Ground War** (February 24–28, 1991), including Schwarzkopf's decisive land campaign, is the story of American land forces' greatest 100 hours.

CHAPTER ONE

The American Civil War

• 1861–1865 •

GETTYSBURG
AND CHICKAMAUGA

High Tide and the River of Death

The bloodiest five days in American history occurred during the summer of 1863, in two locations hundreds of miles apart, and in completely different settings and circumstances. Three of those terrible
days were endured on the bucolic, rolling farmlands of southern
Pennsylvania during the hot, humid days of early July—an unlikely
scene for the greatest battle ever to take place in the western hemisphere. Nevertheless, the battle of Gettysburg marked the high tide
of Confederate military fortune, yet was the greatest defeat ever suffered by one of American's most revered military heroes, Robert E.
Lee.

*Gettysburg, Pennsylvania, 3:00 P.M., July 3, 1863: A mile-long line of gray-clad
infantrymen confidently stepped out of the wood line on Seminary Ridge and strode
across the gently rolling fields, guiding on a small copse of trees at the center of
distant Cemetery Ridge. A half mile away, the soldiers of the Army of the Potomac,
still dazed by the effects of the largest artillery bombardment ever witnessed in North
America, scrambled to take up fighting positions to meet the attack of a Confederate
army that had consistently beaten them during two years of bitter civil war. Pushing
undamaged cannon into firing positions and loading their weapons, the Union*

soldiers grimly settled in to await the single assault that would, more than any other "gallant rush" in a conflict full of such brave, but anachronistic displays of courage, determine the final outcome of the war. Before an hour had passed, the issue would be settled, leaving behind a scene of carnage and human wreckage the likes of which the world had seldom seen. The "high tide" of the Confederacy would be marked that very afternoon by a ragged gray wave breaking along that low ridge, just south of a sleepy little Pennsylvania town.

The other two days of unprecedented bloodshed that summer of 1863 took place in the dense, tangled woods of northern Georgia in the middle of September. The "Great Battle of the West" was a confused, exhausting struggle between desperate men in blue and gray who flung themselves at each other in wild charges and counterattacks through the thick woods bordering a meandering creek. Neither the Union nor the Confederate commander would achieve lasting fame on that tragic battlefield. The vanquished commander was literally swept off the field by the fleeing troops of his routed right wing; yet his victorious opposite number complacently let the fruits of his costly victory slip through his fingers, leaving him to ponder what might have been.

West Chickamauga Creek, Georgia, 11:30 A.M., September 20, 1863: The tightly packed ranks of Confederate troops trudged grimly past the small, rough-hewn cabin of the Brotherton farm situated in one of the few small clearings in the dense woods bordering West Chickamauga Creek. To their right, somewhere among the brush and trees, their comrades had been locked in deadly combat with Federal troops for two hours and the battle hung in the balance. Now it was their turn to engage the enemy and press home the attack. A short distance ahead, somewhere in the tangled wood line, they expected Union troops to be arrayed in battle positions, unseen in the thick trees but ready to deliver a withering fire on their advance. As the Confederates drew closer to the Union lines, they were certain that at any moment bright tongues of flame and billows of dense smoke would appear, followed by the awful sound of thousands of lead bullets buzzing through the air. The men in the front ranks held their breath as they imagined marching headlong into a wall of lead. Incredibly, as they drew nearer, they discovered that the woods in front of them were empty. Instead of smashing into a solid blue wall of dug-in infantrymen, the Confederate division walked right through the Union line of defense. The critical moment of the battle of Chickamauga was at hand.

"Now we are engaged in a great Civil War. . . . "

These two great land battles of the American Civil War represent terrible benchmarks in a struggle that split the nation for four bloody years. But, ultimately, it was also a struggle that ended the coexistence of two separate nations within a crumbling union, and recreated the United States in the form it holds today.

No other war or armed conflict so profoundly affected the development of the United States than did the war Americans waged upon themselves in the middle of the nineteenth century. No other war cost so many American lives or visited such utter destruction on the American population than did the fratricidal bloodletting that began on April 12, 1861. Nearly 10 percent of the 1860 population of the United States, 3,000,000 men out of 31,000,000 people, saw service in the war. One of every five of those died in it. Records from that period are incomplete, especially those from the Confederate side, but one can say with terrible certainty that at least 600,000 Americans were killed—a figure only slightly less than the total of all Americans killed in all the other wars the United States has yet fought. The Civil War battles of Antietam, Chickamauga, and Gettysburg still hold grisly records as the bloodiest one-, two-, and three-day battles Americans have bled and died in. At its end, in April 1865, the Confederacy—the so-called Southern Nation—had not only been defeated, it had been annihilated—its major cities reduced to rubble; its fragile, agrarian economy destroyed; its surviving population placed under the stern hand of martial law by the victorious Federal government. One hundred and thiry years later, the scars of the war have barely healed, and its effects can still be seen.

Weapons and Tactics

The commanders who led the volunteer armies of the American Civil War were educated and trained in the battlefield tactics of Napoleon. Coming of age when Baron Jomini's *Art of War* was the most popular text for military instruction, the commanders of the War Between the States had closely studied the campaigns of the Napoleonic Wars and memorized the tactics. Stressing the utmost importance of maintaining close-packed formations in the face of enemy fire and valuing "mass" over all other principles of war, these tactics had been made horribly obsolete by a deadly invention of the Industrial Revolution—the rifled musket.

The standard infantry arm of the Civil War was the .58-caliber, muzzle-loading, percussion-firing, rifled musket. It fired a hollow-based, conoidal bullet that extended the effective killing range of the infantryman's principal weapon from the old smoothbore musket's mere 100 yards to a bone-shattering, flesh-rending 500 yards; even at 800 to 1,000 yards large formations of troops were still at risk. Mass production and interchangeable parts meant that the new killing tools could be provided to armies in as yet unheard of numbers. Federal armories produced nearly a million of the U.S. Model 1861, 1863, and 1864 Springfield rifle-muskets during the war, while government agents purchased another three quarters of a million similarly designed weapons from civilian contractors. North and South both bought weapons from overseas markets as well, purchasing nearly a million of the excellent British Enfield pattern rifle. Thanks to industrial-age efficiency, the citizen soldiers of the American Civil War did not lack for efficient instruments of death.

Despite the new lethality of the battlefield, Civil War commanders still attempted to storm enemy positions with the "gallant rush" of the Napoleonic frontal assault. More often, such attackers were reduced to piles of corpses by the new rifles which ultimately accounted for nine out of every ten battle casualties. The rifled musket relegated the bayonet, up to that time the reigning queen of battle, and the artillery, historically battle's king and consistently its greatest killer, to second-class status on the killing fields of the American Civil War.

Artillery development in this period of warfare had not kept pace with the dramatic advances in small arms. Even though rifled cannon, including breechloaders, were being produced, the principal artillery piece in battlefield use remained the smoothbore gun-howitzer firing a twelve-pound projectile. It was light enough to move quickly around rough terrain, thus keeping pace with advancing friendly infantry, yet could be loaded and fired fast enough to place several rounds of solid shot, bursting shell, or canister into the advancing ranks of enemy infantry before they closed the intervening gap. In the Mexican War, it was just such smoothbore pieces, served by soldiers organized into "flying batteries," and led by a new class of young, aggressive battery commanders, that saved the day for outnumbered American forces on many occasions. The tragic difference between that earlier war and the Civil War was that by the 1860s, the rifled musket made it possible for enemy infantry to bring unprotected gunners under a devastating and withering fire before the artillerymen could destroy the attacking ranks. Only the ponderous, unwieldy, giant siege guns possessed sufficient range and weight of shell to engage targets effectively at long distances, but their immobility rendered them virtually useless in the typical combat assault that demanded mobility and maneuver, not merely heavy firepower. Artillery, especially when firing canister, made its greatest contribution to the defense.

Tactical employment of the units reflected the commanders' education and training in Napoleonic tactics. The most common maneuver was the frontal assault, conducted by one or more brigades attacking in a closely packed line formation two or three ranks deep. As in the days of Napoleon, officers deployed up to a quarter of the men in the unit as skirmishers in open order up to 500 yards in front of the main body of troops. The skirmish line's mission was to attempt to break up or disrupt the opposing enemy formation by picking off officers or key personnel, then rejoin the ranks when the units closed. One or more regiments (or one or more companies in each attacking regiment) were likely to be kept as a reserve force 300 to 500 yards behind the main force. Weight to the main attack was normally given by brigades or regiments formed in column behind the attacking force at what was presumed to be the decisive point, and by assigning additional artillery batteries to support the assault. Maintaining proper control over these tightly packed ranks of men, walking abreast in long lines for up to a mile, over broken ground and into the teeth of withering fire, was not easy. Many attacks simply fell apart before they got close to the defender's position. To maintain control and prevent an assault from foundering, officers might take the seemingly incredible action of halting their regiment while under the terrible fire and dressing its ranks before once again renewing the advance.

The common-sense response to this blizzard of lead and iron was to disperse and use all available cover provided by the terrain. This dispersion, however, meant loss of control by unit commanders; as a result, the essential tactic of modern warfare—advancing in open order—was never formally adopted. The frontal assault in Napoleonic ranks remained the officially sanctioned tactic (which meant that even in the final year of the war, Grant could order the brutal frontal assault at Cold Harbor in which 7,000 men fell in twenty minutes). Nevertheless, as the war progressed, soldiers began to appreciate the value of digging in, and they would rapidly construct rudimentary field fortifications whenever possible during the attack or defense. Rifle pits or shallow trenches were dug at every opportunity, the soldiers using bayonets, knives, and mess plates when shovels weren't available. Officers began to allow their troops who were waiting to advance against the enemy to lie down in order to gain some protection against the horrible fire, and the defending unit virtually always constructed breastworks, laboring to improve a particular position for as long as they occupied it. Near the end of the war, sieges like Petersburg resembled nothing so much as the horrible trench warfare of World War I, half a century later.

The Battle of Gettysburg

July 1–3, 1863

The greatest battle ever to take place in North America was fought, some say, over shoes. More specifically, the lack of serviceable footwear in Heth's Division of Lee's Army of Northern Virginia sent those Confederate soldiers shuffling along the dusty roads of southwestern Pennsylvania toward the small town of Gettysburg, where it was rumored that plenty of good Yankee leather shoes were to be found. But instead of a brief footwear-foraging detour from their ongoing invasion of the North, Heth's Confederates precipitated the greatest clash of arms of the American Civil War—the three days of Gettysburg.

In the resulting battle more than 150,000 soldiers from North and South engaged in a desperate combat that, more than any other battle of that four-year struggle, helped shape the war's outcome. One of every three men who fought at Gettysburg became a casualty, and 7,000 of those paid the ultimate price. In many regiments, casualty figures of over 50 percent were common, and several units were virtually destroyed. The South's 26th North Carolina lost 714 men out of 800, while the North's 1st Minnesota lost nearly 90 percent. The Union's Iron Brigade lost 1,200 of 1,800 men the first day alone. In some companies, every man was hit. There are few more appalling examples of the horrors of midnineteenth-century warfare than this terrible battle.

After Lee's retreat at the battle's end, never again would the Confederacy muster a force as potent and capable. Never again could the South threaten the North with outright defeat by battlefield actions. And after the Army of the Potomac's stubborn stand against the best the South could offer, never again would it doubt its own prowess or shrink from engaging the army that had been its battlefield master for so long. Lincoln's "terrible swift sword" had finally been forged in the fire of Gettysburg. It needed only a leader with the stubborn resolve of Grant to wield it with devastating effect.

The Road North

Eighteen sixty-three became the decisive year of the American Civil War, although, tragically, it would not be the war's final year. At its beginning, the South still had a chance to win its independence on the battlefield, as Confederate armies in the east and west gained some of the Confederacy's greatest victories. At Chancellorsville in the east and Chickamauga in the west, Confederate forces routed Federal armies and perched on the brink of achieving decisive results. But the might-have-beens of Chancellorsville and Chickamauga were overshadowed by the realities of Gettysburg and Vicksburg. When 1863 ended, the South had missed its last, best opportunities. Their side slowly choking to death from an ever-tightening naval blockade and unable to replace battlefield losses of precious personnel, Confederate commanders settled in to a brutal war of attrition they could not possibly win. Only Northern war weariness and a failure of will in the United States to continue the terrible slaughter could lead to a negotiated peace, and possibly, an independent South.

As 1863 opened, Lincoln made another in what seemed to be an endless series of command changes in the Army of the Potomac. Joseph "Fighting Joe" Hooker replaced the inept Ambrose Burnside after the unmitigated disaster at Fredericksburg, where well-positioned Confederates slaughtered row upon row of Federal troops committed to useless, bloody frontal attacks. By April, Hooker had 134,000 fresh troops moving against Lee's greatly outnumbered Army of Northern Virginia. Hooker devised an excellent plan, which should have worked, to smash Lee once and for all. He sent Sedgwick's VI Corps to fix Lee's forces in front of Fredericksburg, while he maneuvered the rest of the Federal army in a wide, westward sweeping right hook through the Wilderness area to strike Lee in the rear. It was a grand plan, but Hooker was not the commander to carry it out successfully. With everything seeming to go according to plan, Hooker's nerve failed him. In the tangled Wilderness area near Chancellorsville, Hooker halted his forces and ordered them to dig in. Despite the protests of his subordinate commanders, the Federal leader decided to turn the initiative over to Lee and wait to see what would develop. What developed was Lee's most stunning victory of the entire war. With little more than 50,000 troops, less than half Hooker's force, he outmaneuvered and outgeneraled the Federal commander at every turn. Splitting his outnumbered force, Lee crushed Hooker's troops and sent them retreating northward. Only Jackson's mortal wounding on May 2 seemed to mar the battle's remarkable results. Nevertheless, buoyed by this victory, Davis and Lee resolved to take the war once more to the enemy, and invade the North a second time. The Gettysburg campaign had begun.

The military and political objectives of this invasion were essentially the same as those of Lee's previous foray north of the Potomac in September 1862, which was cut short at Antietam. Moving the fighting out of Virginia would save fast-dwindling food supplies, might force evacuation of the Federal capital in Washington, and could lead to foreign recognition. In any case, Lee assumed a serious threat to central Pennsylvania would force the Army of the Potomac to follow him northward, perhaps leading to a climactic battle where his Army of Northern Virginia could crush it once and for all. He fully expected such a pitched battle during this invasion—he just did not know where or when.

During the first week of June 1863, Lee reorganized his 77,000-man Army of Northern Virginia into three corps and began moving them north. James Longstreet continued to command the I Corps, but Jackson's death forced Lee to divide his brilliant subordinate's troops into two units: the II Corps under Richard "Old Baldy" Ewell, and the III Corps with the feisty A. P. Hill in command. Stuart's Cavalry Corps would screen the army's movements. Once again using the natural corridor of the Shenandoah Valley as an express route to western Maryland and Pennsylvania, Lee set out on June 3 with Ewell's corps in the lead.

It took Hooker over a week to realize that the Confederate commander had abandoned his Fredericksburg positions and started on the road north, but eventually he got the 100,000 Federal troops of the Army of the Potomac moving in pursuit. By June 28, the Federal army was centered around Frederick in western Maryland, only twenty-five miles southeast of Lee's main force. Hooker, however, was no longer in command. Annoyed by the general's scheming and backstabbing ways and disappointed by his obvious shortcomings as an army commander, Lincoln accepted Hooker's weak offer to resign, selecting the acerbic, dour George G. Meade to replace him. Meade was not enthusiastic about his appointment, but nevertheless, went about the business of assuming command in a soldierly manner.

When Lee at last learned that the Federal army was close on his heels, he immediately ordered his dispersed corps to concentrate near Cashtown, a few miles west of Gettysburg. Lee's "eyes and ears," Stuart's cavalry, had failed him at the worst possible time. Outnumbered, on unfamiliar terrain, and surrounded by a hostile populace, Lee needed to know exactly where his opponent's army was at all times if his Pennsylvania gambit was to succeed. But Stuart was by then engaged in a dramatic "ride around the Union army," and unavailable to perform his essential scouting and screening missions. Instead of carefully crafting the decisive battle in which he would destroy Meade's army on ground and at a time of his own choosing, Lee's forces literally blundered into the Federal army. Worst of all, their Federal opponents ended up occupying the best terrain. Instead of forcing the Army of the Potomac to destroy itself in futile assaults against well-prepared defensive positions, the Army of Northern Virginia, outnumbered and outgunned, was compelled to assume the tactical offensive.

The First Day—Fighting for Time

When Heth's 7,400 soldiers began their quest for shoes at dawn on July 1, they were completely unaware that between them and their goal waited 2,700 Union cavalry troopers of Brigadier General John Buford's division. Buford's troopers had been shadowing Lee's army, observing its movements and dispositions and keeping the Federal command apprised of its actions—exactly the kind of critical activities Stuart was failing to perform for Lee. Now that part of the Confederate army had turned east toward Gettysburg, Buford had to force it to fight or retire. Alerted to the approaching Confederates, Buford deployed his troopers along McPherson Ridge, about a mile west of town, to block Heth's advance down the Chambersburg Pike leading into Gettysburg.

At about 8:00 A.M., as Heth's advance units were trudging through the dust and humidity immediately west of the ridgeline, they were surprised to find themselves the object of a withering fire from the rapid-firing breechloaders of Buford's troopers. Heth's division suffered the first of the staggering 1,500 casualties it would lose that day, and the three-day battle had now begun in earnest. The Union cavalrymen, despite being supported by a battery of horse artillery, could not hope to defeat Heth's strong infantry force. They could, however, delay it long enough for Federal infantry approaching from south of Gettysburg to arrive and occupy the good defensive positions in and near the town. Buford sent word to Major General John Reynolds, temporarily detached from commanding his I Corps to lead the Federal left wing, to hurry his troops along the roads to Gettysburg before the Confederates overwhelmed his greatly outnumbered cavalrymen.

When Reynolds arrived at Buford's position about an hour later, he immediately realized the potential advantages that would accrue to Union forces if they could develop this initial engagement into a general action, capitalizing on the excellent defensive terrain found in the vicinity of Gettysburg. The problem, however, was which army could concentrate its widely dispersed forces first and seize the best terrain. Federal units had been slowly moving northward, dogging the Confederate advance at a respectful distance, but Lee's earlier order to concentrate west of Gettysburg was causing his three corps to turn south and east, gravitating toward the advancing Federals. Reynolds intended to win this race, and directed his I, XI, and III Corps to hurry forward. He also sent word to Meade that the Confederates were advancing in force, that he would fight them there, at Gettysburg, and that Reynolds's left wing would delay the enemy until Meade brought up the remainder of the army. Thus, while neither Lee nor Meade had planned to fight a major battle at Gettysburg, circumstances had removed that decision from the commanders' hands.

At about 10:00 A.M., Reynolds's leading infantry brigades arrived to support Buford's hard-pressed troopers, just in time to beat back a determined attack by Heth's infantry. More help was on the way as units from I Corps continued to arrive from the south and be placed in the firing line. But Reynolds did not live to see it arrive. A sniper's bullet struck him in the head while he was overseeing the placement of the newly arriving troops, and he fell mortally wounded from his horse. Nevertheless, the concentrating of the Federal army at Gettysburg that Reynolds had set in motion now continued apace. The senior Union leader on the battlefield was now Major General Abner Doubleday, I Corps commander, whose mediocre reputation up to that point in the war seemed to bode ill for Union chances. But with more Federal units already arriving on the field and his soldiers fighting successfully to keep the Confederates at bay, Doubleday performed adequately in a situation requiring little leadership from him.

By 11:00 A.M., Major General Oliver O. Howard of the Federal XI Corps was on the field and, as the new senior officer, was now in command. In the next ninety minutes, Howard rushed his corps through the town and had them in position north and east of Doubleday's troops just in time to meet the next Confederate push. Observing the desperate situation north of the town, Howard hedged his bets by placing Adolph von Steinwehr's division on an excellent defensive position just a half mile south of Gettysburg—Cemetery Hill. That action would soon prove to be one of the most propitious any Federal commander would take during the battle.

Meanwhile, Confederate forces were continuing to arrive in strength. While Heth's corps commander, A. P. Hill, was ordering W. Dorsey Pender's division to continue his advance eastward to Heth's assistance, the leading elements of Richard S. Ewell's corps were sweeping in on Gettysburg from the north. This caused immediate and heavy pressure to be applied to the thin Federal line arrayed in a rough semicircle north and west of town. Although Lee had directed that a general engagement not be conducted prior to the concentration of his entire force, circumstances caused his subordinate to press hard against what appeared to be weakening Union resistance.

At 2:00 P.M., Robert Rodes's division of Ewell's corps launched an uncoordinated attack against one of Doubleday's divisions blocking the Mummasburg road, advancing slowly only after three of its four attacking brigades were cut to pieces. Farther east, Francis Barlow's division of XI Corps was fighting desperately to keep the swarming masses of gray from pushing his outnumbered troops off of a small hill west of the Heidlersburg road. The frenzy of the men locked in combat is illustrated by the fate of Lieutenant Bayard Wilkeson, commanding Battery G, 4th U.S. Artillery. Knocked from his horse by a shell fragment or bullet that nearly severed his leg, Wilkeson had his men set him up against a tree upon a blanket. The gravely wounded lieutenant then took out his pocketknife and finished amputating his own leg, continuing to direct the fires of his battery until he passed out from shock and loss of blood. He died later that night.

At about 2:30 P.M., as the fighting continued all along the line, Lee arrived at Heth's position. The Confederate commanding general was still disinclined to intensify the fight at Gettysburg until Longstreet's corps had arrived and his entire Army of Northern Virginia was assembled in one place. However, even as he was disapproving Heth's request to continue the assault, increased firing from northeast of town indicated that Jubal Early's division had also arrived to add its strength to the Confederate attacks by Ewell's corps.

With the preponderance of forces on the battlefield now firmly in his favor, Lee decided to press home a general attack against the weaker Union line. By 3:00 P.M., all Confederate units were attacking the Union positions to their front. Early's troops soon smashed XI Corps' thin line, sending the Federal right reeling back through the town. Not long afterward, Doubleday's forces succumbed to Hill's reinforced assaults, and troops on the left of the Union line also retired. Fortunately for the Federal troops, they had a good defensive position to withdraw to—Cemetery Hill and Ridge.

Steinwehr's troops of the XI Corps, which Howard had stationed on Cemetery Hill earlier in the day, had prepared some strong breastworks and fighting positions by the time the Union lines north and west of town broke. These works enhanced the natural advantages of the terrain to provide Federal forces with a strong defensive position—if they could place sufficient numbers of troops on this position.

Shaped like an inverted fishhook, the position ran from Culp's Hill, immediately to the right of Cemetery Hill, south down Cemetery Ridge to anchor on the high ground of the two large hills, Round Top and the Little Round Top—a line over three miles long. As the battle-weary, blue-clad soldiers streamed through Gettysburg toward these positions, a fifth Federal officer arrived at Gettysburg and claimed command that day.

Major General Winfield Scott Hancock of the II Corps was, like the recently killed Reynolds, one of the most highly regarded commanders in the Army of the Potomac. He had been dispatched by Meade to rush to Gettysburg and take field command as soon as Meade heard the news of Reynolds's death. Despite being junior in rank to Howard and over Howard's initial resistance, Hancock began, immediately upon his arrival at about 4:30 P.M., to organize the defense of the Cemetery Hill–Ridge position. He realized he had to get the beaten I and XI Corps troops into the best possible defensive posture to meet the inevitable renewed Confederate attack. Like his four predecessors in command that day, Hancock's mission was to delay Lee's troops long enough for the rest of the Army of the Potomac to arrive and strengthen the Union position. Luckily for Han-

Ewell's Corps CSA
2:00 P.M.
Ewell's Corps
CSA
Ewell's Corps CSA
2:30 P.M.
Hill's Corps CSA
8:00 A.M.
Mummasburg Road
Carlisle Road
Heidlersburg Road
Oak
Hill
Chambersburg Pike
York Pike
Rodes CSA
Early CSA
I Corps USA
(After Buford)
XI Corps USA
Heth CSA
USA Positions
Morning - Afternoon
July 1
GETTYSBURG
Hagerstown Road
Hanover Road
Cemetery Hill
XI Corps
Culp's Hill
XII Corps
USA
I Corps
Seminary Ridge
Cemetery Ridge
III Corps
USA
USA Positions
Night of July 1-2
Little
Round
Top
Round
Top
Baltimore Pike
Tangytown Road
III, XII Corps USA
5:00 - 6:00 P.M.
Emmitsburg Road
Gettysburg
July 1, 1863
1 Mile
(Scale Approximate)
— CSA Units
— USA Units
— Wheat Field
— Peach Orchard

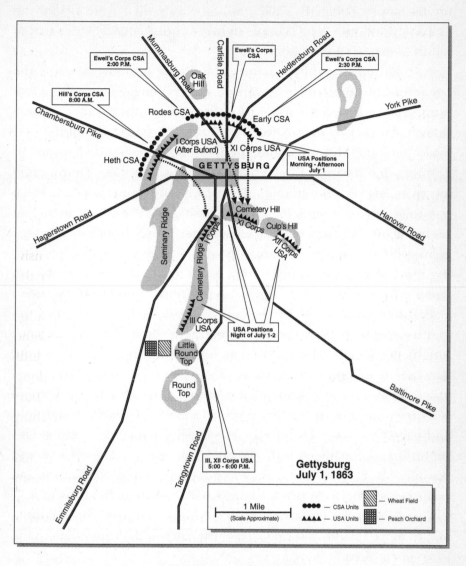

Gettysburg, July 1, 1863

cock, Dan Sickles's III Corps and Henry W. Slocum's XII Corps were rapidly approaching. By 5:00 P.M., Slocum's men were occupying fighting positions on the Union right. An hour later Sickles's troops fell in along Cemetery Ridge.

Lee realized that the Cemetery Hill–Ridge position was now the key terrain if he intended to fight a general engagement at Gettysburg, and he ordered Hill and Ewell to press forward their attacks against Hancock's forces before reinforcements arrived. But the normally sanguine Hill was disinclined to ask his exhausted troops to do more that day, and Ewell was not Stonewall Jackson. Despite urging from his division commanders, Early and John Gordon, Ewell was reluctant to assault the strong positions Steinwehr's men had prepared on Cemetery Hill. Likewise, when scouts from Ewell's newly arrived division under Edward Johnson timidly probed Culp's Hill, the few Federal troops there drove them back. By the time Slocum and Sickles's reinforcements got into position around 6:00 P.M., Lee's opportunity to seize the key terrain had vanished.

After seeing to the disposition of the Federal troops, Hancock sought out Meade, still a dozen miles to the south in Taneytown, and convinced him that the strong Union position at Gettysburg was just the place for the Army of the Potomac to fight Lee's Army of Northern Virginia. Meade arrived on Cemetery Hill about midnight and called for a council of war. His corps commanders and senior subordinates concurred with Hancock's judgment. The army would complete its concentration on the good ground at Gettysburg and await Lee's attack—Meade's soldiers had won their fight for time.

Throughout the night of July 1–2, troops from both sides continued to move steadily toward Gettysburg, adding their numbers to the weary men already there.

The Second Day—Fury on the Flanks

Lee's plan of attack for July 2 was to strike Meade's forces on both flanks, rolling up the Union position from the south where Lee presumed his enemy was weaker. Longstreet, whose I Corps divisions were still arriving from the west, continued to stubbornly resist fighting the well-defended Federal army on the Gettysburg battlefield. Lee's ablest subordinate commander now that the eccentric, brilliant Jackson was dead, the "Old Warhorse" Longstreet, tried to persuade Lee to maneuver around the Federal left, get between Meade and Washington on some defensible terrain, then crush the Army of the Potomac as it attacked their own. Lee demurred. The enemy was right there in front of them, and the Confederate commander intended to smash the Army of the Potomac, once and for all, in its present positions. After all, the Army of Northern Virginia had consistently beaten their Northern foes up to this point, and Lee was certain that his troops could do it again.

Despite Longstreet's opposition, Lee issued his attack orders for the day at about 10:00 A.M., July 2. The assault Lee envisioned was not simple. Two of Longstreet's three divisions (Hood's and Mc-Law's—Pickett's was still on the road from Chambersburg) would work their way, under cover, to attack positions south of Cemetery Ridge along the Emmitsburg road. Longstreet was then to attack, in echelon of brigades, northeast toward Cemetery Ridge. When Longstreet began rolling up the Union left flank, Anderson's division of Hill's corps, supported by Pender's division, would attack Cemetery Hill from Seminary Ridge to the west. As soon as he heard Longstreet's guns, indicating the I Corps attack was under way, Ewell was to demonstrate in front of Cemetery and Culp's hills. If conditions permitted, Ewell could launch a full-scale attack on the heights. The battle plan was complex, poorly coordinated, and as it turned out, abysmally executed. Nevertheless, two critical Federal errors caused it nearly to succeed.

The New York politician-turned-general, Dan Sickles, was not satisfied with his III Corps troops' defensive position on the southern part of Cemetery Ridge. The ground here was very low, almost level, and Sickles observed what he thought was higher, better ground to his front, about a half mile west. Without orders or permission, Sickles moved his corps forward and out of direct contact with the main Union line, creating an L-shaped salient bordered by a wheat field, a peach orchard, and the Emmitsburg road. The result was a dangerous bulge in the Federal line, open to deadly Confederate artillery fire from two directions, and unconnected to the main Union defensive line. Sickles's men now sat directly in the path of Longstreet's planned attack.

The other Federal error further jeopardized the Union left flank. The two dominant hills—Round Top and Little Round Top—had been left undefended, an incredible blunder that meant Meade's line of defense had no anchor in the south.

Longstreet, however, was taking a frustratingly long time to get his divisions into attack positions, and Lee was losing patience. Starting late and taking a roundabout route to avoid detection, Longstreet's troops got lost, countermarched, and eventually took hours to arrive at their jumping-off point. It wasn't until 3:30 P.M. that Hood and McLaws had their divisions in place and ready to begin their assaults. Nearly a day had been wasted. When they did attack, however, Sickles's exposed corps was caught in a deadly vise. Hood's division quickly shattered Sickles's left flank, rapidly moved through the jumbled, boulder-strewn terrain at the base of Round Top called Devil's Den, and started up the slopes of Little Round Top. If the Confederates occupied the dominant terrain of this hill, the entire Union line could be brought under devastating artillery fire.

Fortunately for Meade, his army's chief engineer officer, Brigadier General Gouverneur K. Warren, had arrived at the crest of Little Round Top. Warren realized, in horror, that this key position lay undefended, and he took immediate action. Acting on his own, Warren ordered two passing brigades of Sykes's V Corps rushed to occupy Little Round Top. The Northern troops arrived only moments before Hood's soldiers assaulted the hill from the south and west. In desperate, hand-to-hand combat, the Federal troops repulsed Hood's men and saved the heights. Typical of the terrific efforts of the troops on both sides were the actions of Colonel Joshua Lawrence Chamberlain's 20th Maine Regiment. Occupying the far left of Meade's long defense line, Chamberlain's regiment struggled desperately to fend off the continued assaults of Hood's troops. Finally, nearly out of ammunition, weakened by heavy casualties, and on the verge of being overwhelmed by another Confederate attack,

Mummasburg Road
Carlisle Road
Heidlersburg Road
Oak Hill
York Pike
Chambersburg Pike
Heth CSA
GETTYSBURG
Pender CSA
Early CSA
Johnson CSA
Hagerstown Road
Seminary Ridge
Cemetery Hill
XI Corps
Culp's Hill
Hanover Road
Anderson CSA
I Corps
XII Corps USA
II Corps USA
Cemetary Ridge
McLaws CSA
III Corps USA
Longstreet's I Corps Attack 4:00 P.M.
Little Round Top
V Corps USA
Hood CSA
Round Top
2 USA Brigades (V Corps) arrive on Little Round Top just in time to stop Hood's attack.
Baltimore Pike
VI Corps USA
Emmitsburg Road
Tangytown Road
Gettysburg July 2, 1863
1 Mile
(Scale Approximate)
— CSA Units
— USA Units
— Wheat Field
— Peach Orchard

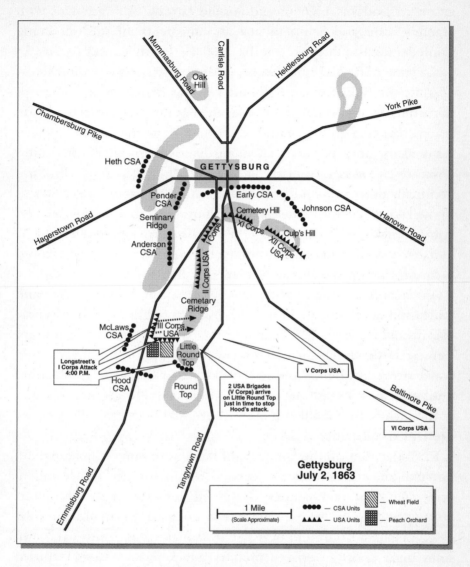

Gettysburg, July 2, 1863

Chamberlain made the completely unexpected and unorthodox decision to lead his men in a do-or-die bayonet charge. The 20th Maine's surprising counterattack into the teeth of the oncoming Confederate assault broke the back of the nearly overwhelming attack by the 15th Alabama and saved the far left of the Union line.

While the fight for Little Round Top was raging, Sickles's troops remaining in the salient were savagely assaulted by Longstreet's divisions. Brutal fighting in the wheat field and the peach orchard resulted in those positions changing hands many times that afternoon. Over the course of the next several hours, Sickles's line was eventually overcome and forced back onto Cemetery Ridge. Sickles himself was gravely wounded when a cannonball smashed his leg and knocked his horse from under him. His III Corps, shattered as badly as its commander's leg that terrible afternoon, was nearly destroyed before regaining the refuge of Cemetery Ridge.

Anderson's division of Hill's corps was next in line to attack, and joined in the assault late in the day. But it could make little headway except for one brigade's foray into the heart of the Union line on Cemetery Ridge. The penetration was unsupported, however, and was destroyed by Union counterattacks. Accordingly, it produced no positive results. Longstreet and Hill's attacks finally ground to a halt as darkness set in about 8:00 P.M.. There had been no rolling up of the Union left flank.

Ewell's actions on the Union right flank were uncoordinated, half-hearted, and also produced no good results for Lee. The Confederate II Corps commander contented himself with a two-hour artillery barrage as his only support to Longstreet's attack, then decided belatedly at around 6:30 P.M. to launch each of his three divisions on a poorly prepared infantry attack against Cemetery and Culp's hills. These assaults, lasting well into the darkness, put substantial pressure on Meade's right flank but were all failures. Lee's complicated, ambitious plan to destroy the flanks of Meade's army, late to start, uncoordinated, and poorly executed, had failed. At another late-night council of war, Meade's corps commanders voted to remain in place and fight Lee's next attack. Meade suspected it would be directed at his center.

The Third Day—High Tide at Pickett's Charge

Surely, Lee reasoned, after forcing his opponent to shift his troops to his threatened flanks all day on July 2, his line must be fatally weak at its center. With this as his basic assumption, he formulated his plan of attack for the final day of the battle. Ewell's corps would once again assault the heights of Culp's Hill while Longstreet's troops, supported by Hill, would carry out the main attack, which would be aimed at the Federal center on Cemetery Ridge. Yet Longstreet still argued for a sweep to the right around the Federal left flank. He considered it suicidal to launch a frontal attack at the center of the well-positioned Federal army and remonstrated with his commanding officer. His arguments and objections did no good, for Lee had made up his mind to attack Meade where he stood. Longstreet was only able to get Lee to excuse the battered survivors of Hood and McLaws's divisions from the coming assault. His final uncommitted division, Pickett's fresh troops, reinforced by two divisions from Hill's corps—somewhat less than 15,000 men—would undertake the attack. Longstreet remained unenthusiastic, recording in his postwar memoirs that he told Lee "the fifteen thousand men who could make successful assault over that field had never been arrayed for battle."

Ewell's supporting attack on Culp's Hill was precipitated early on the morning of July 3 by Federal cannonading on Johnson's division as it occupied attack positions at the base of the hill. Since Johnson could not remain under the galling fire, he launched his attack early, about 8:00 A.M. The resulting attack broke up and ground to a halt before it could achieve any useful gains. Finally, then, only Longstreet's attack remained to be undertaken.

"Pickett's Charge," the most famous assault in American military history, is really a misnomer, since Major General George E. Pickett commanded only one of three principal units making up the main attack. To acknowledge the other division commanders and their soldiers' contributions to the history-making charge, later historians have taken to referring to the Confederate attack on the center of the Union line on the final day as the Pickett-Pettigrew-Trimble attack. Regardless of their attempts, however, it will likely always be known simply if incorrectly as Pickett's Charge.

The largest artillery bombardment ever to take place in the western hemisphere preceded the attack. At about 1:00 P.M. on an oppressively hot July 3, nearly 170 Confederate guns concentrated along Seminary Ridge broke the silence and opened fire on Meade's positions, raining deadly shells on the Northern troopers for two solid hours. Despite the tendency of much of the Confederate shot and shell to fall well behind the front-line Union positions, this barrage caused many casualties among the defending troops. Henry Hunt, Meade's chief of artillery, wisely ordered his Federal guns to quit returning fire, suspecting that every round of ammunition they had would be needed to repel the Confederate infantry attack he thought would surely follow the bombardment. When the Union guns fell silent, Confederate commanders wrongly assumed that their heavy cannonading had achieved their desired effect. With the defense now presumed fatally weakened, now was the time, Longstreet was advised, to send in Pickett. Longstreet, overcome by the heavy responsibility of ordering what he knew in his soldier's heart to be a futile and ill-advised attack, could not even bring himself to speak to Pickett, merely nodding his head when the latter asked, "Shall I advance?"

At about 3:00 P.M., the mile-long line of Confederate infantry moved out of the wood line on Seminary Ridge and began marching toward the Union center, over a half mile away. The stifling, humid air seemed to lie over the battlefield like a blanket as the men followed their officers across the wide field separating the two armies. Almost immediately, the Confederate ranks came under Federal artillery fire from the now unsilenced guns. Solid shot and bursting shell caused some casualties, and holes began to appear where men had been only a split second before. Here and there a man with a missing arm or leg, or one who had been disemboweled, began to scream piteously. Most men, however, were still up and moving well in formation. With the attackers closing in to about 600 yards, the

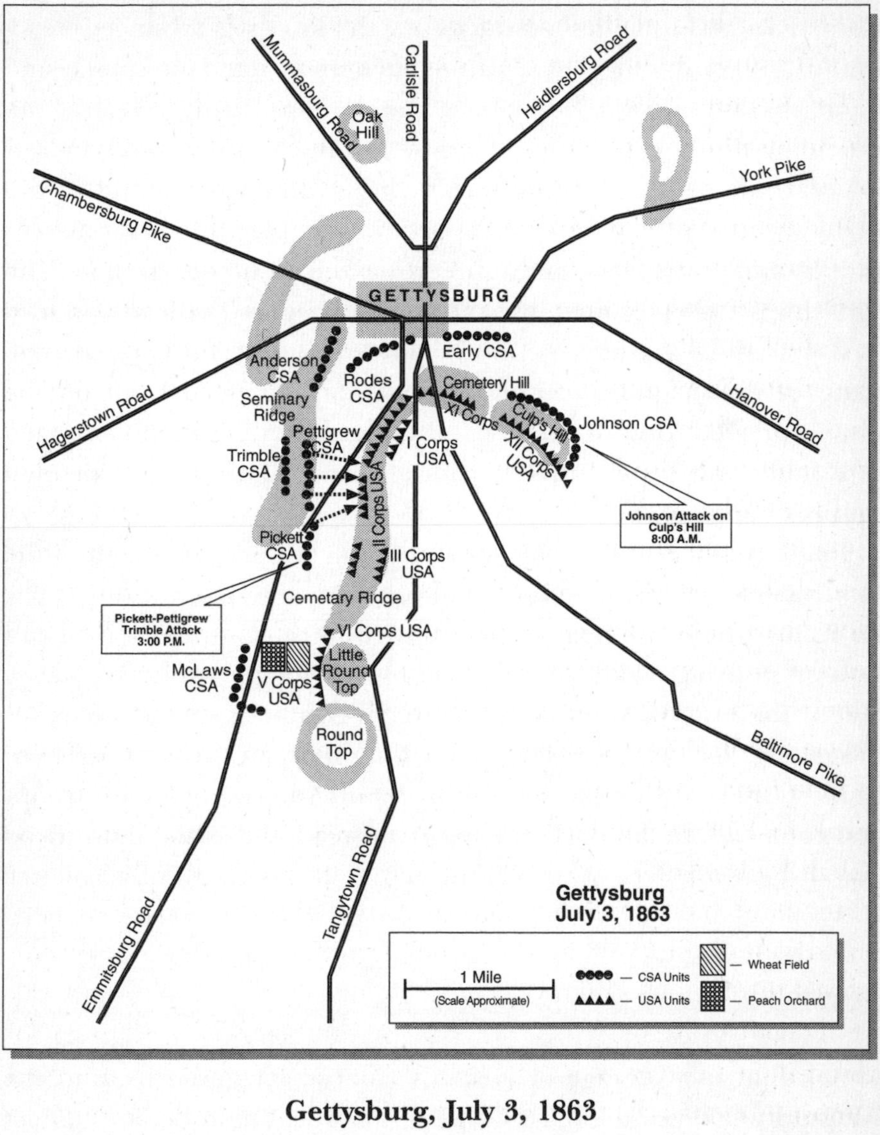

Mummasburg Road
Carlisle Road
Heidlersburg Road
Oak Hill
York Pike
Chambersburg Pike
GETTYSBURG
Early CSA
Anderson CSA
Rodes CSA
Cemetery Hill
Hagerstown Road
Seminary Ridge
XI Corps
Culp's Hill
Johnson CSA
Hanover Road
Pettigrew CSA
XII Corps USA
Trimble CSA
I Corps USA
II Corps USA
Johnson Attack on Culp's Hill 8:00 A.M.
Pickett CSA
III Corps USA
Cemetary Ridge
Pickett-Pettigrew Trimble Attack 3:00 P.M.
VI Corps USA
McLaws CSA
V Corps USA
Little Round Top
Round Top
Baltimore Pike
Tangytown Road
Emmitsburg Road
Gettysburg July 3, 1863
1 Mile
(Scale Approximate)
— CSA Units
— USA Units
— Wheat Field
— Peach Orchard

Gettysburg, July 3, 1863

shelling intensified as more and more of the Union guns, intentionally kept silent during the barrage, began to rain shells down on the Confederates. Casualties mounted, but the lines still advanced steadily. At 300 yards, the entire Union center erupted in smoke and flame, as aimed rifle fire joined the artillery firing, creating an unending din of explosions. Men now fell in clumps as thousands of Federal riflemen, each firing two or three rounds per minute, whittled away at the gray ranks. At 200 yards, canister and shrapnel cut wide swaths, yards at a time, shredding the Confederate line. The surviving attackers leaned into the almost solid wall of lead and iron as if marching into the teeth of a howling gale. The tattered remnants of the magnificent line of men that had started out on the assault pressed forward the last few yards. Federal gunners rammed in double and triple loads of canister, and whole squads of men simply disappeared.

Finally, upon reaching the low stone wall at the Union center, the survivors of the mile-long line were reduced to a space of only a few yards, the whole milling mass surrounded by the Union riflemen and cannon pouring deadly fire into the horribly depleted ranks. Maybe 200 of the original thousands followed Brigadier General Lewis Armistead up to the Union line; fewer than that got through it. Those who did make it that far were hit by counterattacking Union troops and soon had to fall back, leaving Armistead and many more dead and dying at the feet of the Union victors. It was all over by 3:50 P.M.

Aftermath

As the human wreckage of Pickett's Charge staggered back to the temporary safety of the main Confederate line, Lee rode out to meet them, saying to some that "the fault is all mine." And, primarily, it was Lee's stubborn determination to end the battle and the war with a massive frontal assault that gave Meade the victory. Despite the missed opportunities of the previous two days, the slowness of Longstreet's attack on the second day, and the overall ineptness of Ewell's corps throughout the battle, it was the failure of the commander in chief of the Army of Northern Virginia to devise a simple, workable plan of attack, then force his commanders to carry it through to success, that doomed the South's chances on this battlefield. Lee became a Southern icon after the war, making criticism of any of his actions sacrilege, but he himself never evaded his own responsibility for the Confederacy's greatest defeat.

Lee's final effort to gain victory at Gettysburg had been broken, but his army was still not destroyed. The Confederate commander withdrew his forces to Seminary Ridge and had them prepare breast-works and fortifications in anticipation of a massive Federal coun-terattack. None came. Meade's troops may have won the battle of Gettysburg, but the Army of the Potomac had been badly mauled in some of the most intense fighting ever seen. And although Meade still had some forces that had not been heavily engaged during the previous three days, he considered that his army, overall, was too exhausted to take the offensive against a still-dangerous Army of Northern Virginia. All day on July 4, 1863, Lee's army sat unmolested by Meade's forces. That night, in a driving rainstorm, Lee's troops began the long road back to Virginia.

Meade slowly followed Lee's retreating army, but made no con-certed effort to cut it off and destroy it. Much to Lincoln's dismay, Lee escaped across the Potomac during the night of July 13–14. Re-duced to about half of its campaign strength, the Army of Northern Virginia had nevertheless been saved to fight again—and prolong the agony for two more years.

The toll of the battle's human misery is unequaled in any other three days in this nation's history. Federal records show that 23,049 men of the Army of the Potomac were either killed, wounded, or cap-tured, with 3,155 of those killed outright or dying later of their wounds. Most of these casualties occurred in only about half of Meade's corps, so the overall Union casualty rate of 25 percent is much higher in those units most hotly engaged. Sickles's and Rey-nolds/Doubleday's corps suffered so heavily that they simply ceased to exist for the remainder of the war. Confederate record-keeping was much less tidy, so the official casualty figures of 20,448 are highly sus-pect. More likely, the Confederates lost 28,000 (3,500 killed), closer to

40 percent. Individual regiments took appalling losses, and Pickett's division was destroyed. Two of his three brigade commanders were killed, and the third crippled for life. Thirteen of fifteen regimental commanders were killed, and all were wounded. Of the nearly 6,000 troops in his division setting out from Seminary Ridge on July 3, Pickett could barely muster half of them at the battle's conclusion.

The Confederate loss at Gettysburg ended the South's hopes of winning independence through offensive battlefield action. It did not, however, end the war. Davis could still hope to delay Union victory long enough to make the war-weary North quit. Perhaps, Davis hoped, a decisive victory in the Western Theater could salvage Southern fortune and destiny.

The Battle of Chickamauga

September 19–20, 1863

By all rights, the battle fought along Chickamauga Creek on the outskirts of Chattanooga, Tennessee, should have been a great Union victory. Federal Major General William S. Rosecrans had brilliantly maneuvered the four corps of his 65,000-man Army of the Cumberland to a point south and west of Chattanooga that obliged the Confederates to evacuate the important city with hardly a shot being fired. But in his haste to trap what he falsely believed was the fleeing Confederate army, Rosecrans committed a near-fatal blunder. Spreading his army over an impossibly wide forty miles, the Federal commander invited a disastrous Confederate counterattack. What should have become a stunning Union victory was turned into a golden opportunity for the South to redeem its sagging battlefield fortunes and save middle Tennessee (and perhaps the entire mid-South) for the Confederacy.

It was equally likely, therefore, to have been a great and decisive Confederate triumph—a Gettysburg in the west with gray-clad soldiers victorious, instead of those in blue. The Confederate Army of Tennessee commander, Braxton Bragg, was presented with the chance to hurl his 62,000 troops against the widely scattered Federal corps, defeating them in detail, one after the other. After the humiliation of his long retreat from Murfreesboro, such a decisive victory would have been remarkable.

The battle of Chickamauga was, in effect, one of the greatest might-have-been battles of the entire Civil War. Had it ended as decisively as either of the two opposing commanders wished, it might have had as great an impact on the outcome of the war as Gettysburg. In reality, however, it was a decisive victory for neither side. Bragg failed to capitalize on his tactical victory and destroy the fleeing Union army, instead allowing it to reach the safety of Chattanooga. Later, reinforced with fresh troops and led by Grant and Sherman, the Union army in the west used Chattanooga as the starting point for one of the most devastating campaigns yet seen in modern war—Sherman's Atlanta campaign and brutal March to the Sea. Chickamauga has, as a result, merely gone go down in history as the bloodiest two-day battle of the Civil War, fought along a sluggish creek whose Indian name means, ironically, "River of Death."

Murfreesboro, Tullahoma, and Crossing the Tennessee

Despite the Federal victories at Forts Henry and Donelson, Shiloh, Pea Ridge, and New Orleans earlier in 1862, it was the Confederacy that seized the initiative in the last half of the year. Braxton Bragg led his Army of Tennessee in an invasion of Kentucky, attempting to win that border state for the Confederacy. At Perryville, Kentucky, however, Buell's Federal army fought Bragg to a standstill on October 8, and the Confederates withdrew. Buell's successor, William S. Rosecrans, attacked Bragg's Confederates on December 31 near Murfreesboro, Tennessee, at Stones River, gaining a costly Federal victory. After three days of heavy fighting, Bragg conceded the battlefield to Rosecrans and withdrew. The 12,000 casualties Rosecrans suffered, however, prevented him from decisively following up his victory for several months. When Rosecrans did move, he initiated the campaign that led to his historic confrontation with Bragg's forces on the battlefield at Chickamauga, Georgia.

The campaign that ended at Chickamauga actually began in January 1863, with the Federal and Confederate armies camped in or near Murfreesboro, scene of the recent Union victory in the battle of Stones River. Rosecrans's army had suffered over 12,000 casualties in the near-Pyrrhic victory over Bragg's army and needed time to recover its strength. Despite daily prodding from the War Department, Rosecrans seemed uninterested in leading his Army of the Cumberland against Bragg's Army of Tennessee. Bragg, defeated at Stones River, yet responsible for protecting the important communications center at Chattanooga, was unable to take the offensive, and was forced by circumstances to keep his army on the defensive.

Instead of initiating major campaigns against each other, both commanders launched their cavalry corps on a series of ultimately fruitless raids. Confederate Major General Joseph "Fighting Joe" Wheeler's cavalrymen attacked Union-held Fort Donelson without success in February. The diminutive Wheeler succeeded only in enraging his fellow Confederate cavalry commander, the dynamic, aggressive Nathan Bedford Forrest, by senselessly causing some of Forrest's troopers to get killed. Forrest swore never again to serve under Wheeler's command, forcing Bragg to reorganize his cavalry units into two separate wings and keep the two bickering cavalrymen apart.

Rosecrans's cavalry corps struck next, losing a detachment trying to cut Bragg's lines of communications in March. Forrest tried a similar maneuver against Rosecrans's lines of communications shortly afterward and failed to achieve any decisive results. Finally, Confederate cavalry raider Brigadier General John Hunt Morgan conducted his famous raid into Ohio and Pennsylvania, but it ended, disastrously, in his capture. Between January and June 1863, the Confederates lost 4,000 cavalrymen and the Federals lost 3,300 in these debilitating raids with little positive results to justify their losses.

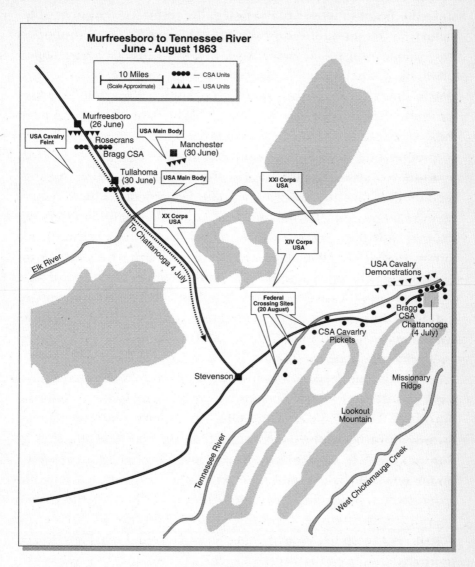

Murfreesboro to Tennessee River, June–August 1863

Despite his procrastination and frustratingly slow start, when Rosecrans did begin to move against Bragg, the results proved to be spectacular. In late June 1863, Rosecrans sent his cavalry corps, supported by Gordon Granger's Reserve Corps, in a move against Bragg's open left flank at Shelbyville. Convinced that this was the Federal main attack, Bragg took the bait, thereby permitting Rosecrans to move the bulk of his troops around Bragg's right flank. This compelled the outmaneuvered Confederate commander to withdraw southward and set up a defensive line around Tullahoma. Four days later Rosecrans moved again against Bragg's supply lines by seizing crossings over the Elk River in Bragg's rear. The Confederate officer's situation was then completely untenable. Fearing the likelihood of being trapped with the Tennessee River at his back, Bragg withdrew his forces back across that major river line, centering his defense on Chattanooga. In only nine days of brilliant maneuvering and at a cost of only 560 casualties, Rosecrans had forced his opponent to withdraw completely from the formidable Tennessee River. But Rosecrans wasn't finished quite yet. He had more unpleasant surprises for the Confederate commander.

Assuming that Rosecrans would now shift his axis of advance eastward in order to facilitate cooperation with Major General Ambrose Burnside's Federal Army of the Ohio in eastern Tennessee, Bragg focused his army's attention on guarding possible crossing sites in front and east of Chattanooga. Bragg had Wheeler's and Forrest's cavalry establish screens all along the Tennessee River, but failed to order them to picket the north side of the river. Although the screening effort was extensive, it proved to be of little use in discovering Rosecrans's intended crossing sites since it kept exclusively to the Confederate side of the river.

Rosecrans, on the contrary, used his own cavalry very effectively to deceive Bragg as to his main crossing sites. Although he waited more than a month before moving south, he again skillfully outmaneuvered the stationary Confederate forces. Keeping the main body of his force well away from the river to conceal his intentions, Rosecrans used mounted troops in a series of demonstrations across from and northeast of Chattanooga. The Federal troopers were kept busy making large and numerous campfires each night, loudly hammering boards, and frantically cutting timber in a great show of preparing to cross the river north and east of Chattanooga in force. This drew Bragg's attention away from Rosecrans's intended main crossing site, near the town of Stevenson, well to the southwest of Chattanooga. The Federal demonstrations were so effective and Bragg's pickets so ineffective that it was not until a week after Rosecrans had pushed his XIV, XX, and XXI Corps up to the river and nearly completed their crossing that his opponent discovered the truth. By then it was too late to oppose the Federal main effort.

Once his army had gotten safely across the Tennessee River by the first week of September 1863, Rosecrans began to move south and east against Bragg's main supply link, the Western and Atlantic Railroad. In a bold attempt to duplicate his earlier successes at Tullahoma and Elk River, Rosecrans sent his three corps along parallel but widely dispersed routes to threaten the railroad. Major General Alexander McCook's XX Corps swung the farthest south, near Alpine on the Alabama–Georgia border, while Major General Thomas L. Crittenden's XXI Corps followed the Tennessee River north of Lookout Mountain, hoping to occupy Chattanooga. In the middle, Major General George H. Thomas pushed his XIV Corps over the low spots on the rugged ridges euphemistically called "gaps" in this rough country. More than forty miles of heavily wooded, steep ridges containing only a few poor roads separated the flanks of Rosecrans's army. The territory traversed by the Union columns is unbelievably rugged, resembling nothing so much as a giant washboard covered by a carpet of thick woods and brush. It can swallow up whole formations of troops, and even if the entire opposing army were just over the next ridgeline, it would be invisible until one's own forces blundered into it. Nevertheless, concentrating his cavalry, his army's eyes and ears, only on his extreme flanks, Rosecrans left his center blinded. Ominously, there was nothing in front of Thomas's XIV Corps in the center except the forbidding terrain—and, as it turned out, Bragg's Confederate army.

Ironically, these maneuvers, which would soon bring the Federal army to the brink of disaster, actually accomplished their intended purpose. Once Bragg discovered Rosecrans's true movements, he was obliged to evacuate Chattanooga, beginning to pull his troops out of the city on September 8. Bragg was forced to give up the city without a fight and began concentrating his forces near Lafayette, Georgia, about twenty miles south. But the Confederate commander was soon provided with some good news. Thanks to the aggressive patrolling of Wheeler's and Forrest's cavalry units, Bragg was apprised of the great dispersion of Rosecrans's army. With his own army relatively well concentrated near Rosecrans's unsupported center, he perceived his great opportunity to smash the Federal corps one at a time.

With no cavalry to scout the hills in front of him, Thomas blindly pushed his lead division, commanded by Major General James S. Negley, far forward into the vicinity of McLemore's Cove and Dug Gap on September 9. Like the exposed neck of a turtle protruding out of its shell, Negley's division lay vulnerable for two agonizing days while Bragg tried in vain to order his recalcitrant subordinates to attack. Unfortunately for the Confederates, however, neither Major General Thomas C. Hindman's division nor Lieutenant General Daniel Harvey Hill's forces could be badgered, bullied, or cajoled into launching a determined assault. A unique opportunity to destroy Rosecrans's center and fatally split the Union army was lost.

This near disaster to Negley did, however, finally alert Rosecrans to his army's precarious position. Belatedly recognizing that his forces were much too widely spread out to support each other, he began a scramble to concentrate before Bragg could strike. For the next several days the Federals frantically raced northward, concentrating their forces to meet the inevitable Confederate attack. McCook, on the far right flank, drove his XX Corps troops mercilessly over the dust-choked tracks in a forced-march race to close on the left. Thomas, starting from the central position, had a better chance to arrive on the left flank before Bragg struck—and the Confederate commander was trying very hard indeed to strike.

Bragg, meanwhile, was becoming increasingly frustrated with his subordinate commanders as he once again failed to get an attack going against a part of Rosecrans's vulnerable forces. This time it

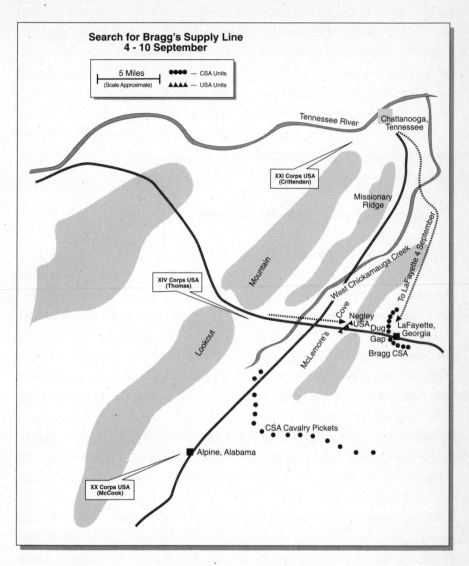

Search for Bragg's Supply Line, September 4–10, 1863

was Lieutenant General Leonidas Polk who could not be persuaded or ordered to attack with his corps. By the time Bragg began moving his army across Chickamauga Creek on September 18, Rosecrans had nearly succeeded in getting the bulk of his troops concentrated just to the west and south of Bragg's crossing points. After overcoming stiff resistance from two Union cavalry brigades guarding the bridges over Chickamauga Creek, the vanguard of Bragg's army also camped that night on the west bank. The main forces of both armies now lay in close proximity to each other.

The First Day—Confederate Attack

As September 19 dawned, Bragg had great hopes of cutting Rosecrans's army off from its supply base in Chattanooga and destroying it. Mustering about 62,000 men, Bragg's Army of Tennessee, now organized into four corps, was just then being reinforced by Longstreet's corps from Lee's Army of Northern Virginia. Taking the long way around by rail from Virginia, Hood's division had arrived on September 18 and gone immediately into the line. Longstreet and two more brigades would arrive that day while the battle was in progress, and the remainder of his corps was due on September 21. But Bragg wouldn't wait for all of Longstreet's unit to arrive. He intended to attack that day, expecting to find Rosecrans still concentrating his forces. The bulk of Bragg's army was that morning now across Chickamauga Creek.

Bragg's plan was to attack Crittenden's XXI Corps, what he presumed to be the Federal left, with the Confederate corps of Walker, Buckner, and the newly arrived Hood. But before these units could strike, Brannan's division of Thomas's XIV Corps, after hard marching now located on Crittenden's left, ran into Bedford Forrest's dismounted cavalrymen guarding the Confederate right flank. This contact precipitated a general engagement, which soon spread throughout the battlefield.

The resulting fighting on September 19 was a nightmare of confusion, countermarching, and brutal combat through the tangled woods and thick brush, with neither Bragg nor Rosecrans fully certain of the other's dispositions. Hardest hit of Rosecrans's units was Thomas's XIV Corps, which endured onslaught after onslaught from successive Confederate units. But while most of Bragg's forces were engaged in assaulting Thomas's corps, the rest of the Federal army was arriving on the battlefield, McCook's XX Corps reaching the area about midday.

Throughout the afternoon and into the evening, Bragg's subordinates launched attack after attack at the Union forces filling the dense woods in front of them. At about 4:00 P.M., Hood led a two-division attack at what was, by then, the right of the Federal "line." Smashing into the division of the unfortunately named Union general Jefferson C. Davis, Hood's troops threatened to break through the Union line. Fortunately for Rosecrans, fresh troops of Brigadier General Thomas J. Wood arrived just in time to strike Hood's exposed flank and turn the Confederates back. When the division of Major General Philip Sheridan arrived shortly thereafter, Rosecrans's right flank was secure for the day. But even as darkness fell, the Confederates were massing for one more major attack.

Confederate General Patrick Cleburne's division had waded across Chickamauga Creek at dusk, and took attack positions opposite Thomas's exhausted brigades. After dark Cleburne's gray ranks came howling through the woods and grappled with Thomas in a horrible, confused firefight. Late into the terrible night the fighting continued, never dying out completely. Thomas's units were severely battered, but the line held.

The Final Day—Rock of Chickamauga

Rosecrans held a council of war the night of September 19–20, obtaining the consensus of his corps commanders that the army should remain on the field and await Bragg's certain renewal of the attack the next day. Despite Bragg's intention of the last several days to destroy the Federal army before it could concentrate, every Union division save James B. Steedman's in the Reserve Corps had gotten into the action on September 19. Given its desperate straits only a few days earlier, Rosecrans's army was not then in such a bad position. Ordering some final adjustments to his troops' dispositions, Rosecrans prepared to see what his opponent had in store for the following day.

Bragg was still intent on crushing the Federal army, and his plan was to strike its left flank, driving it southwest away from Chattanooga. To execute this plan, Bragg once more reorganized his army. This time, without paying much attention to the existing corps organization, he grouped his men into two wings—the right under Polk, and the left under the just-arrived Longstreet. Polk would attack first, followed near midday by Longstreet.

At about 9:30 A.M., and after considerable delay, Breckinridge's division of Polk's wing finally assaulted Thomas's left flank. Just about the time the Confederates were turning Thomas's flank, reinforcements arrived and, after hard fighting, stabilized the line. Next to attack was Cleburne's division, which slammed into Thomas's front about 10:00 A.M.. Firing from behind hastily constructed breastworks, the Federals halted Cleburne's attack. At 11:00 A.M., Polk threw two more divisions into the attack, but, though hardpressed, the Federal line held. The constant attacks on Thomas caused Rosecrans to continue shifting troops around in order to send the XIV Corps some badly needed help. While most of this activity was helping his cause, one ill-timed movement proved disastrous.

Rosecrans, misinformed about the existence of a serious gap in his line just south of Major General Joseph J. Reynolds's division, ordered the division of Thomas J. Wood to "close up on Reynolds as fast as possible." Shortly after 11:00 A.M., Wood obeyed, pulling his division out of the line and marching it north. Before Davis's division could arrive to fill the gap left by Wood's departure, all hell broke loose.

Precisely at the worst moment for Rosecrans and at the exact point where Wood had left the line, Longstreet's wing proceeded to launch its attack. Led by the divisions of Bushrod Johnson and Hood, and meeting no organized opposition, the Confederate assault lit-

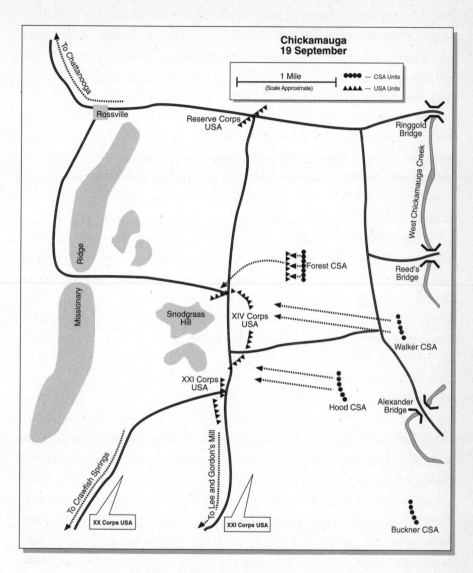

Chickamauga, September 19, 1863

erally destroyed Rosecrans's defensive line. Continuing through the gap, Longstreet's troops struck the divisions of Davis and Sheridan, both on the move and unprepared to receive an assault. The resulting panicked retreat swept Rosecrans and two of his corps commanders, Crittenden and McCook, all the way back to Chattanooga. Only the battered but steady Thomas remained on the field.

The unrelenting attacks against Thomas's XIV Corps had beaten the unit's line back on both sides, so that it resembled a horseshoe centered around Snodgrass Hill. Despite being left alone on the battlefield, the Federal corps continued to repulse the repeated attacks of Bragg's army. Reinforced by the reserve division of Steedman, and including the divisions of Johnson from XX Corps and Palmer from XXI Corps, Thomas's troops held their position throughout the day. Their epic stand prevented the Federal loss from turning into a complete disaster, and earned for Thomas the lasting nickname "Rock of Chickamauga." Finally, after countless attacks all day long from Bragg's weary troops, Thomas withdrew his men in good order to the safety of Chattanooga in the darkness.

Aftermath

The fiery cavalryman Bedford Forrest thought the battle should have been far from over. Following the retreating Federal troops all the way to Chattanooga, he sent frantic messages back to Bragg's headquarters that the whole army must be brought forward at once to crush Rosecrans's remaining troops. Chattanooga, Forrest claimed, lay wide-open, and the Federal army could be completely annihilated. After Bragg failed to respond to his call, Forrest went to his army commander's headquarters in person. Finding Bragg in bed, he woke him and demanded that he follow up on the victory. Bragg refused, asking how he could move an army without supplies. Forrest replied that their army could find all the supplies it needed in Chattanooga, if only it would go there and take them. When Bragg failed to reply, Forrest left in disgust.

Bragg's failure to follow up his tactical victory on the battlefield

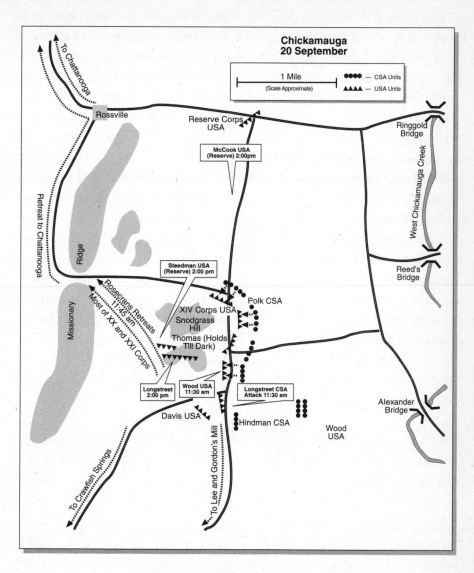

Chickamauga, September 20, 1863

of Chickamauga with a determined move on Chattanooga killed any chance the Confederacy had to retake middle Tennessee and, possibly, save the Deep South from the later ravages of Sherman's March. Even if Bragg had borrowed a page from Rosecrans's book and quickly maneuvered his forces around Rosecrans's lines of communications, he might still have forced the Union general to evacuate the key city. As it happened, Bragg contented himself with investing Chattanooga, deciding to besiege the town. He chose the worst available option. Within a month Grant and Sherman were sent to Chattanooga, and Federal reinforcements had arrived. Bragg's chance had clearly vanished. Within a year, Sherman had captured Atlanta and was gutting the Confederacy in the west while Grant bludgeoned it in the east. The might-have-been of Chickamauga had disappeared in smoke and blood.

Casualties on both sides of this terrible battle were appalling. The beaten Union forces lost an official 16,170 out of approximately 57,000 who fought on the field, one in ten of those casualties being killed. The tally for the victorious Confederates was a sickening 18,454, with 2,312 of those dying out of the nearly 66,000 present. Some think Bragg lost many more. Surely, though, it was pure horror.

CHAPTER TWO

The Franco-Prussian War

• 1870–1871 •

THE BATTLE OF SEDAN

The End of *"La Gloire"*

The crushing Prussian victory at Sedan over the French forces led by Napoleon III was a beginning as well as an end. With the humiliating surrender of 82,000 French survivors trapped in the fortress on the Meuse River, any French pretensions to a return to Napoleonic glory died ignominiously. At the same time, the battle opened the way for the victorious Prussian troops to besiege Paris and seal France's fate, and marked the beginning of Germany's reign as the premier power on the European continent. Victory in the Franco-Prussian War brought Otto von Bismarck, the Iron Chancellor, his ultimate triumph when his sovereign, Kaiser Wilhelm I of Prussia, was crowned emperor of a new, united Germany in the Hall of Mirrors of the Palace of Versailles on January 18, 1871.

Floing, near Sedan, France, 2:30 P.M., September 1, 1870: As the pitiful wreckage of two gallant, but utterly useless French cavalry charges lay sprawled across the uneven ground leading up to the Prussian-held village of Floing, French General Gallifet rallied the remnants of his shattered division for yet another attempt to break out of the trap of Sedan. Dead and maimed horses lay in heaps among the dead and maimed French cavalrymen under the clear skies and hot sun of a beautiful summer day. Sixty years earlier, on the battlefields of the first Napoleon, either of the two attacks by thousands of helmeted, breastplated cavalrymen mounted on their magnificent horses might have successfully overwhelmed the Prussian infantrymen deployed in front of the small provincial village, trampling them under their mounts' slashing hooves. But new technology had long since replaced the inaccurate muzzle-loading muskets and short-ranged bronze cannon of Napoleon's time with deadly accurate breech-loading rifles and long-ranged steel Krupp artillery pieces, forever changing the character of the battlefield and making the classic cavalry charge a suicide mission.

Nevertheless, despite the bloody failures of the first two charges, General Ducrot, the dashing cavalry general's commanding officer, turned once again to General Gallifet and asked if he could repeat the charge. Gallifet replied, "As often as you like, General, so long as there is one of us left." When Gallifet formed his surviving horsemen into two long ranks and began moving out to face the exploding shells and storm of lead of the Prussian line for the third time that afternoon, Kaiser Wilhelm, observing the action from the heights above Floing, could not help remarking, "Ah! the brave men!" But bravery was of little practical value in the face of modern firepower—the gallant but futile charge failed again, and more corpses of Frenchmen and carcasses of horses were added to those of the previous attacks. The slaughter was so one-sided that as Gallifet gathered up his few survivors and began to withdraw to the French positions, the Prussian troops spontaneously held their fire, allowing their brave enemy to leave the field of death unmolested. The Prussian officers saluted as Gallifet passed.

The French army's failure to break out of the Prussian trap at Sedan ended any hopes of winning the war France had declared only six weeks earlier. Although the war would not officially end until the devastating siege of Paris, the crushing defeat at Sedan effectively removed any doubt as to its outcome. The Prussian victory brought a final end to the Napoleonic empire. Caught in the trap at Sedan along with his army, Napoleon III surrendered his sword and his dreams of empire to Kaiser Wilhelm I. Sick and humiliated, he went into exile in England, surviving his former imperial domain by only three years.

Weapons and Tactics

There is no question that the primary French infantry weapon, the Chassepot rifle, was technically superior to the Prussian infantryman's Dreyse needle gun. Although the two were of similar design, the French had ingeniously used a rubber seal to overcome the needle gun's major defect, a breech mechanism that failed to prevent the rearward escape of the gases produced when the combustible cartridge was fired (a dangerous situation that reduced the needle gun's range and endangered the firer). The more properly sealed breech of the Chassepot increased the weapon's effective range to over 1,200 yards, about twice that of the needle gun's. Both weapons, however, permitted the user to load and shoot rapidly from the prone position, reducing his own exposure while pouring forth a deadly stream of lead. If the battlefields of the American Civil War were highly lethal because of muzzle-loading, relatively slow-firing rifled muskets, then the killing fields of the Franco-Prussian War were made even more lethal by the greater efficiency and enhanced rate of fire of the Chassepot and the needle gun.

The greatest advantage in weaponry the Prussian army enjoyed over its French opponent was the superior quality of its field artillery. After being pounded and blasted by the excellent steel, breech-loading, rifled fieldpieces of the Austrian army in the 1866 war, the Prussian gunners and their field commanders rapidly redressed this serious error by adopting similar artillery of their own. By 1870, the Prussians had armed their artillery units with weapons that could outrange, outshoot, and generally outclass their French opponents' in every regard. For their part, French artillery units continued to be supplied with obsolete, muzzle-loading, bronze guns, such as the twelve-pounder "Napoleon"—so called because Napoleon III had personally supervised its design and production. French commanders preferred such weapons since they thought that these relatively light, mobile guns, principally firing canister, could better support the violent, massive infantry attacks they assumed would constitute the French army's standard battlefield maneuver. What they did not evidently anticipate was that the longer-ranged, quicker-firing Krupp guns would simply blast the French cannon to bits while sweeping the French infantry and cavalry attacks from the field. Prussian artillery dominated the battlefield of the 1870 war, more than compensating for the superior range of the French Chassepot rifle.

The tactics employed by both sides in this war were of a transitional nature, mixing the anachronistic grand maneuvers of massed troops in the Napoleonic manner with the more practical and sensible advance in open order and fighting from behind field fortifications or in rifle pits. Infantry quickly learned that any advance in mass formation was suicide, and both armies usually fought in widely separated "skirmisher" (open order) formations. Nevertheless, firepower did not yet completely dominate, and the mass movements of troops on and around the battlefield still occurred. When attacking units closed on each other, however, the volume of bullets and shellfire typically caused them to spread out.

The prominence of cavalry was shattered by the extended range and firepower of infantry and artillery weapons in this war. Massed charges by mounted troopers wielding swords and lances did little more than litter the battlefield with dead cavalrymen and horse carcasses, and none proved to be decisive as they had in the days of the first Napoleon. Cavalry became more and more relegated to a reconnaissance role, useful for scouting enemy movements and probing enemy positions, but unsuited for fighting a well-positioned enemy armed with rifled cannon and muskets. Horse soldiers were completely out of place in the increasingly common street and house-to-house fighting of battles in towns and urban areas.

The Battle of Sedan

September 1, 1870

"Nach Paris! À Berlin!"

Prior to the stunning Prussian victory over the Austrian army at Königgraetz (the battle of Sadowa) in 1866, France was the major power in Europe. The Prussian defeat of the Austrians cast a large shadow over that assumption. The creation of the North German Confederation under Prussia's leadership confirmed that the Prussian chancellor, Otto von Bismarck, was determined to unite the fractious Germanic states and principalities under one banner. Should this be accomplished, France realized, the balance of power on the European continent would be changed forever. It seemed inevitable that France and Prussia would challenge each other for hegemony and that such a challenge would be decided on the battlefield. With the stunning defeat of Austria a few short years after beating Denmark and adding Schleswig-Holstein to Prussia's growing territory, Bismarck was two thirds of the way toward accomplishing his goal. He lacked only the occasion for initiating the war with France.

In 1868, Queen Isabella of Spain was dethroned, leaving a void at the head of that country's government that was still unfilled in the summer of 1870. In July of that year, France was appalled to learn that Prince Leopold of Hohenzollern-Sigmaringen had accepted the offer of the Spanish crown. If Leopold ever sat on the throne of Spain, France would be faced with a hostile Germanic confederation on its eastern border and a Spanish head of state sympathetic to its Prussian enemies on its west. France immediately protested vigorously and Leopold withdrew his candidacy for the throne. But Kaiser Wilhelm was not willing to assure France that the effort would never be renewed. Aided by the behind-the-scenes machinations of Bismarck, who saw this as the perfect opportunity to start a war with France, the diplomatic notes and exchanges surrounding the incident enraged public opinion in both nations, raising war fever to the boiling point.

Everyone now expected France to declare war on Prussia, and that is exactly what happened. France ordered mobilization on the afternoon of July 14, 1870, and Prussia followed suit the next day. With hundreds of thousands of reservists recalled to the colors and active-duty units beginning their movement to border areas on the countries' frontiers, the two war machines were now in motion. Five days later, on July 19, 1870, France formally declared war on Prussia.

Like its plans for mobilization and concentration of its armies, France's plan for the actual conduct of the war was haphazard, poorly prepared, and badly executed. Indeed, except for a vague idea of "invading Prussia" and "attacking and rapidly defeating the Prussian army," French leaders had no real systematic plan. The French High Command considered several specific schemes for attacking and defeating the Prussians, but all involved the rapid concentration of available French forces on the Franco-Prussian frontier in either Lorraine, or Alsace, or both, then launching an *attaque brusquée* on the Prussian forces (and their north and south German allies) before the Prussians could complete their own mobilization. French leaders assumed they could mobilize faster than their Prussian enemies, invade Germany in the Strasbourg area to force neutrality on the south German states, and thereby fatally split the Germanic military confederation. Prior to the actual outbreak of the war, there was even hope that Austria would enter the war on the French side. When the Austrians declined, the French determined to execute their plan alone.

There were several obvious flaws in the plan, the most serious being its basic assumption. The disorder and lack of a thoughtful, guiding hand on French mobilization efforts meant that it was virtually impossible for the French to mobilize faster than their Prussian enemies. Forced by the layout of the French national railway system to concentrate in only two principal areas on the frontier (Metz and Strasbourg), the French leaders were able to put a total of only 250,000 troops at the two locations, while the Prussians amassed 400,000 troops in three strategically placed armies.

Further complicating French efforts were serious problems in command organization and supply. As initially envisaged, French forces (optimistically assumed to be as many as 490,000) would be organized into three armies based in Metz, Strasbourg, and Châlons, all operating under the overall command and direction of French imperial headquarters. A not unreasonable organization (it was very similar to the successful Prussian command arrangements), it was completely changed by Napoleon III on the eve of the war. On July 11, he directed the creation of one large field force consisting of eight individual corps under imperial command. This unwieldy, awkward organization was quite beyond the capacity of the emperor to control, and resulted in a fragmented, piecemeal conduct of operations that played right into Prussian hands from the start.

The French army's supply and provisioning problems compounded the errors of basic unit organization and destroyed any chance French subordinate commanders may have had of compensating for the abysmal command situation. Provisions and supplies were forwarded to mobilization points and troop concentration areas with little thought as to what was actually needed, almost no prior planning for subsequent distribution, and scant regard even for how they would be off-loaded from the railcars. As the mobilization progressed, hundreds of railcars loaded with badly needed equipment and provisions sat abandoned on sidings or blocked busy railway stations. French soldiers, nearly starving and desperate for everything from boots to bullets, looted railcars and supply wagons. The resulting situation was appalling.

On the Prussian side of the frontier, the mobilization efforts went more smoothly, but mistakes were also made by Prussian commanders and staff officers and their German confederation allies (especially the Bavarians). However, compared with the French, these Prussian mistakes fade into insignificance. The Prussians, at least, had a plan based upon a reasonable analysis of the situation, the mission, and the enemy. Drawn up by the Prussian general staff, the plan had been created over three years.

The Prussian and allied forces were deployed in three armies plus a reserve over a frontage of approximately 100 miles centered on Saarbrücken. In the north, around Wittlich, was the 60,000-man First Army, commanded by General von Steinmetz and consisting of two corps and a cavalry division. In the center, fifty miles farther south at Homburg, was the Second Army, 131,000 men in three corps, a guards division, and two cavalry divisions commanded by Prince Frederick Charles. Farthest south, near Landau, was the Prussian crown prince's Third Army, 130,000 men in four corps, two infantry divisions, and a cavalry division. Kaiser Wilhelm personally commanded a two-corps reserve of 60,000 men. Moltke envisioned the three armies operating in two "wings," the First and Second under overall command of Frederick Charles as the northern wing, and the

Third as the southern wing. Despite the seemingly disadvantageous contrast between the widely dispersed Prussian forces and the more tightly concentrated French forces, Moltke's dispositions were carefully planned to minimize supply and provisioning problems while on the move, but maintain a reasonable supporting distance between each major wing to enable rapid concentration against any French effort while simultaneously permitting the outflanking of any enemy force. Reminiscent of the successful Prussian dispositions against the Austrians at Königgraetz (Sadowa), Moltke's overall plan was to advance on a main axis from Saarbrücken to Paris, attacking and defeating with superior forces and maneuver any French force he encountered.

Opening Battles—French Disasters

As the disorganized French mobilization and troop concentration continued through the remainder of July and into the first days of August, Napoleon found it necessary to group his subordinate units into two large forces—one around Metz and the other centered on Strasbourg. Although he retained overall command of all French forces, the emperor appointed Maréchal MacMahon, hero of campaigns in North Africa and the Crimea, as commander of forces in the vicinity of Strasbourg, about 100,000 troops. Farther north, at Metz, Napoleon ordered Maréchal Bazaine, also a veteran of many battles in North Africa, Mexico, and the Crimea, to assume command of the five corps and 150,000 French troops assembling at that city until he arrived to take over.

The fighting portion of the Franco-Prussian War began with a much-trumpeted, but ultimately hollow, French "victory" at Saarbrücken on August 2. On that date and, it seems, for want of anything better to do, the French II Corps under General Frossard advanced nearly unopposed into the city, pushing out the two Prussian companies that had garrisoned it. The major French forces did little to exploit this initial success or to continue operations against the Prussian troops moving to the frontier. On August 6, however, the Prussians moved against Saarbrücken in force, precipitating the first of the war's two real battles.

Despite Moltke's carefully thought-out dispositions, his obstinate subordinate General von Steinmetz moved his First Army against Saarlouis, in the face of specific orders to the contrary and directly across the path of Frederick Charles's Second Army. Ignoring Moltke's orders, Steinmetz continued, pushing two of his corps toward Saarbrücken, clashing with Frossard's French forces west of the town and precipitating the Battle of Spicheren. By day's end, Prussian victory was assured, although Frossard's troops managed to hold off poorly coordinated Prussian attacks for most of the battle. Although well within supporting distance of his beleaguered colleague, Bazaine never attempted to come to Frossard's aid. A pattern of French failure was set at Spicheren that continued throughout the war.

Meanwhile MacMahon was repeating the Spicheren experience farther south, at Fröschwiller. Also on August 6, the Prussian Third Army, having already crossed the Franco-German border, engaged MacMahon's troops in another sharp fight that they would ultimately win. Just as at Spicheren, French troops fought off successive Prussian attacks for most of the day only to be forced to retreat. And once more, French forces within easy supporting distance failed to come to their comrades' aid. Napoleon ordered Failly's V Corps to assist MacMahon in the Fröschwiller fighting, but Failly refused, sending only one division. The unit arrived in time to cover MacMahon's retreat. Although French forces had demonstrated bravery, superb fighting qualities, and tactical skill in both of these sharp fights, French senior commanders had demonstrated equally well that they were incapable of utilizing their fine troops for any larger purpose. French commanders seemed to fail to grasp any overall strategy or operational purpose, and they seemed extremely reluctant to march to the sound of the guns once battle had begun.

French disorganization continued unabated as MacMahon withdrew his forces to Neufchâteau, then to Châlons, while Bazaine and the emperor remained in the vicinity of Metz. Fearing public reaction in Paris if it was learned that he had abandoned Metz, the emperor rescinded the order for the armies to fall back and concentrate on Châlons. But while Bazaine remained in Metz, MacMahon completed the withdrawal of his forces to Châlons. The two halves of the outnumbered French army were now separated by ninety miles. Moving between the two forces and beginning to surround Bazaine at Metz was a concentrated Prussian army.

Two more Prussian victories in the middle of August sealed Bazaine's fate, trapping him and his men in Metz. On August 16, Prussian forces struck the French advance-guard units at Mars-la-Tour, preventing Bazaine from withdrawing from Metz to Verdun and causing about 16,000 casualties on each side. The Prussians followed up this narrow victory with a more substantial one on August 18 at St.-Privat-Gravelotte, forcing Bazaine to seek the safety of Metz's fortifications and abandon any chance of escape.

Meanwhile Napoleon III had left Bazaine on August 16 to join MacMahon and the other French forces forming at Châlons. Called the Army of Châlons, this force of 130,000 men included raw recruits, completely untrained in warfare, some even unfamiliar with how to fire their rifles. Nevertheless, Napoleon expected this army to strike the Prussian forces surrounding Bazaine, break the siege of Metz, and sweep the invaders from French soil. Instead, it ended its brief existence as a field force at Sedan on the Meuse River, never getting within fifty miles of Metz.

The Road to Sedan

MacMahon, rather sensibly, never intended the Army of Châlons to end up at Sedan. Rather, he wished to protect Paris from the advancing Prussian troops by repositioning his 130,000 men at Rheims, from which point he could better receive fresh troops while covering Paris from any Prussian advance. But on August 21, he was informed that to prevent his emperor's government from falling, Bazaine and the Army of the Rhine must not be permitted to rot inside Metz.

It was always assumed—and this assumption was supported by dispatches from Bazaine—that the latter would attempt to break out of the Prussian encirclement and rejoin the emperor's forces. No one on the French side imagined that Bazaine would passively sit in Metz until he surrendered his army to the Prussians on October 19. On August 23, therefore, the only question was in which direction Bazaine would move to effect a breakout. In a dispatch Napoleon received on August 23, Bazaine announced his intention to strike northward to Montmédy to escape the Prussian trap. On that day, MacMahon's Army of Châlons was put in motion toward the northeast to meet Bazaine and reunite the French forces.

Abandoning Châlons, MacMahon made a wide swing to the north, avoiding the Prussian forces situated between his army and Metz, but uncovering the direct route to Paris in the process. The Prussian forces, which now included a fourth army, the Army of the Meuse under the Crown Prince of Saxony, took full advantage of this extraordinarily bad move to swing their forces not engaged in the siege of Metz in behind the French commander. The farther north and east MacMahon's forces moved, the deeper they fell into the jaws of a Prussian steel trap. On August 30, the forces of the Crown Prince of Saxony slammed the trap shut. At Beaumont the Saxons fell on the by now exhausted French troops and proceeded to inflict 5,000 casualties while capturing about forty guns. By this time it was clear to all that Bazaine would make no concerted effort to break out of Metz and could certainly not assist MacMahon in a combined attack against the superior Prussian forces. Although he still intended to take the offensive against the Prussian forces, MacMahon saw only one immediate course of action given the exhausted state of his outnumbered troops and Bazaine's refusal to cooperate—retire into Sedan.

An End at Sedan

Sedan was hardly a state-of-the-art fortress. Situated on the marshy valley floor near a sharp bend of the Meuse River and surrounded on all sides by dominating hills, this small provincial border town had some seventeenth-century fortifications remaining from the Vauban era, but little else to recommend it. The wooded hills to the north and east sloped sharply upward to merge with the rugged Ardennes region of France and Belgium. On August 31, MacMahon's four corps began filing into Sedan and occupying positions in and around the town. The Prussian forces were close behind them.

Situated on the northwest sector of the French positions, between the villages of Floing and Illy, was Douay's VII Corps. Stretched out along the Givonne River, a small tributary of the Meuse, was Ducrot's I Corps, linking up with Douay at Illy and extending southward along the river to La Moncelle. Lebrun's XII Corps occupied the southeast sector, tied in with Ducrot at La Moncelle and ending at the marshy banks of the Meuse south of Sedan. MacMahon kept the V Corps as a centrally located reserve. The V Corps, originally commanded by Failly, came under the command of General de Wimpffen when the latter arrived from Paris with instructions to relieve Failly just as the army was retiring into Sedan. Also arriving in Sedan that day was Napoleon III.

The town contained insufficient supplies to support so large a force, and there were only about 200,000 rations stockpiled when the French troops moved in. This was not particularly alarming to MacMahon, however, because he intended to remain only a short time before taking the offensive. The enemy, however, had other ideas. Almost as soon as the French units arrived, the Prussian troops closed up behind them and began attempting to force crossings over the Meuse. Despite the fact that the French engineers lacked the equipment to destroy the bridges, French troops were initially able to prevent the Prussians from capturing crossing sites over the river. At day's end, however, Prussian forces not only completely ringed the French positions, they held several bridges leading into the French lines as well.

On September 1, the day after the French troops' arrival, the Prussian forces began the preliminary bombardment that signaled their intention to attack and seize the town. On the east end of the French positions, Saxon and Bavarian troops crossed the Meuse and attacked the French positions, penetrating some distance before being pushed back. Prussian artillery easily silenced the French guns and continued to batter the city and surrounding area. Throughout the

CHANNEL
Brussels
BELGIUM
FRANCE
GERMANY
XXXX
FIRST
P
Wittlich
Frankfurt
Rhine River
Moselle River
LUXEMBOURG
Mézières
Sedan
XXXX
SECOND
P
XXXX
THIRD
P
Saarlouis
Homburg
Reims
Vesle River
Gravelotte
Meuse River
Saarbrücken
Landau
Verdun
Metz
XXXX
Spicheren
Mars-la-Tour
BAZAINE
F
Seine River
Paris
Marne River
Châlons
Wissenburg
XXXX
Strasbourg
MAC MAHON
F
Sedan
September 1, 1870
50 Mile

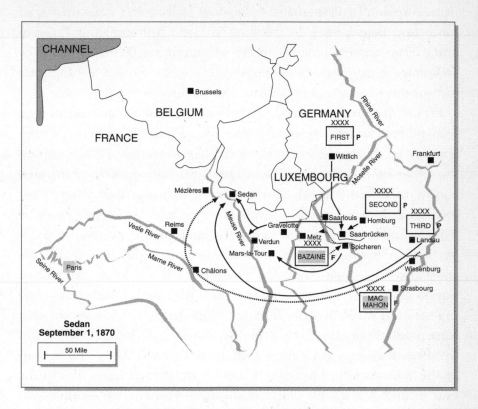

Sedan, September 1, 1870 #1

morning Prussian forces continued assaults upon the French positions surrounding the now beleaguered fortress but were unable to
force any large breach in the French lines. Although the Prussian
and German confederation forces outnumbered French troops by
90,000 men, they were being kept at bay by the bravery and fighting
skill of French soldiers and small unit leaders.

French troops were aided in their defense of Sedan and its outlying villages by armed civilians, who, enraged at the invasion of their
country by the hated Prussians and their Germanic allies, took up
the rifles of the dead and wounded and joined their uniformed
countrymen in the largely house-to-house fighting. This rising of the
local populace against the invaders was a small-scale precursor of
what would take place several weeks later in the defense of Paris
against the besieging Prussian forces. Although the armed mobs of
the Paris Commune could not possibly hope to defeat disciplined
enemy troops, they demonstrated clearly that nations were now making total war on each other. The age of the private little wars between
European princes employing small, isolated, professional armies was
finished. For their part, the Prussians were enraged by the actions
of the civilians around Sedan. At the small village of Bazeilles to the
east of Sedan, they immediately shot any French civilian they captured who was bearing a weapon (and probably quite a few who were
unarmed). The Prussian and, later, German army became quite
adept at this, and continued to shoot civilians in this part of France
and nearby Belgium in 1914, 1940, and 1944.

Shortly after the Prussian shelling of Sedan began on September
1, the French commanding officer became a casualty. At about 7:00
A.M., Maréchal MacMahon was wounded by an exploding shell while
riding forth to rally the troops. Although the wound was not serious,
he was forced to turn over active command of the army to General
Ducrot, I Corps commander. Ducrot had quickly grasped the seriousness of the situation when the army began retiring into Sedan
the day before, remarking, "We are in a chamber pot!" and providing a rather earthy description of exactly what material in the pot
the French forces represented. Ducrot at once ordered the I and
XII Corps to break out of the Sedan trap and move westward toward

St. Menges
XI Corps
Illy
V Corps
Cavalry
Floing
VII Corps
Douay
Givonne
Meuse River
XII Saxon Corps
I Corps
Ducrot
Sedan
V Corps (Res)
de Wimpffen
To Mézières
IV Corps
Balan
Lebrun XII
Corps
La Moncelle
II Bavarian Corps
Bazeilles
I Bavarian Corps
Sedan
September 1, 1870
2 Miles
— French Positions
— Prussian/German Positions

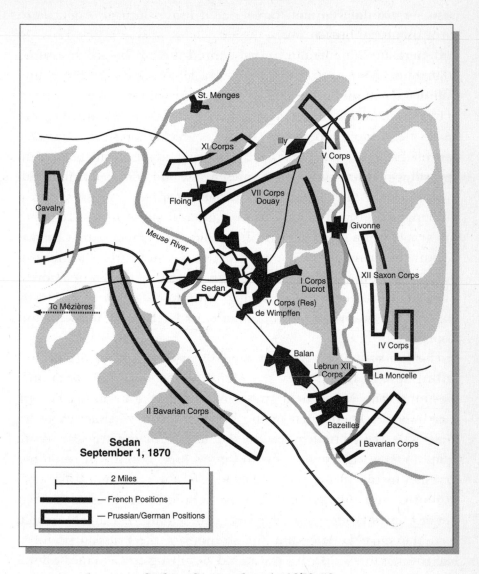

Sedan, September 1, 1870 #2

Mézières. But before the units could attempt to execute a sensible escape from the Prussian trap, French leadership was once more thrown into confusion.

General de Wimpffen, who had arrived the day before to assume command of the V Corps, produced a letter signed by the prime minister (General Count Palikao) instructing him to take command of the army if anything happened to MacMahon. Flourishing the letter, De Wimpffen replaced Ducrot as MacMahon's successor and canceled the proposed breakout. Abysmally ignorant of the tactical and strategic situation of the French army, and completely misreading the minor repulse of the Bavarian attack as a precursor to a monumental French victory, De Wimpffen thought he was rescuing the army from a gigantic error. Informing the emperor that he was now in command and that a great victory would be won "within two hours," he prevented any coordinated action by the French corps. The command confusion continued into the late morning, and by 10:30 A.M., Prussian troop movements had rendered the situation hopeless.

The Prussian Third Army crossed the Meuse west of Sedan and linked up with the Army of the Meuse to the north of the French positions. With Krupp field guns now ringing the town, the French were mercilessly pounded by the Prussian artillery. Although it appears that De Wimpffen remained ignorant of the true situation, Ducrot had not given up trying to force a breach in the surrounding Prussian forces. In the early afternoon, he directed the cavalry division of General Margueritte to smash a hole in the Prussian line in the northwest sector near the village of Floing. During his initial reconnaissance to determine the strength of the Prussian position, Margueritte was killed, his command devolving to General Gallifet. The gallant cavalryman bravely led three hopeless charges, none of which had a chance of saving the French army from certain defeat.

De Wimpffen still refused to admit the situation was lost and attempted to mount a final counterattack to break out of the ring of deadly artillery. Pleading with Napoleon III to join him and the troops, he tried to rally the increasingly demoralized French soldiers. Napoleon refused to join in the futile attack and had already ordered the white flag to be raised over the town. De Wimpffen used threats and cajolery to convince the troops to mount one more effort, even lying to them by shouting, "Bazaine approaches!" Finally, he was able to collect an unorganized group of about 1,200 men and two guns, which he led in the direction of Balan. The ill-conceived and desperate counterattack quickly broke up when it met stiff fire from Prussian troops lining both sides of its route of advance. Amid the wreckage of his failed counterattack, De Wimpffen met XII Corps commander, Lebrun, and attempted to turn overall command of the French army to him. Lebrun sensibly refused.

By 6:00 P.M. that day, the battle was over and De Wimpffen was forced to begin negotiations with the kaiser to surrender the French army. The negotiations were, of course, completely one-sided, as the French had little left to bargain with. The result was a virtual unconditional surrender, and De Wimpffen led 100,000 French soldiers into captivity. Napoleon offered his sword to Wilhelm the next morning, then left for exile in England. With fewer than 9,000 casualties, the Prussian forces had inflicted a stunning and costly defeat on France. In addition to 3,000 French soldiers killed and 14,000 wounded, 104,000 marched into captivity in Prussia.

Aftermath

Sedan was the watershed victory for Prussia in the 1870 war and destroyed any chance French forces may have had to stave off humiliating defeat. Prussian forces moved virtually unopposed to Paris and began a successful siege of the French capital on September 20. Napoleon's surrender at Sedan was the downfall of the empire, and the Third Republic was proclaimed in Paris on September 4 under Léon Gambetta. Despite the fact that the defenders of Paris outnumbered the besieging Prussians, they made no concerted attempt to break out of the trap and lift the siege until it was too late. Bazaine's army of 170,000 in Metz remained surrounded and did not try to escape and come to the aid of the capital. On October 29, Bazaine surrendered Metz and all French forces trapped within the fortress city to the Prussian forces, an act for which he was later court-martialed and imprisoned. Paris surrendered at the end of January 1871, ending the military operations of the war (except for the bloody suppression of the revolt of the Paris Commune by French troops in May 1871—about 30,000 communards were killed by their own countrymen when the government recaptured the city).

While the siege of Paris still proceeded, Kaiser Wilhelm was crowned emperor of a united Germany at Versailles on January 18, 1871. This act emphasizes the real significance of the Franco-Prussian War of 1870, which was not France's humiliation on the battlefield, but the unification of Germany and its rise to the position of the reigning power in Europe. France was left smoldering with resentment at the defeat and subsequent loss of Alsace and eastern Lorraine, but would have to wait forty long years for its revenge. In the meantime, the professionalism, skill, organization, and expertise the Prussian army demonstrated on the battlegrounds of 1870 became the model for all the world's first-class military establishments.

CHAPTER THREE

The Russo-Japanese War

• 1904–1905 •

THE BATTLE OF PORT ARTHUR

East Versus West

The first serious conflict between major powers in the twentieth century was fought in the Far East, an area that, in recent centuries, had seen a nearly unbroken succession of colonial Western powers pick over the bones of faded empires. Until the beginning of the Russo-Japanese War in February 1904, any clash of East versus West almost inevitably led to the humiliation of the Eastern power through the modern firepower and technological superiority of the West. If a Far Eastern nation did achieve battlefield success during this era—as Japan did against China in 1894—it was likely to be against another Eastern country more backward than itself. The Japanese defeat of Russian forces in China, Manchuria, and the surrounding seas in 1904 and 1905, therefore, shocked the Western powers, and gave hope to colonized peoples from Africa and India, to the Philippines. A non-Christian, non-Caucasian, Asian state had grappled with and soundly defeated one of the greatest imperial nations in the world. The fact that the Russian empire was rotting from the inside and teetering on the brink of revolution was largely ignored by subject nations who sought hope from any quarter they could find. The rising sun of Japan had burst upon the East with a power and energy not seen since the glory days of ancient China. The world had changed forever.

Port Arthur, Manchuria, Night of February 8, 1904: The most famous land battle of the Russo-Japanese War began with a surprise-attack naval engagement two days before any formal declaration of war. In an action that presaged the more famous Japanese sneak attack, also before a declaration of war, thirty-seven years later at Pearl Harbor, the naval forces of Admiral Togo Heihachiro struck elements of the Russian Far East Fleet in the waters immediately outside of the harbor of Port Arthur. About midnight on the night of February 8–9, Admiral Togo's ten torpedo-armed, light destroyers swept in on the largely unsuspecting Russian ships, launched their deadly underwater missiles, and severely damaged the two newest and best Russian battleships in the Far East as well as holing a Russian cruiser below the waterline.

Although the attack struck only these three ships, its unexpectedness combined with a series of follow-up Japanese naval attacks on Russian vessels in Port Arthur and the Korean port of Chemulpo (Inchon), shocked the Russian Far East Command and caused them to keep their naval striking power bottled up inside Port Arthur and Vladivostok harbors. Seemingly safe behind the protective fires of the Russian shore batteries, the Russian ships made only a few timid attempts to challenge Japanese control of the sea-lanes. When the attempts quickly turned into further Russian disasters, even these halfhearted ventures were abandoned. Skulking in the shallow, confined waters of Port Arthur Harbor, the Russian vessels not only willingly turned over mastery of the seas in the entire zone of operations to the Japanese, they also ensured that the Japanese land forces would undertake a ground assault to capture Port Arthur and root out the Russian ships sheltered there. By their daring actions on that dark, cold night of February 8, 1904, Admiral Togo and his Japanese naval forces seized the initiative from their Russian opponents. In so doing, they made the ground campaign against Port Arthur (and, indeed, all subsequent ground operations in Manchuria) inevitable.

Weapons and Tactics

With the exception of the tank and the airplane, and of course, atomic weapons, virtually all the major weapons systems later employed in the twentieth century were used in the Russo-Japanese War. These included magazine-fed rifles firing smokeless powder and high-velocity, small-caliber bullets; machine guns operating with efficient, belt-fed or magazine-fed mechanisms; hand grenades and high explosive artillery shells that fragmented into a thousand or more steel segments; quick-firing, long-range fieldpieces with recoil-absorption mechanisms; heavy guns of large caliber, firing huge, high-explosive shells capable of collapsing entire sections of trench lines and destroying massive bunkers; and field telephone systems that linked observers to masked, protected guns, permitting artillery to destroy targets through indirect fire. Also in extensive use were field entrenchments, sandbags, and barbed wire to provide soldiers a means of escaping, however temporarily, the lethal fire of bullets and shells.

Both the Japanese and the Russian infantryman were armed with small-caliber, magazine-fed rifles. Japanese weapons fired a small, high-velocity, .256-caliber bullet, and the Russian rifle used a similar bullet of .299 caliber. Both weapons were capable of sighting out to 2,000 meters, but were most effective at about 300 meters, or less. Still revering its seemingly mystical power and spirit, the Russian soldier was more adept at wielding his two-foot, triangular bayonet at close quarters than he was at hitting a man-sized silhouette at 300 meters. Russian troops were notoriously poor marksmen—their officers trained them to deliver volley fire—and were well behind their Japanese opponent in this critical combat skill.

Each side began the conflict with machine guns, although, like the French in the Franco-Prussian War, they tended to employ them in batteries and use them like artillery support weapons. As the war ground on, the lessons of the battlefield taught the troops of both sides that the Russian Maxim and the Japanese Hotchkiss machine guns were better suited to direct infantry support in the attack and defense. They took particular note of the devastating effect machine guns, when fired from fortified positions, had on exposed, attacking troops.

As if in a bloody preview of the killing fields of Europe ten years later, artillery in this war demonstrated that it had achieved an unchallenged prominence it would never entirely yield (although the tank and the armored fighting vehicle joined it in importance during World War II). Modern artillery weapons on both sides established themselves as the deadliest weapons system available. Longer ranges and indirect fire techniques allowed unseen and protected artillerymen to shoot at enemy troops, equipment, and positions with deadly accuracy and at virtually no risk. Only other artillery weapons, using observed and well-directed counterbattery fire, could strike back effectively. The two types of artillery featured most prominently in the Port Arthur campaign were the quick-firing field gun of approximately three-inch caliber and the Japanese heavy howitzers of eleven-inch caliber, firing a 500-pound projectile. The huge Japanese eleven-inch howitzers became the weapon that finally broke the siege of Port Arthur and won the battle, once they were moved into position in sufficient numbers and Japanese observers gained promontories from which they could accurately direct their fire.

Much of the fighting in Manchuria, and virtually all of it at Port Arthur, was characterized by the attack and defense of fortified positions, closely resembling the trench warfare of World War I. Defenders dug into hillsides and reverse slopes to escape enemy artillery fire, and burrowed deeply into extensive trench systems and well-sandbagged bunkers and "bombproofs." Attackers dug approach trenches, laid and exploded mines under enemy positions, and stormed isolated sectors of enemy trench lines in sudden, violent rushes, using small units, frequently at night, and preceded by an artillery barrage intended to pin the defenders inside their protective bunkers.

The Battle of Port Arthur

May 1904–January 1905

Japan began its climb to major-power stature with the Meiji restoration in the 1860s, more out of motives of self-preservation than the desire to build an empire. At that time, it began industrializing and modernizing with astonishing rapidity. During the last quarter of the nineteenth century, Japanese interests outside the home islands centered on Korea and Manchuria. Korea, then a nation of weak rulers and decidedly unwarlike people, lies only 100 miles from the coast of Japan and, if controlled by a power hostile to Japan, could present a grave threat to the island nation. Manchuria was a land poor in people but rich in natural resources. Hegemony over both of these areas, nominally under the loose control of a weak, corrupt China, became a primary goal of Japanese foreign policy. From the 1880s onward, this brought Japan increasingly into conflict with Russian interests.

Already humiliated by the much-stronger Russia over possession of Sakhalin Island in 1875, Japan became deeply suspicious of Russian intentions in Korea and Manchuria when Russia announced its plan to build the Trans-Siberian Railway in 1891. There seemed to be no economic justification for the Russian government to undertake so costly a project, and the Japanese rightly feared this was the first of several Russian moves into Manchuria and, possibly, Korea. As if to underscore the implied threat, two of the Russian ships accompanying Czarevitch Nicholas on his official visit to Japan that year were named *Koreyetz* (Korea) and *Manjour* (Manchuria). Whether intentional or not, the message was not lost on Nicholas's Japanese hosts, and a Japanese naval officer attacked the Czarevitch with a sword and attempted to assassinate him. Although he escaped with only a small wound on his forehead, Nicholas never forgave the Japanese for the attempt. In 1895, this confirmed Japan-hater became czar of all the Russias.

In the meantime Japan found an excuse to start a war with the incompetent Chinese in order to occupy Korea and secure the country for "protection" of Japanese interests. With the eruption of a rebellion in Korea in 1894 came the excuse the Japanese needed to intervene on the Asian mainland. China naturally resisted the Japanese military movements and an eight-month-long war ensued. On the seas, then-captain Togo won a stunning victory over the weak Chinese fleet, using naval tactics similar to those he would use to destroy the Russian Baltic Fleet in the Tsushima Straits in 1905. On land, the Japanese ground forces easily defeated the Chinese armies in Korea, Manchuria, and China. Forced to the peace table on April

10, 1895, China recognized the "independence" of Korea (under Japanese protection, of course), gave Japan the island of Formosa, and ceded Japan the Liaotung Peninsula at whose southern tip lies the warm-water harbor of Port Arthur. Russia was appalled.

Japan had little time to enjoy the fruits of this victory, as Russia convinced the other Western colonial powers that the island nation must be stripped of its new possessions. With the assistance of France and Germany, Russia notified Japan on April 20, 1895, that the peace treaty ending the Sino-Japanese War must be abrogated and the territory returned. Not nearly strong enough to take on all three world powers, the Japanese emperor acquiesced. Bitter and resentful, Japan was left with little positive gain from the war except a large cash indemnity. The money was almost immediately invested in warships and arms.

Russian motives for all this are obvious. Russia itself wanted control over the resources of Manchuria—and, if possible, Korea—and the unrestricted use of the warm-water harbor of Port Arthur. It seemed obvious that a weak China was about to be carved up by the Western imperial powers, and Russia wanted to position itself to take full advantage of it. In 1896, China had agreed to permit Russia to build a 1,000-mile shortcut to Vladivostok; any threat to the completion of this rail line would give Russia a perfect excuse for intervening in Manchuria. In addition to the direct line across Manchuria, Russia began constructing a spur from Harbin, through Mukden, to Port Arthur in 1898. The nation of the czars was now in Manchuria in force, resisting Chinese requests to leave.

The year before, 1897, a Russian fleet began operating in the waters immediately off Port Arthur, flexing its muscles in preparation for an occupation of the Liaotung Peninsula. Early in 1898, Russia "persuaded" China to lease it Port Arthur on a long-term, renewable basis. Immediately upon taking over the port, Russian ground forces were moved in and began constructing extensive fortifications. The Russians intended to stay.

Increasingly, Russians began appearing in Korea, too, especially at the port of Chemulpo, but also along the Yalu River. In 1903, Russian logging interests were awarded a contract to begin work in the valley of the Yalu River separating Manchuria and Korea. At Yongampo, near the mouth of the Yalu, the Russians even built a fort. Throughout the remainder of 1903 and into the first month of 1904, Russian and Japanese diplomats struggled to reach a compromise. Japan sought to force Russian recognition of its legitimate sphere of influence in Korea, even at the cost of recognizing Russian supremacy in Manchuria. The Russians, however, were not inclined to allow Japan much satisfaction in this area, primarily, it seems, because they never expected that the upstart Asian nation could successfully challenge them. Czar Nicholas, who liked to refer to the Japanese as the "Yellow Peril," refused to accommodate Japanese entreaties, even when the nation recognized Russian hegemony in Manchuria.

On February 4, 1904, the time limit on the final Japanese proposal on the disposition of each country's interests in the region lapsed with no Russian reply. On February 6, the Japanese ambassador at St. Petersburg was recalled, effectively breaking off diplomatic relations between the countries. When informed of this, the Russian Far East viceroy, Admiral Alexeiev, confidently told the czar that the Japanese were bluffing. Two days later Togo's warships attacked Port Arthur.

The Fortress of Port Arthur

When Admiral Togo's ships delivered the opening blows of the Russo-Japanese War on the night of February 8, 1904, Russian engineers and soldiers had been fortifying Port Arthur and its immediate vicinity for six years. An excellent natural harbor, the port was protected from direct access to the sea by a narrow channel only 400 yards wide and over 1,000 yards long. Togo's numerous failures over the next several weeks to plug this channel meant that the Russian warships sheltering there could continue to threaten the Japanese sea lines of communications between the home island and mainland Asia. Additionally, the Russians could make a dash for Vladivostok, linking up there with other ships from the Russian Pacific Fleet in the Far East and presenting Japanese naval forces with the threat of combined action. Overarching these legitimate military reasons for capturing Port Arthur was the burning desire by Japanese commanders to erase the humiliation of the forced relinquishment of the port after they captured it from the Chinese in 1894. A full-garrisoned, well-defended Port Arthur was a direct challenge to Japanese interests in the entire region, as well as a dangerous threat to Japan's successful conduct of the present war. It had to be reduced, captured, and returned to Japanese control.

Port Arthur lay in a natural bowl at the far end of the Liaotung Peninsula, surrounded by a ring of bare hills that jutted 300 to 600 feet above sea level. To protect its seafront, which extended for five miles along the inside of the sheltered harbor, the Russians built twenty-two batteries of 150mm–280mm guns, siting most of these at the 300-foot level. Located on a cliff near the outer entrance to the harbor was an electric power station that ran four searchlight batteries for night illumination.

A system of interlocking defensive works several miles in circumference were constructed in the hills surrounding the port. The most important of these were Fort Chi-kuan-shan to the northeast, Fort Erh-lung-shan and Fort Sung-su-shan on the north, and the dominating and most important position, 203-Meter Hill on the northwest approaches. Farther out, about twelve miles from Port Arthur, an eighteen-mile-long defensive line ran across the entire neck of the peninsula, including strongpoints at Ta-ku-shan and Sia-gu-shan facing Dalny. Between this outer line and the close-in defenses of the inner ring of forts was an intermediate line, lying about six miles from the port.

The strongest of these fortifications were permanent structures capable of withstanding hits from heavy artillery up to 280mm and incorporating extensive and elaborate outerworks. Russian defenders employed such innovations as electrically charged barbed wire and fences, searchlights and star clusters to illuminate night attacks, and early trench mortar devices. Numerous redoubts, trenches, bomb-proof shelters, and other fortified positions made the entire complex a formidable one to carry by infantry assault. The Russian defenses bristled with about 600 medium- and small-caliber cannon.

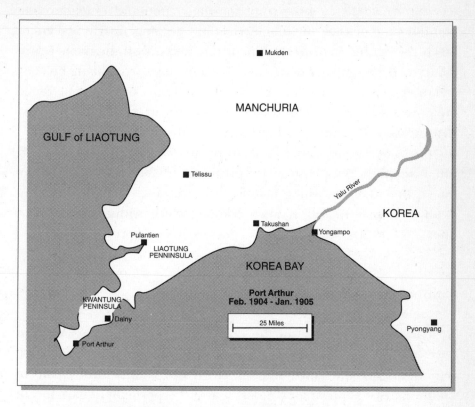

Port Arthur, February 1904–January 1905

Although the defenses of Port Arthur appeared strong to an attacking army, the sustenance of its many thousand defenders depended upon either the single rail line coming nearly 500 miles down the peninsula from Harbin (where it spurs off the main Trans-Siberian Railway), or on waterborne transport brought in bulk by freighter or in small bundles by Chinese junks or sampans. Since Japanese naval vessels already controlled the waters surrounding Port Arthur, once Japanese ground forces cut the rail line from Harbin, the port's defenders were in serious trouble in regard to rations and other supplies. As the siege wore on, the defenders would be reduced to a diet consisting mainly of horsemeat, and the resulting sicknesses, mainly scurvy, were commonplace within the Russian lines.

Combatants at Port Arthur

To conduct the defense of the Port Arthur area the Russians had fewer than 40,000 soldiers and sailors. This represented about 24,000 infantrymen of the Third Siberian Army Corps under command of Lieutenant General Anatoli Stoessel and the permanent garrison of Port Arthur, commanded by Lieutenant General Smirnov. The remaining force was made up of sailors from the ships anchored in the harbor. Since Smirnov was responsible for the defense of the Port Arthur garrison, while Stoessel was in command of the overall fortified zone, the two men were required to work in close harmony or risk serious command and control problems. Unfortunately, they despised each other, and their frequent conflicts interfered with the coordinated defense of the area and sapped the morale of the defending troops. Some subordinate commanders, such as the popular General Kondratenko, emerged as true heroes of the fighting, but Stoessel was court-martialed and sentenced to death.

The Russians' opponent at Port Arthur was General Count Nogi Marosuke, a tenacious fighter and cold-blooded commander who had few qualms about sending his brave men in one frontal assault after another against the stout Russian defenses. Nogi's besieging force eventually reached about 80,000 troops, but was considerably smaller than that when the battle began. Commander of the Japanese Third Army, Nogi had two of his own army's divisions plus a third division from the Japanese Second Army. Later a fourth division was added to Nogi's force as well as a significant number of artillery pieces (including the giant Krupp eleven-inch howitzers) to give him the manpower and firepower he required to reduce and capture the fortress. Initially attempting to storm the sturdy Russian defenses with bayonet attacks supported by only about seventy guns, Nogi was forced to gather reinforcements and then engage in more systematic efforts—true siege warfare—in order to prevail. Nevertheless, he required over six months of brutal fighting to do so.

Opening Moves

On April 13, 1904, another naval action took place in the waters surrounding Port Arthur, which made it possible for the Japanese to initiate the land actions that led directly to the siege of the city. Russian Admiral Stefan Makarov, popularly known as the "Cossack Admiral," gathered the elements of the bottled-up fleet and attempted to break the Japanese admiral's stranglehold on the port and bring Russian naval power to bear on Japanese lines of communication. The sortie ended in disaster when the Russian admiral's flagship, the battleship *Petropavlovsk*, struck a mine shortly after clearing the harbor and sank with the loss of 600 crewmen, including Makarov himself. With the popular and capable leader dead, the Russian ships retreated once more into the safety of Port Arthur, refusing to venture forth again until the heavy guns of the Japanese land forces closing on Port Arthur threatened to sink them.

With the Russian fleet once again securely bottled up in Port Arthur, the Japanese were free to begin the land campaign on the Liaotung Peninsula to isolate, then surround and capture Port Arthur. Earlier in April, Japanese troops had come ashore at Chemulpo in Korea and, after advancing overland to the Korea–Manchuria border, won the battle of the Yalu River against a smaller Russian force.

At about the same time—early May 1904—the Japanese landed five divisions on the Liaotung Peninsula north of Port Arthur and moved to cut the harbor's rail link with Manchuria by capturing the important heights around Nanshan. This hill formed the key to the Russian defenses on the narrow neck of land separating the smaller Kwantung Peninsula (at whose southern end lies Port Arthur) from the larger Liaotung Peninsula, which connects the smaller peninsula to Manchuria proper. Stoessel's troops at Nanshan, commanded by General Fock, an irritable shouter who possessed no great skill as a tactical battlefield commander, were eventually forced to withdraw in the face of continuing Japanese attacks against their rather poorly sited guns and entrenchments. On May 26, the Japanese captured the hill at the cost of about 4,500 casualties, cutting off the Port Arthur defenders to the south from any assistance from the main Russian forces in Manchuria (commanded by General Kuropatkin).

By the first week of June, Nogi's forces were in position to begin operations against the Port Arthur fortified area. Unless Kuropatkin could break through the Japanese lines with a relieving force from Manchuria or until the Russian Baltic Fleet arrived and opened the sea lines of communication with the port, the Russian defenders were completely on their own.

On July 26, the Japanese attacked the outermost Russian defensive positions (the so-called Green Hills lie twelve to eighteen miles north of Port Arthur) and over the next five days lost about 4,000 men in massed charges. Russian resistance on the outer line, and the intermediate line just behind it, was not aggressively pursued, and Russian commanders showed themselves quick to withdraw their troops into the safety of the main defenses of the port in the face of the determined Japanese attacks. However, the relatively large number of Japanese casualties suffered in capturing these haphazardly prepared, and indifferently defended, positions should have sent a message to Nogi. Apparently it did not, for in his assault on Port Arthur's main line of defenses, the Japanese commander used the same reckless methods.

Kinchou
Nanshan Hill
May 26
Nangalin
KWANTUNG PENINSULA
Dalny
June 27 - July 28
June 28-30
Wolf's Hills Line
June 1-26
Green Hills Line
Port Arthur
July 30
Aug 8
July 30
Port Arthur
May - Aug. 1904
10 Miles

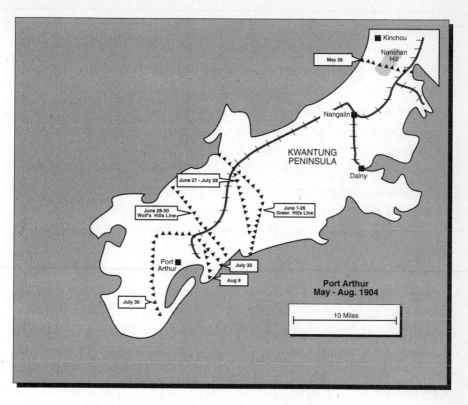

Port Arthur, May–August, 1904

The Siege Begins—Frontal Assault

On August 7, 1904, the first of tens of thousands of Japanese shells began falling on the buildings, houses, and people in the town of Port Arthur, and continued to fall until the garrison finally capitulated the following January. In the hills northeast of the town, Japanese forces launched the first assault against the main defensive line and its immediate outlying positions that evening when they stormed up the slopes of Big Orphan and Little Orphan hills. Initially stopped by Russian shellfire from the hills and some supporting naval vessels, the Japanese finally succeeded in capturing the positions the following day, losing 1,280 troops.

The fortifications facing the Japanese attackers was not as strong as they could (or should) have been. Despite the fact that the Chinese had constructed numerous fortifications in the surrounding hills before the Russians took over the port in 1898 and began their own efforts to strengthen the defenses, the defensive lines were still incomplete when the war broke out. Most of the Russian guns were medium- or small-caliber fieldpieces, and only a few of the larger, six-inch guns were available. Most batteries were situated on the very tops of hills, many without overhead protection, leaving them vulnerable to Japanese counterfire.

The most competent of the Russian subordinate commanders, General Kondratenko, had been working tirelessly to dig more trenches, construct more substantial bunkers, and lay wire entanglements in front of the approaches to the principal positions. He was hampered, however, by lack of sufficient barrier materials (especially barbed wire) and the short time he had before the Japanese assault. To make up for this lack, he employed a number of ingenious weapons and makeshift devices such as electronically detonated land mines, explosive flame weapons, staked pits, and booby traps. These expedients were somewhat crude, but they proved surprisingly effective against Nogi's next major effort—a suicidal frontal assault.

Worried that the Russian positions must be quickly overrun before reinforcements from the west could be rushed in to strengthen the czar's forces, and probably influenced by the fact that as a regimental commander he had led a daring frontal assault that wrested the port from the Chinese with only a dozen casualties in 1894, Nogi was determined to throw his forces at the Russian defenses in a massed frontal attack. His objective was to seize the Wantai Heights ("Watcher's Terrace") at the center of the northeast sector of the Russian lines. From here, Nogi could then push his men on to capture the commanding forts of Erh-lung-shan and Sung-su-shan, which would serve as the jumping-off points for an attack on the town proper. Before proceeding, Nogi sent a surrender demand to the Port Arthur garrison on August 17, promising safe conduct for noncombatants. Stoessel curtly refused.

At dawn on August 19, Nogi's troops began the general attack after a preliminary bombardment of the Russian line. During the next five days, their suicidal frontal assaults failed to breach the Russian lines to any significant degree, and succeeded principally in littering the hillsides with heaps of dead Japanese soldiers. The Russian defenders, who possessed ten times the number of machine guns as the attacking Japanese, put these weapons to good use, mowing down the attackers. The Japanese night attacks were disrupted by the Russian searchlights and illuminating flares, blinding the assaulting troops in a harsh glare and pinpointing their locations for the machine guns and artillery observers.

After a final, gallant effort on the night of August 23–24 to capture the commanding heights on Wantai, Nogi called off the attacks for the time being. His soldiers had captured two outlying forts during five days and nights of terrible combat, and those positions remained under constant Russian shellfire (the forts' new Japanese occupants suffered 100 casualties each day). This initial major effort to storm Port Arthur had cost Nogi about 18,000 casualties. Russian losses were about 3,000. Nogi needed to reconsider his tactics.

The Siege Continues—The September Attacks

On September 19, Nogi resumed his concerted efforts to capture the Russian defensive positions with simultaneous attacks upon the Waterworks Redoubt to the north of the main line and the dominating heights of 203-Meter Hill on the northwest side of the town. Since the difficult August fighting had demonstrated the inappropriateness of purely frontal assaults in storming well-defended positions, the Japanese resorted to sapping and mining techniques more properly suited to siege warfare. The attack on the Waterworks Redoubt was preceded by the laborious digging of 650 yards of covered trenches and tunnels, work not considered temperamentally suited to the "Banzai!" attack mentality of the Japanese soldier. However, the subsequent attack succeeded in capturing the redoubt, at the cost of 500 Japanese casualties.

203-Meter Hill proved a tougher nut to crack. Japanese attacks against it cost them 2,500 casualties, but failed to win them possession. A multiaxis attack up the hill on September 20 was repulsed with great loss to the attackers, but Nogi's men succeeded in gaining a tiny toehold on the southwest side. They staunchly maintained possession of a Russian bombproof under constant fire from the Russians occupying the remainder of the hilltop. On September 22, General Smirnov, exercising personal command of this most critical sector, managed to locate the Japanese reserve forces awaiting word to continue the assault and reinforce the detachment in the bombproof. Secretly moving fieldpieces to within point-blank range, Smirnov's gunners opened up on the unsuspecting Japanese and annihilated them. This success was followed up later that night when Russian sappers managed to toss handmade mines into the bombproof, killing most of the Japanese inside and scattering the survivors. Nogi was forced to give up attempts to capture 203-Meter Hill for now. Despite this failure, the Japanese had, nonetheless, succeeded in wresting from the Russians several more important positions, including the Waterworks Redoubt, the Temple Redoubt, and Namako-yama Hill.

Now that the Russian ships lying at anchor in Port Arthur Harbor were in range of Nogi's artillery, the Japanese gunners began lobbing long-range fire at the still-unobserved targets. Until they could take possession of 203-Meter Hill, which would give them unobstructed observation of the harbor, however, the Japanese could fire only harassing rounds.

Time Runs Out—The Big Guns Arrive

During the last few days of September and the first weeks of October 1904, the Japanese landed and began moving into position the giant Krupp eleven-inch howitzers. Transporting these monsters to their firing positions and preparing them for bombardment required the expenditure of considerable effort. Each of the 500-pound shells had to be towed to the giant guns' firing positions, and tiny rails were constructed from the ammunition dumps to the guns to facilitate this. Emplaced in well-concealed positions, the howitzers soon began lobbing their deadly projectiles (nicknamed "express trains" by the troops after the roaring whoosh of the rounds' flight) against the Russian lines. No fortification the Russians had yet built could withstand the pounding of such a weapon, at least not indefinitely. The reinforced-concrete-and-steel construction of the fort of Chi-kuan-shan was subjected to 100 rounds on October 1, and although it initially withstood the pounding, one of the shells finally burst through, killing the defenders. Even when the massive projectiles failed to explode on impact, the momentum of the huge piece of metal was often sufficient to smash the target. Nogi at last had the means to take 203-Meter Hill.

The Japanese divisions surrounding Port Arthur now began sapping and mining in an effort to move the jumping-off points of the assault troops to within a reasonable distance of the intended objective. The previous efforts, characterized by thousands of unprotected troops milling about in groups through an extended kill zone, had forced Nogi to adjust his tactics before he literally ran out of troops. With his sappers inching ever closer to the Russian positions and the new eleven-inch guns ready to smash the enemy fortifications to bits, the Japanese commander was confident that the capture of Port Arthur was within his grasp.

Yet Nogi remained reluctant to abandon the frontal assault altogether. He ordered another massive attempt to break into the Russian lines from the north and northeast, targeting the forts of Chi-kuan-shan and Erh-lung-shan. The attacks began on October 24 and continued for most of a week, ending by the close of day on October 31. Despite the approaching trenches that, before this attack, Nogi's sappers had dug to within a few hundred yards of the Russian lines (at Chi-kuan-shan battery, the troops only had to cross forty yards of open ground), the Japanese lost about 4,000 more casualties. They were only partially successful in seizing the Russian positions.

Before giving up the frontal assault tactic, Nogi subjected his troops to one more brutal ordeal. Launching a brigade-sized attack against the northeastern sector of the Russian lines on the night of November 26–27, Nogi lost 4,000 more men and failed again. At last, under mounting criticism from his immediate superiors and lambastings in the popular press in Japan, he relinquished the frontal assault and returned his attention to the key to the Russian defense: 203-Meter Hill.

End of the Battle—203-Meter Hill Falls

The assault that finally gave Nogi victory at Port Arthur began with a barrage on November 27, 1904, conducted by four of the eleven-inch howitzers and hundreds of field guns surrounding three sides of the hill. After three days of intense artillery shelling alternating with infantry assaults, the hill remained in Russian hands. On November 30, the infantry attacks were temporarily suspended while the big guns pulverized the Russian trenches into unrecognizable scars on the rocky hillside. Over 4,000 of the 500-pound projectiles

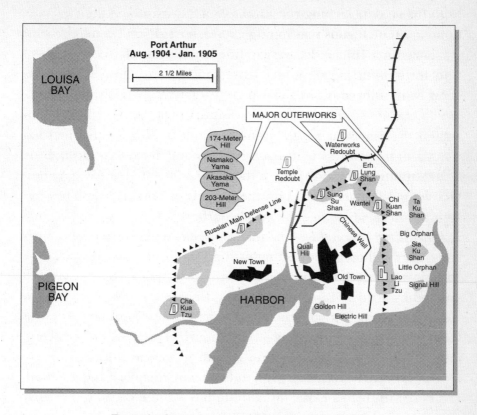

Port Arthur, August 1904–January 1905

were used to blast the Russian trench lines into oblivion.

At 2:30 P.M. on November 30, the Japanese resumed their infantry attacks, simultaneously assaulting 203-Meter Hill and its neighboring Akasaka-yama Hill. For the next five days the battle seesawed back and forth, with Japanese attackers gaining footholds on the hills, then being shoved off by Russian counterattacks. Finally, on December 5, Japanese units reached the summit of 203-Meter Hill and eliminated the few remaining Russian defenders. Nogi's units had lost 14,000 more soldiers in taking the hill, and the Russians had lost 5,000 troops attempting to stop them. By 5:00 P.M. that day, Japanese troops stood unchallenged on the heights of Port Arthur. They had an unobstructed view of the entire harbor.

On the very next day, Japanese observers sited on the summit of 203-Meter Hill began directing artillery fire onto the Russian ships in Port Arthur Harbor. Within days, the principal Russian ships were blasted by artillery fire and abandoned by their crews (save the battleship *Sevastopol*, which was towed out to sea by her crew and scuttled). Well before the Russian Baltic Fleet arrived to challenge Togo's warships, the Port Arthur squadron was destroyed.

The capture of 203-Meter Hill did not immediately bring the battle for Port Arthur to a close, for, although it was the key to the Russian defenses, Russian troops still held other substantial fortifications and defended them stoutly. The forts of Erh-lung-shan and Chi-kuan-shan still resisted all Nogi's efforts, somehow holding up to the merciless battering of the eleven-inch rounds. But in mid-December Japanese miners succeeded in detonating two huge explosive charges under Chi-kuan-shan, which paved the way for the fort's capture. Similarly, on December 28, a mine destroyed Erh-lung-shan, after a bitter struggle, it, too, fell to Nogi's forces. Methodically, the Japanese troops attacked one Russian position after another, moving ever closer to the town itself. On December 31, the last remaining major Russian fort, Sung-su-shan, was captured after its primary defenses succumbed to another Japanese mine. The following day saw the capture of the heights of Wantai. Nevertheless, most Russians remaining in Port Arthur were determined to hold out for as long as possible, and Nogi fully expected that the completion of his campaign, although now assured, would require the expenditure of many more Japanese lives. But to the surprise of both Russians and Japanese, Stoessel sent an emissary to Nogi on New Year's Day to offer surrender.

Stoessel's officers and soldiers were alarmed and angry that after all they had suffered, their commander had surrendered without fighting to the bitter end. Despite the widespread incidence of scurvy, dysentery, and typhoid, the garrison contained ample supplies of ammunition and food, although rationed and, as we said, consisting mostly of horsemeat, was sufficient for several more weeks. Although the defenders had suffered 31,000 casualties, over 20,000 reasonably able-bodied men remained. Even Nogi's troops were astonished that so many Russians who were apparently fit to continue fighting had agreed to surrender.

Stoessel's surrender became effective on January 2, 1905. Two weeks later, on January 14, 1905, Nogi assembled his forces for a memorial service to honor the nearly 100,000 Japanese soldiers who had fallen during the campaign. Sixty thousand had become casualties on the field of battle, the rest stricken by disease.

Aftermath

The fall of Port Arthur was only one in a series of disasters befalling the czar's forces in the Far East during this first major war of the twentieth century. While Nogi's troops were conducting the half-year-long siege, other Japanese ground forces were smashing Russian General Kuropatkin's troops farther north in Manchuria. In battle after battle, Japanese commanders beat their Russian opponents, although these victories were as costly to the winning side as they were to the losers'. Kuropatkin, fearing that the fall of Port Arthur would release Nogi's troops for operations against his own forces, initiated an offensive against his opponent, Field Marshal Oyama, on January 26. The subsequent battle of Sandepu was notable only for the ineptitude of the Russian commanders, who ordered their troops to withdraw when they might have carried the day. The end for Kuropatkin, and for Russian hopes to salvage a ground victory, came at the two-week battle of Mukden, fought from the end of February to the beginning of March 1905. The war's largest battle, Mukden involved over 300,000 troops on each side. The Japanese won, but allowed Kuropatkin and the bulk of his troops to escape a trap they had created around them. At any rate, events at sea soon proved decisive.

The battle of Tsushima Straits, in which Admiral Togo completely destroyed the Russian Baltic Fleet under the command of Admiral Rozhdestvenski, is one of the most decisive sea battles in the history of warfare, and ended any hope Czar Nicholas had of salvaging anything from the wreckage of his armed forces in the Far East. With his forces on land and sea destroyed or neutralized and with strong elements in revolt against his government, Nicholas sued for peace. The treaty ending the Russo-Japanese War was negotiated in Portsmouth, New Hampshire, by U.S. President Theodore Roosevelt, and was signed by the emissaries of the warring factions on September 5, 1905. Roosevelt was awarded a Nobel Peace Prize for his efforts.

By the end of the conflict, Japan was firmly established as a major Asian, and, subsequently, world power, while Russia was exposed as having significant political and military difficulties. German observers paid especially close attention to the military problems of the czar's forces, and adjusted their own war plans accordingly. In this way, Russia's poor showing in this war helped precipitate the one brewing for 1914.

Major General George G. Meade, Federal commander of the Army of the Potomac beginning in June 1863. His troops won the battle of Gettysburg for the Union (National Archives photo no. 111-B-16).

General Robert E. Lee, Confederate commander of the Army of Northern Virginia and loser at Gettysburg. Lee always accepted full blame for the Confederate loss (National Archives photo no. 111-B-1564).

Lieutenant General James Longstreet, Confederate corps commander at Gettysburg and Chickamauga. Although his troops failed to accomplish Lee's plan to envelop Meade's left flank on the second day's fighting at Gettysburg, one of his divisions made the battle-winning breakthrough at Chickamauga two months later (National Archives photo no. 111-B-2028).

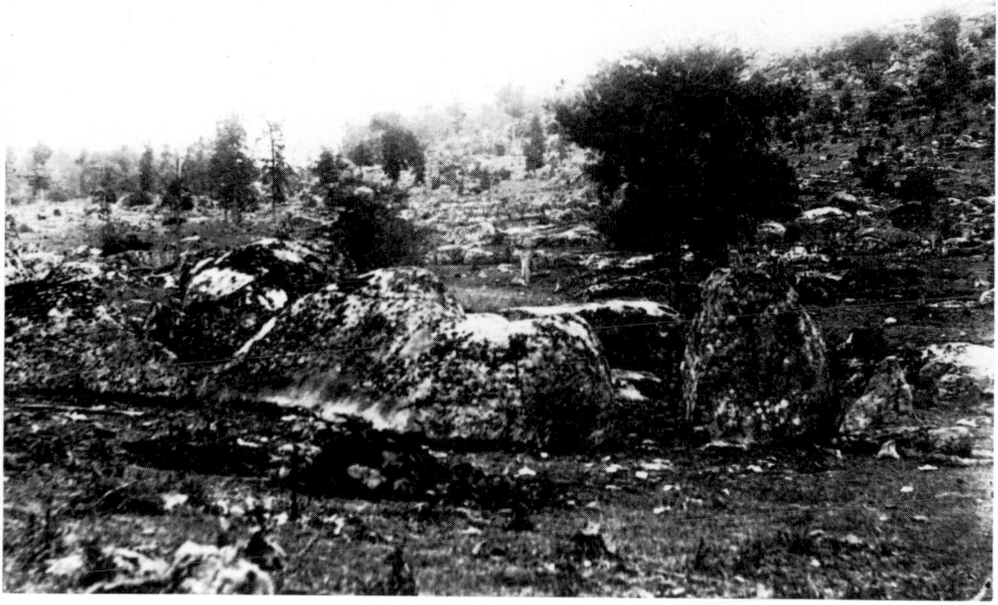

Little Round Top, Gettysburg battlefield. Key terrain on the Federal left flank, barely saved by the timely arrival of Union troops (National Archives photo no. 111-SC-114776).

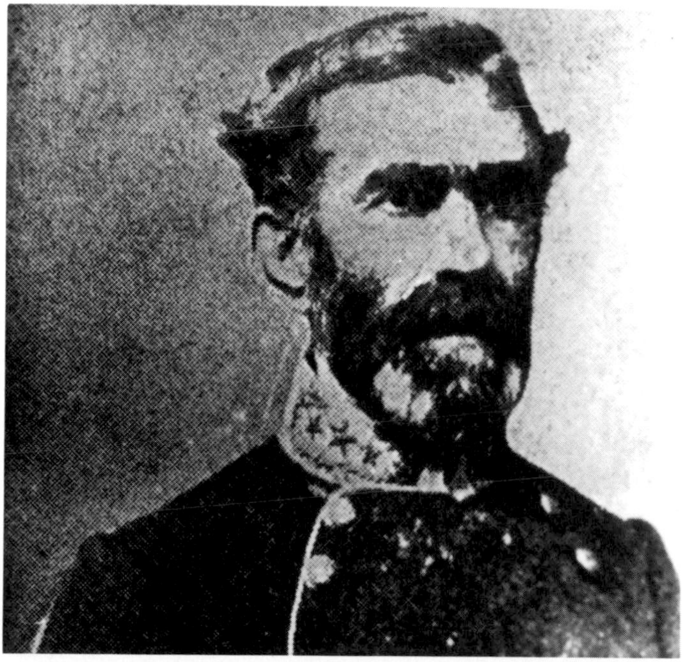

General Braxton Bragg, Confederate commander of the Army of Tennessee. Acerbic and unpopular, Bragg failed to follow up his victory at Chickamauga with a timely drive on Chattanooga, allowing Federal troops to retain the strategically located city that later served as a base for the 1864 Atlanta campaign (National Archives photo no. 111-BA-1927).

Major General William S. Rosecrans, Federal commander of the Army of the Cumberland, defeated at Chickamauga. Rosecrans accomplished some brilliant maneuvers during the weeks leading up to the battle of Chickamauga, but was literally swept from the battlefield as his routed troops fled the victorious Confederate advance (National Archives photo no. 111-B-2505).

Major General George H. Thomas, commander of the Federal XIV Corps at Chickamauga. The stand of Thomas's men on Snodgrass Hill prevented Rosecrans's army from being completely annihilated and earned Thomas the lasting nickname of the "Rock of Chickamauga" (National Archives photo no. 111-BA-2251).

Chickamauga battlefield. Typical of the terrain bordering West Chickamauga Creek, although much of the surrounding land began the battle as heavily wooded (National Archives photo no. 111-B-7040).

The "Iron Chancellor." Count Otto von Bismarck's dream was to create a united Germany under Prussian leadership. The Prussian victory at Sedan in the 1870 war ensured that his dream would be realized. His monarch, Kaiser Wilhelm, was crowned emperor of a united Germany in the palace of Versailles on January 18, 1871 (National Archives photo no. 111-B-4422).

Japanese infantry marching through a Chinese field. Taken in 1900, this photograph of Japanese troops shows them marching as allies of czarist Russian soldiers in the China Relief Expedition during the Boxer Rebellion. In four years Japanese and Russian troops would face each other at Port Arthur and Manchuria (National Archives photo no. 111-SC-80771 C).

Field Marshal Paul von Beneckendorf und von Hindenburg came out of retirement to take command of the German Eighth Army in East Prussia and win the battle of Tannenberg (National Archives photo no. 111-SC-98433).

General Erich Ludendorf, chief of staff to Hindenburg at Tannenberg. The Hindenburg-Ludendorf team, created at Tannenberg, became the most famous of the Great War, and they ended that conflict leading Germany's armies (National Archives photo no. 111-SC-98435).

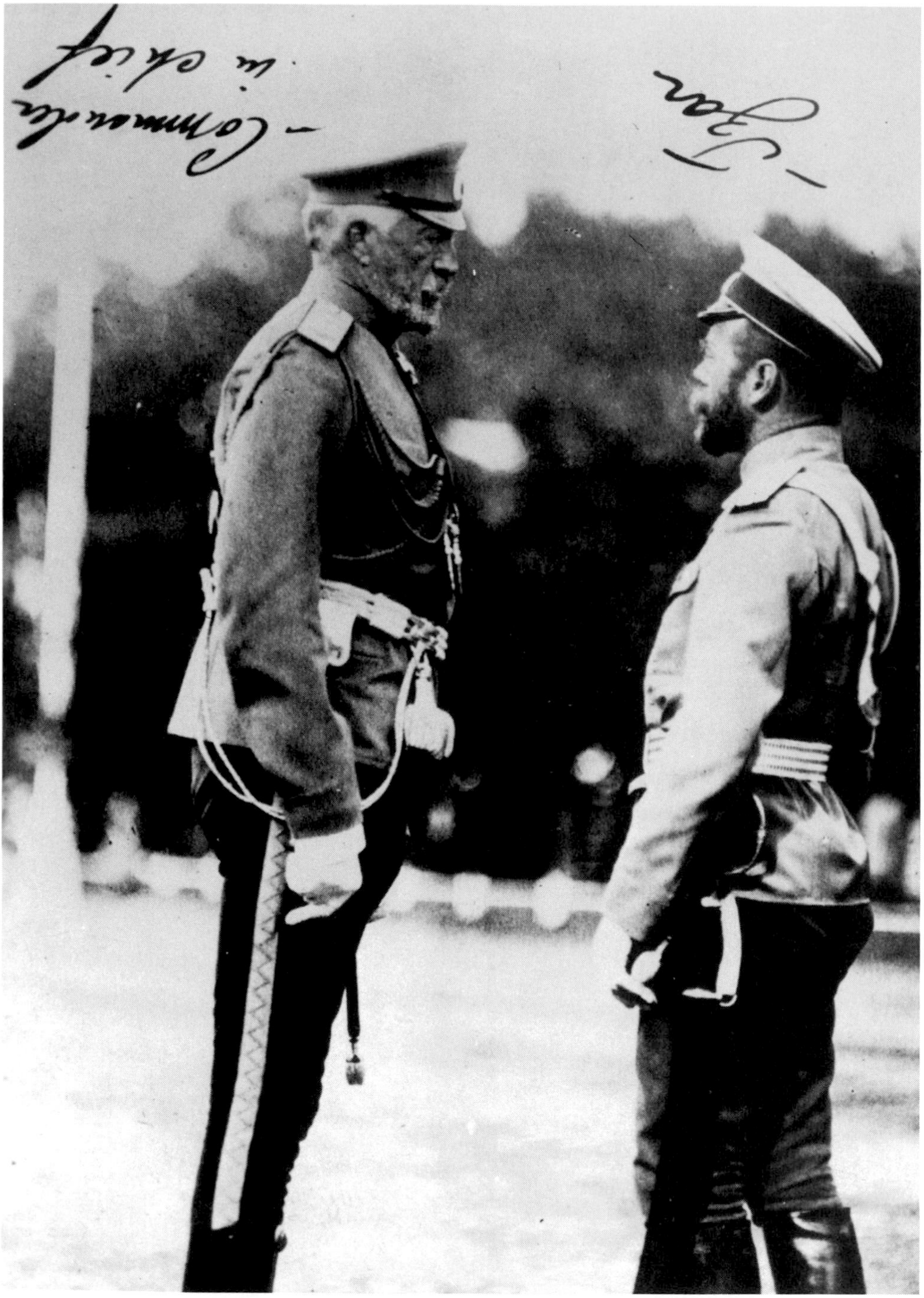

Czar Nicholas II of Russia and his armies' commander in chief, his cousin Grand Duke Nicholas. The manpower available to the czar and his field commander was awesome, but the inefficiencies and defects in the Russian military system were too formidable for their sturdy peasant soldiers to overcome (National Archives photo no. 111-SC-89249).

General Aleksandr Samsonov, commander of the Russian Second Army at Tannenberg. Distraught over the tremendous disaster that overcame his troops, Samsonov killed himself on the eve of the battle's final day (National Archives photo no. 111-SC-89255).

German infantry, August 1914. Troops such as these won Tannenberg for the Hindenburg-Ludendorf team (National Archives photo no. WC 637).

General Joseph Joffre, French commander in chief during the 1916 battle of Verdun. Joffre's stubborn insistence on holding the ancient fortress city, regardless of casualties, was exactly the attitude his German opposite number was counting on to turn Verdun into a giant "mincing machine" (National Archives photo no. 111-SC-98407).

General Henri-Philippe Pétain. Sent to take command of the French defenses at Verdun during the darkest hours, Pétain lived up to his emotional battle cry, *"Ils ne passeront pas! (They will not pass!)"* (National Archives photo no. 111-SC-98408).

Field Marshal Erich von Falkenhayn, chosen to succeed the unfortunate younger Moltke as chief of the German General Staff after Moltke's failures in the opening battles of 1914. Falkenhayn decided to "bleed the French Army white" at Verdun (National Archives photo no. 111-SC-98434).

French *poilu* of 1914-18. French commanders expended a generation of these men on the Western Front during four years of brutal war (National Archives photo no. WC 646).

Soldiers of a French infantry company, 1916-18. Steel helmets and horizon blue greatcoats replaced the wool kepis and *pantalons rouge* (red trousers) of 1914-15 (National Archives photo no. WC 619).

German gun crew wearing gas masks prepares a heavy-artillery piece (5.9-inch naval gun) for firing. Over 1,200 artillery pieces of all sizes fired the opening barrage at Verdun on February 21, 1916. By the battle's end the following December, 37 million artillery rounds had been expended (National Archives photo no. 111-SC-97172).

German Krupp heavy gun being prepared for action on the Verdun front. A giant 340mm heavy-artillery piece mounted on a railcar is placed into position under camouflage netting prior to firing. Such "heavies" were able to blast holes through even the thickest walls and protective earthworks of the Verdun forts (National Archives photo no. 111-SC-97220).

German infantry, 1916-18. Wearing gas masks and occupying a hastily dug trench, these soldiers are much like their comrades who died at Verdun by the hundreds of thousands (National Archives photo no. 111-SC-97207).

Village of Vaux, France, near Verdun, after the battles of 1916 and 1918. Nearby Fort Vaux held out for a week against intense German bombardment and ceaseless attacks before finally succumbing to the giant German guns (National Archives photo no. WC 704).

General John J. Pershing, commander of the American Expeditionary Force in France, 1917-18, and overall U.S. commander for the Meuse-Argonne campaign at GHQ, Chaumont, France. Pershing's insistence on maintaining U.S. forces under American command frustrated his French and British allies, but permitted the U.S. Army to begin its evolution into a modern, world-class fighting force (National Archives photo no. 111-SC-26646).

General Pershing pins an American Distinguished Service Medal on the tunic of French General Pétain while a French honor guard presents arms, November 13, 1918 (National Archives photo no. 111-SC-31496).

Kaiser Wilhelm II studies aerial photographs of the Western Front as Hindenburg and Ludendorf look on. By this point in the war (summer-fall 1918), Germany's chances to win had vanished. The Meuse-Argonne campaign, spearheaded by the tens of thousands of fresh American troops, marked the beginning of the end (National Archives photo no. 111-SC-90716).

CHAPTER FOUR

The First World War

• 1914–1918 •

TANNENBERG, VERDUN, MEUSE-ARGONNE

Victory in the East, Abattoir, Defeat in the West

It was supposed to be the "war to end all wars," but of course it was not. What it truly became, however, was a horror of gigantic proportions theretofore not witnessed. To the generation that fought in it, it was known simply as the "Great War," the first modern global conflict, involving all but a few of the world's major nations, and conducted on a global battlefield. Born of the competing European nations' dreams of empire and rooted in the entangling alliances and secret treaties of that era, this terrible conflict turned large portions of Europe into charnel houses and created surreal landscapes of death and destruction. At least 10 million human beings died in the war and 20 million were wounded and/or maimed. Millions more became casualties of the violence, starvation, disease, and disruption that occurred in its wake. In the end, the war changed everything and it changed nothing, for while it destroyed forever the imperial monarchies that had so enthusiastically entered it, it failed to alter the nationalism, militarism, greed, mistrust, and imperialism that would plunge the world into another paroxysm of violence only two decades later, validating Maréchal Foch's prediction that the treaty ending the Great War promised little more than a twenty-year armistice.

The war was fought in the air, on sea, and on land, and the "greatness" of the battles was often a simple reflection of the unprecedented size of their casualty lists. Three of its great land battles, however, represent significant phases of the conflict—its hopeful beginning in a stunning German triumph at Tannenberg on the Eastern Front; its interminable stalemate in the abattoir that was the Western Front and Verdun; and its bitter end in a massive advance by rejuvenated Allied forces in the Meuse-Argonne.

Near Willenberg, East Prussia, Dusk on August 29, 1914: *On a warm summer evening during the final stages of the battle of Tannenberg, General Aleksandr Samsonov, commander of the quarter-million-man Second Imperial Russian Army, vanguard of the much-feared "Russian Steamroller," rode silently and alone through a deathly-still forest a few miles outside the remote German town of Willenberg. As he nudged his horse deeper into the dense woods, Samsonov contemplated the dramatic swing of events over the past several days.*

Only nine days earlier, his bitter rival within the czarist forces, General Pavel Rennenkampf, had achieved a modest victory when his First Imperial Russian Army defeated the Eighth German Army in the battle of Gumbinnen. Two days after Rennenkampf's success, Samsonov had advanced confidently against what he assumed to be a defeated and retreating German army, intending to occupy East Prussia for the czar and win an early and, presumedly, bloodless campaign. But on August 26, things went tragically wrong for the Russian forces. Instead of sweeping aside the remnants of German resistance and occupying all of East Prussia, Samsonov's Second Army was trapped and destroyed by a resurgent German force in a modern reenactment of Hannibal's famous double envelopment at Cannae. Rennenkampf, Samsonov's professional enemy, took no action to aid the Second Army, and 122,000 Russians entered German captivity—at least 30,000 more were killed.

Samsonov, reflecting gloomily on his responsibility for this tragedy, dismounted and walked a few more steps across the blanket of pine needles and soft, sandy soil of the forest. Halting in the now darkening woods, the Russian general drew his service revolver, thumbed back the hammer, then slowly turned the muzzle on himself. The heavy silence of the East Prussian woods was broken by the sharp crack of his pistol. Some distance away, his staff, hearing the shot and realizing its significance, did not trouble to search for or recover the general's body.

In 1916, eighteen months after their remarkable triumph at Tannenberg, the German High Command launched a prolonged offensive on the Western Front at Verdun, where they hoped to decimate the French army and tip the balance of forces in the west in Germany's favor. At the battle's end the following December, a million men— French and German—had become casualties in the war's longest battle, and both armies, not just France's, had been decimated.

Verdun, France, Dawn of February 21, 1916: Modern artillery primarily owes its reputation as "the greatest killer on the battlefield" to the engagements of World War I. While the overwhelming majority of battle deaths and wounds in the American Civil War and other conflicts of the preceding fifty years were caused by small-arms fire, most of the killing of World War I was accomplished by artillery. Verdun would prove to be no exception to this general rule. To open the ten-month slaughter, the Germans had secretly massed 1,220 artillery pieces, giant mortars, and mine throwers along their side of the Verdun sector of the front, stockpiling 2,500,000 high-explosive shells for a saturation bombardment of the French positions. These German guns included huge monsters, such as the 420mm "Big Bertha" Krupp mortars, which had been used to flatten the Belgian forts at the beginning of the war, as well as 380mm Krupp naval cannon, which fired a projectile nearly as big as a man. Other "heavies," hundreds of fieldpieces of smaller caliber, and mine throwers capable of lofting powerful 100-pound, trench-leveling explosives, silently awaited the signal to open the most intense barrage yet experienced in this, or any other, war.

Suddenly, as dawn broke on the first clear day since February 12, the long-awaited command, "Feuer!" was passed over field telephones all along the German front lines. Within minutes hundreds of tons of iron and steel thundered down on the French positions. Smashing everything underneath it to pulp, the German barrage continued unabated for nine hours. Though only the first of many such barrages fired by both sides during the ten-month struggle for Verdun, this cannonading began the process of turning the once beautiful countryside into a lunar landscape. Blasting, smashing, even disintegrating its targets, the relentless rain of shells turned carefully constructed fighting positions into shapeless mounds of earth, steel, and concrete dust, and buried alive entire trenchfuls of men.

By December 18, 1916, the opponents at Verdun had fired 37 million artillery and mortar shells. The ossuary at Douaumont, erected a few years after the battle's end, contains bits and pieces of skeletons and bone fragments collected from the Verdun battlefield, representing the remains of at least 150,000 human beings. These fragments are, of course, the principal product of those 37 million rounds.

In September 1918, nearly two years after the horrendous slaughter at Verdun, the Great War was finally winding down. Rejuvenated by the influx of large numbers of fresh, eager American troops onto the battlefields of the Western Front, the Allies launched the Meuse-Argonne offensive, the final great battle of the war.

Near Brieulles, France, September 29, 1918: *The Meuse-Argonne offensive was three days old as Private Richard L. Longren and three of his comrades from F Company, 131st Infantry Regiment of the U.S. 33rd Infantry Division, lay in a shell hole somewhere in the middle of this particular section of "No-Man's-Land." The men had been there since early morning of the day before when they had crawled into the empty crater to gain some cover from the increasingly heavy rain of German artillery shells and machine-gun fire directed at them from positions on the higher ground just across the Meuse River on their right flank. Unfortunately for Longren and his companions, their enthusiastic advance against the German positions leading up to the main defenses of the so-called Hindenburg Line had proven somewhat too successful for their own good. Fearing that these mostly isolated forward positions were too exposed to German counterattacks, General John J. Pershing, still exercising direct command of the American First Army, ordered the most exposed of the positions given up and the units pulled back to a more defensible line prior to renewing the general offensive on October 4.*

Longren and his three company mates, however, had remained trapped in their shell hole in No-Man's-Land, unable to evade the German fire and work their way back to their own lines. As the hours wore on, it became obvious that something would have to be done. Out of water and cut off from the rest of their company, the men decided that one of them would have to attempt the dangerous journey back to friendly lines. Finally, Longren spoke up. "I'm the only single guy of the four of us, and you all have wives and families to go back to. It's only right that I try to make it back and get help." The others reluctantly agreed, wished him luck, and shook his hand. Easing himself out over the lip of the crater, Longren began crawling on his stomach across the broken ground toward the 33rd Division's main positions. Dragging himself over the rough, shell-pounded terrain, he had moved only a few dozen yards from the crater when he heard the screaming sound of an "incoming" German artillery shell that seemed to be hurtling directly toward his exposed position. Longren covered his ears, hugged the ground as closely as he could, and braced himself for the shell's fatal, bone-smashing impact.

The explosion of the large caliber projectile was deafening; its force sucked the air out of Longren's lungs, tossed him into the air, then slammed him back on the ground. As the smoke and dust cleared, he dimly realized that despite the proximity of the shell's impact, he had been spared its full force. Peering behind him, he gasped in horror: the deadly projectile had exploded in the middle of the crater he had so recently left. Longren's unselfish effort to save his buddies had ironically saved only himself, and his comrades had become just three of the 993 men of the 33rd Division who would die on the battlefield in France. Wearily and resignedly, Longren continued his long crawl back to the temporary safety of the American lines.

The First World War was filled with countless such ironies, and none of its belligerents were able to take much satisfaction when it finally concluded in November 1918—even the "winners" suffered horribly. France lost an entire generation in the mud and blood of the Western Front, and Great Britain suffered 1 million dead and another 2 million wounded and maimed. Even the United States, a late entry into the slaughter, suffered over 300,000 dead and wounded on the battlefield in only about five months of active fighting. The worldwide influenza pandemic of the final year of the war killed even more soldiers before they could get to the fighting front (nearly 30 million people died worldwide). The armistice of November 11, 1918, came none too soon.

By the summer of 1914, the principal players had arrayed themselves generally into two opposing camps: the Central Powers of Germany and Austria-Hungary, supported by Bulgaria and Turkey, on one side; and France, Russia, Great Britain, and Japan on the other. A miscalculation by any of the great powers would tip the whole teetering mass into the abyss of war. Europe had gone to war many times before; but this time, with massive national armies supplied with the latest wonders of technology, the scale of slaughter would be immense.

Weapons and Tactics

The artillery piece and the machine gun were the true masters of the World War I battlefield. The "state of the art" results of the previous fifty years' technological progress, these two weapons systems dominated the World War I battlefield—indeed, the failure of the belligerents to adapt their war-fighting doctrine to these technological innovations turned a war of several weeks or months into a bloody stalemate of several years.

Fifty years earlier, the American Civil War had clearly demonstrated the dominance of defense and the fact that massed attacks of successive lines of troops disintegrated in the face of intense rifle fire from troops occupying rifle pits or dug-in positions. The opposing trench lines of Petersburg, Virginia in 1864–65 were chilling presages of the No-Man's-Land trench lines of 1914–18. The speed with which Germany defeated France in the 1870 war, however, masked the advances in small arms and, especially, artillery, and the lessons of 1861–65 (if the European powers ever learned them at all) were forgotten. The Prussian victors and the French losers of 1870 drew similar "lessons" from that short war. They assumed that a mass of highly motivated, disciplined troops, led by competent and well-trained leaders, could overcome any obstacle, no matter how stoutly defended, with an enthusiastic and hard-pressed attack. No hail of bullets from an entrenched machine gun or storm of exploding steel from an artillery barrage could prevent a courageous and determined attacker from taking any position. Morale, discipline, and bravery, they were certain, were more powerful than modern bullets and bombs. Doomed to repeat the mistakes of the Union and Confederate commanders of the American Civil War, the European commanders of the Great War attempted to win victory on the twentieth-century battlefield using offensive doctrine more suited to the eighteenth.

The greatest killer on a battlefield choked with a wide variety of killers was modern artillery. During the American Civil War artillery was only a second-class killing tool, the overwhelming majority of casualties (90 percent) being caused by rifle fire. But the artillery of that earlier war was much closer in design, construction, and functioning to the artillery of Napoleon than it was to the lethal killing machines of World War I. Great technological advances had occurred in the fifty years separating the two wars which now placed artillery at the top of the hierarchy of instruments of death, replacing the once dominant rifle. These advances included smokeless powder, breech-loading, improved rifling, and a recoil system. These improvements led to the development of rapid firing, long-range, accurate weapons, which, when linked by another technological development—the telephone—could rain thousands of shells onto masses of troops from miles away. The shells themselves were much improved over their Civil War counterparts, modern high explosives with steel casings replacing the primitive black-powder, cast-iron cartridges of the earlier battlefield. Instead of being subjected to a bombardment of a relatively few, smallish shells that burst into only four or five large shards, the soldier of the Great War was subjected to a torrent of thousands of high-velocity, powerful explosive shells that burst into hundreds of steel fragments, saturating the area he occupied. Thousands of these guns, firing millions of shells, churned the battlefield into a hellish, nearly impassable morass.

The other master of the World War I battlefield was the machine gun—a rapid-firing, automatic weapon that could sweep aside masses of attacking troops as easily as a broom sweeps a kitchen floor. With cyclic rates of fire in the hundreds of rounds per minute, a single machine gun might hold up the advance of huge bodies of troops if well sited in an entrenched position. The result of technological advances in small-arms weapons and, especially, smokeless-powder, jacketed, cartridge ammunition, the machine gun was, in the words of Liddell Hart, "concentrated essence of infantry." Although the German, like the French and British, army initially allocated only two machine guns to each of its line infantry battalions, it possessed more of the automatic weapons (as it possessed more artillery weapons) in the supporting battalions of corps troops and cavalry regiments. By the end of the war, machine-gun companies would be standard formations in each army's order of battle. France, for example, which began the war with only 2,500 machine guns (to Germany's initial 4,500), manufactured and fielded 315,000 automatic weapons by the war's end.

Linking these weapons of war were other technological advances that served to increase the killing efficiency of the battlefield. The telephone (and, later, rudimentary radios) provided an unprecedented means of exercising command over the new weapons systems, allowing World War I commanders to extend the range and scope of their control while maximizing the effect of modern staff systems. Railroads, motor transport, and the internal-combustion engine permitted the belligerents to vastly expand the scope of the battlefield and deploy, or redeploy, huge bodies of troops and war equipment over continental distances. Although the horse remained the principal mover for artillery and supply wagons, it was increasingly displaced by machines (whose appetite for gasoline actually required less use of transportation resources than the fodder for the horses they replaced).

The war-fighting doctrine employed by the belligerents was sadly out of synch with the advances in weapons technology. At the war's beginning, all of the warring powers assumed to one degree or another that the offensive was the strongest form of warfare, and that the new weapons had only served to strengthen the power of the attacker. It would be, they assumed, a violent but short war, and victory would go to the side executing its offensive plan with the greatest spirit, energy, and courage. But when the initial battles failed to produce a quick victory, the soldiers reverted to trenches, barbed wire, and massive fortifications. Massed infantry assaults against each other's trenchworks, preceded by tremendous artillery barrages, failed to produce the final breakthrough that would end the stalemate of the trenches and turn the war into a battle of maneuver (although British commanders kept massed horse cavalry divisions at the ready for most of the war waiting to exploit this).

The technological developments of poison gas and the tank, both utilized in conjunction with the orthodox fighting doctrine of the first three and a half years of the war, also failed to produce the breakthrough for which both sides so ardently wished. The ruptures in the opposing trench line and the subsequent small gains these weapons did produce were wasted by the small scope of the undertakings, the lack of strategic vision by the commanders using them, and their abysmal failure to follow up the breakthroughs with adequate reserves. The only truly significant advance in doctrine and tactics to appear during the war that could have turned the tide of battle in favor of one of the belligerents was launched by Germany on the Western Front in March 1918—too late to be decisive. Referred to as "Hutier Tactics," after German General Oscar von Hutier, who first utilized them in his offensive at Riga on the Eastern Front in 1917 (they were also used against the Italians at Caporetto), this new tactical concept emphasized surprise, penetration of enemy weak points by infiltration, bypassing strong points, rapid exploitation of penetrations, maximizing fire support (automatic weapons, mortars and grenades, artillery, and aircraft), and maintaining the momentum of successful attacks. These revolutionary tactics, when the power and speed of tanks and armored vehicles were added a few years later, would develop into the "blitzkrieg" of World War II, and ultimately become the basis for all modern war-fighting doctrine. But German supplies and logistical support capabilities by 1918 could not sustain the momentum of this new type of intense, violent offensive, and the Allies—now under the common direction of one supreme commander, Maréchal Foch, and bolstered by millions of fresh American troops—kept the German attack from driving a fatal wedge in the front. In July 1918, the Allied counterattack began.

The Battle of Tannenberg

August 26–31, 1914

On July 24, 1914, the Russians instituted a "period preparatory to war," which was followed the next day by Austria-Hungary's declaration of "partial mobilization." France recalled all troops on leave on July 26, and three days later Germany sent a telegram to Russia warning that "further Russian mobilization would cause German mobilization." That same day, July 29, the czar signed the partial mobilization decree. The next day, fearing that failure to fully mobilize would fatally delay the concentrating of Russian forces on the frontiers, "full mobilization" was announced in Russia. On July 31, the day following Russia's full mobilization announcement, Austria-Hungary declared "general mobilization," Germany issued a "state of imminent danger" announcement, and France sent a "mobilization warning order." August 1, 1914, saw France and Germany declare "full mobilization" and Great Britain announce "full naval mobilization." When, in accordance with the modified Schlieffen war plan, Germany invaded Luxembourg, then Belgium, on August 2 and 3, Great Britain declared war on Germany and announced full mobilization of all British forces. The major powers of Europe were now hopelessly enmeshed in what would be the greatest land war yet seen. Mobilizing much faster than the Germans and Austrians predicted, Russia launched an early offensive into German East Prussia (August 1914), winning early successes against the outnumbered German army.

The stunning German victory in the dark, vast pine forests of East Prussia during the opening month of the Great War accomplished two important things. The immediate effect was a quick end to the early (and surprising) Russian threat to German territory in the east, creating a pattern of German domination over Russian forces that would continue on the Eastern Front throughout the war. The vaunted Russian steamroller, while promising the eventual provision of several millions of sturdy troops to the battlefield, was generally regarded by the major European powers as too backward and too technologically inferior to mount a timely and effective offensive within the first month of general mobilization. The disasters suffered by the Russian forces in the Russo-Japanese War of 1904–05 exposed the inherent weaknesses of the czarist military structure, and the subsequent civil unrest seemed to confirm that those weaknesses were present throughout all echelons of civilian as well as military establishments. The progress of reforms in the intervening years was generally invisible to outside observers like the Germans, who based their war plans on the inability of Russia to mobilize rapidly and threaten the weak German forces remaining in the east. When two Russian armies, therefore, pushed aggressively forward into German East Prussia in the middle of August 1914, the unexpected situation appeared dangerous and threatened to disrupt overall German plans. Only the overwhelming German victory at Tannenberg prevented early disaster on the Eastern Front, preserving German territory in East Prussia and salvaging hopes for an even greater success.

The second accomplishment of the Tannenberg victory, however, was more important. The victory raised to prominence and firmly established the reputations of the two men who would lead Germany's main armies during the last, decisive years of the war, becoming the virtual military dictators of Germany in the process. Colonel General Paul von Hindenburg and Major General Erich Ludendorff rushed to East Prussia in the latter days of August to rescue the faltering fortunes of Germany's outmanned forces and entered into combat as little-known leaders in a second-rate theater of war against a third-rate enemy. Within six months the two men had become heroes of the German nation. Later, after they had taken over direct command of the main German forces on the Western Front and assumed responsibility for overall direction of the war, the two became the most influential leaders in Germany.

Hindenburg and Ludendorff—The Great War's Most Famous Team

An aristocrat and a commoner, joined together by the accidents of war, Hindenburg and Ludendorff became a commander–chief-of-staff team by accident. The younger Ludendorff had made a recent impression on the chief of the general staff and was, therefore, immediately thought of when the issue arose of sending some bright, capable officer to rescue the faltering situation in the East. The other, retired for several years and living in obscurity, was only dimly remembered by a junior staff officer who suggested that since the old general lived conveniently close to the main rail station in Hannover near which the train carrying Ludendorff must pass on its route east, perhaps he would be an appropriate choice as the figurehead commander. The choices could not have proven more propitious for German fortunes.

Colonel General Paul von Beneckendorf und von Hindenburg (only after he gained his fame in 1914 would he be consistently known as Von Hindenburg) was born in 1847 to Prussian aristocrat parents. After receiving the standard Prussian education, he was commissioned in the prestigious 3rd Foot Guards in 1866, seeing action in the Austro-Prussian War of that year and the Franco-Prussian War of 1870. He was decorated for bravery in both wars (Order of the Red Eagle, Iron Cross), then selected to represent his regiment at Wilhelm I of Prussia's coronation as Emperor of Germany in Versailles. Between 1870 and his retirement in 1911, Hindenburg gained a reputation as a steady, though not necessarily brilliant officer, and was promoted regularly, but not quickly, reaching the rank of general in 1904. Although there were rumors that he had been considered to replace Schlieffen in 1905, there is no indication that the undistinguished Hindenburg was a serious candidate. In 1908, he ended any chance he may have had for future advancement in the peacetime German army by defeating Kaiser Wilhelm II in that year's summer war games. Hindenburg retired from active duty in 1911 "to make way for younger men," as he said.

On August 22, 1914, Hindenburg received a telegram from the general staff asking if he was ready for immediate active service. "I am ready," he replied. He was rapidly recalled, promoted to colonel general, and sent to assume command of the German Eighth Army. Assigned as his army chief of staff was Erich Ludendorff.

Erich Ludendorff was born nearly twenty years after Hindenburg in Kruschevia, Prussian Poland, where his father was a small landholder. Lacking an aristocratic name and money, Ludendorff was commissioned in a rather commonplace infantry regiment (57th Infantry in Wesel) following completion of cadet school in Plön. However, he managed to transfer eventually to the more prestigious 8th Grenadiers while still a junior officer and after service with a marine unit at the sea base in Kiel. In 1893, however, Ludendorff attended the Prussian Staff College and began establishing a reputation as an outstanding staff officer, which he kept for the remainder of his army career. Winning a place on the general staff through his superior performance at staff college, he was posted to army headquarters in Berlin in 1904, serving under Schlieffen. In 1907, he was promoted to head of the Operations Section of the German general staff, the premier staff position and a plum assignment. He caused some controversy over the next few years, however, when, after raising eyebrows by marrying a divorcée, he meddled in the Reichstag's affairs. Ludendorff was dismissed from the general staff in 1913 and exiled to the Rhineland. The war saved him from exile, however, and he was appointed deputy chief of staff to Von Bülow's Second German Army, a critical unit in the main German attack in the west. Assuming personal command of an important and successful assault on one of the Liège fortresses (where his bravery won him a Pour le

Mérite, Germany's highest award), he had a similar striking success in the battle of the Sambre a short time later. When Moltke needed a bright, proven leader to send east, Ludendorff was fresh on his mind. Not senior enough, however, to be placed in command of the Eighth Army, he would be the brains and the driving force while a suitable figurehead would actually exercise command.

Instead of a dynamic subordinate supporting a figurehead, however, the Hindenburg-Ludendorff duo became an unmatched team whose strengths—Hindenburg's character and Ludendorff's brains—complemented each other.

Eastern Plans—Setting the Armies in Motion to Tannenberg

Germany's plan for the Eastern Front, of course, counted on a slow Russian mobilization to produce little early activity in East Prussia, while the bulk of German forces smashed France and the Western Allies in a six-week campaign. Once victorious in the west, Germany could send its armies eastward, where, assisted by the Austro-Hungarian forces, they could subsequently defeat Russia. In support of this plan, Germany maintained a deliberately weak force of only one army—the Eighth—to defend all of East Prussia. The 135,000 soldiers of the German Eighth Army (initially commanded by General von Prittwitz) consisted of three active army corps, a reserve corps, a cavalry division, landwehr brigades, and fortress troops (most located in Königsberg). The dense forests of much of this frontierlike region, combined with a rudimentary road network, and dotted with a chain of 2,700 lakes (the Masurian Lakes and Marsh District), made the defensive mission of the troops of the Eighth Army somewhat easier to accomplish, even against a greater number of Russian soldiers.

Germany also counted on its ally, Austria-Hungary, to launch an early offensive in the east, in Galicia and Russian Poland, which would serve to keep the Russians occupied farther to the south on the vast Eastern Front. The Austro-Hungarian plan, based like the German plan on the assumption of a fatally slow Russian mobilization, called for an offensive from two Austro-Hungarian armies in Galicia to the northeast, toward Lublin and Chelm, to cut off the salient of Russian Poland. The Austrian commander, Field Marshal Conrad von Hötzendorff, assumed, without sufficient reason, that his attack would be assisted and complemented by a corresponding German offensive out of East Prussia on the north side of the salient. A third Austro-Hungarian army would face eastward, prepared to attack toward Russia proper. Hötzendorff had a fourth army, but as a result of his bungling and contradictory orders to it after the fighting began with Serbia, this force was hopelessly tangled in rail traffic gridlock between Galicia and the Balkans and therefore unavailable for the first three weeks of the war.

Russian war plans were based on the unpleasant prospect of facing two enemies on the vast Eastern Front. If Germany threw the weight of its armies early against Russia, the czar's forces were to conduct an orderly withdrawal to defensive positions farther east (à la the strategy used against Napoleon in 1812). However, if Germany held fast in the east and attacked with its full weight against France and the Western Allies, Russia was to take the offensive, occupy East Prussia, and prepare to drive on toward Berlin. Russian dispositions in August 1914 were essentially the same for both eventualities. Opposite East Prussia in the north, two Russian armies—Rennenkampf's First and Samsonov's Second—were deployed. In the Polish salient, the Russian Ninth, Fourth, and Fifth Armies faced south toward Austro-Hungarian forces, while the Russian Third and Eighth Armies bordered Hötzendorff's forces on the east. Russian forces facing the Austro-Hungarians were also to attack into Galicia if Germany attacked France first. Under the terms of an agreement with France, Russia was committed to launching 800,000 troops against Germany and Austria-Hungary within fifteen days of the beginning of full mobilization. Although full compliance with this commitment was essentially impossible given the primitive state of the Russian transportation system and the country's inadequate mobilization plans, the czar was nevertheless anxious to honor the promise to the fullest extent possible.

On August 17, 1914, General Pavel Rennenkampf's First Russian

Imperial Army began its advance into German East Prussia, headed directly for Königsberg. Intended to comprise five corps, made up from six and a half infantry divisions and five cavalry divisions, the First Army began the war in the east far from completely mobilized. Understrength, since reservists had not yet arrived, and further depleted because line infantry companies had to be detached to guard depots and lines of communications, Rennenkampf's army lacked adequate supplies of food and ammunition, had insufficient supply trains with which to move the few supplies it did have, and contained no field kitchens to cook the little food the soldiers carried. Russian fieldpieces and howitzers, fewer in number than those in their corresponding German units, entered the war zone with only about 850 rounds per weapon—and little prospect for timely resupply. Nevertheless, the Russian columns advanced, principally due to Prittwitz's instructions to give up territory instead of becoming involved in a decisive engagement. Grudgingly withdrawing in front of the advancing Russians, the German subordinate commanders were reluctant to obey Prittwitz's orders, and sought to fight Rennenkampf's forces wherever they could. At Gumbinnen, on August 19–20, eight of Rennenkampf's First Army divisions attacked seven of Prittwitz's divisions, forcing the Germans to retreat once more. Gumbinnen was a small affair (Russian losses were about 16,000) compared with the immense battles yet to come, but its impact on German fortunes in the east was far in excess of its limited scope.

Meanwhile, on August 19, General Aleksandr Samsonov's Second Russian Imperial Army had begun its stumbling advance into East Prussia farther to the south. Ordered to wheel to the west of the Masurian Lakes, Samsonov's five corps of 200,000 men pressed forward amid the same chaotic supply and support conditions that confronted Rennenkampf. Crossing the East Prussian–Polish border on August 21–22, Samsonov's weary troops—who had been conducting forced marches for nine days on scant rations—moved even farther away from their nearest friendly forces, Rennenkampf's First Army, far to the north beyond the chain of lakes. Unable to provide mutual support to each other, the two armies conducted, essentially, two separate campaigns. Samsonov's advance, however, coupled with that rather minor Russian victory farther north at Gumbinnen, put Prittwitz into a panic.

Interpreting his orders as permission to stage a massive withdrawal from East Prussia if the Russians launched a full-scale offensive, Prittwitz informed Moltke and the general staff in Berlin that he intended to move the Eighth Army behind the line of the Vistula River—this meant he intended to completely abandon East Prussia to the advancing Russians and move his defense nearly all the way back to Danzig.

Already at wit's end about the progress of the war in the west, Moltke panicked upon receiving Prittwitz's report. The general staff chief ordered that two corps be detached from the western armies and immediately sent to reinforce the Eighth Army in East Prussia. He took these corps from the right wing, however, supposedly the force making the decisive attack in the west. Although the actual impact of removing these two corps from the right wing in France and Belgium just at the decisive point of the war's initial offensive is problematic, the fact that these corps arrived too late to have any positive impact on the German victory at Tannenberg means that Moltke's precipitous action had no positive effect on either front.

Prittwitz's announcement that he intended to evacuate East Prussia did, however, have one overwhelmingly positive effect. It convinced Moltke to relieve him as Eighth Army commander and replace him with the Hindenburg-Ludendorff team. Despite the fact that Prittwitz was dissuaded by key members of his staff (including his deputy chief of operations, Lieutenant Colonel Max Hoffman) from actually ordering the general withdrawal behind the Vistula, it was too late to save his job. Hindenburg and Ludendorff arrived at Eighth Army headquarters on August 23 and took charge. Upon arrival, they found that Colonel Hoffman had been busy devising a means of turning the initial Russian successes into an overwhelming German victory.

BALTIC SEA
Tilsit
RUSSIA
XXXX
RU FIRST
Rennenkampf
Königsberg
Gumbinnen
XXXX–
GE EIGHTH
XXXX
GE EIGHTH HQ
Prittwitz
(Hindenburg)
To Danzig
Bischofsburg
Allenstein
MASURIAN LAKES
XXX
GE XX
Willenberg
RUSSIA
Tannenberg
Heidenburg
Usdau
Soldau
POLAND
XXXX
RU SECOND
Samsonov
To Warsaw
Tannenberg
Aug. 19 - 23, 1914
25 Miles

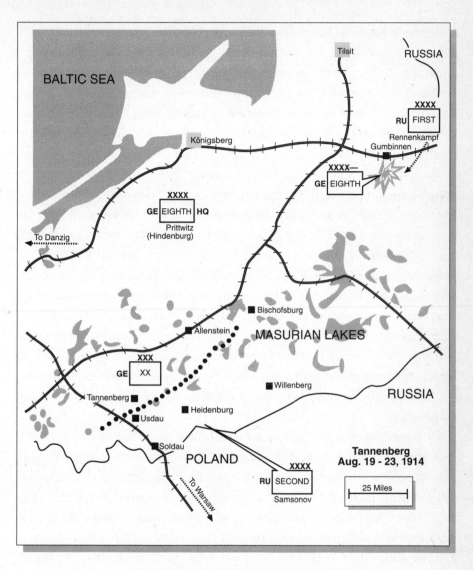

Tannenberg, August 19–23, 1914

Cannae Redux—The "Classic" Double Envelopment

Ever since the great Carthaginian general Hannibal destroyed an entire Roman army in a single afternoon—at Cannae in 216 B.C.—military commanders have dreamed of duplicating his classic double envelopment. Fixing an enemy force in place by actions to his immediate front while sweeping around both of his flanks simultaneously to utterly crush him—the ultimate battle of encirclement—represents the pinnacle of military tactics and demonstrates the highest form of the military art. Its essence is incredibly simple, yet its attainment is difficult. No enemy commander worthy of the name will knowingly allow his force to be placed in a position where an opposing force can freely enfilade both his flanks. And few commanders have the skill (or luck) to place their own forces in a position where carrying out such an attack is even a possibility. All the conditions must be just right. All of the players must cooperate (knowingly or unwittingly). Lieutenant Colonel Hoffman, who had been listening to Russian radio transmissions of orders in clear text for several days, thought the conditions (and the players) were close to perfect.

Hoffman sought to capitalize on the lack of cooperation and mutual support between Rennenkampf's and Samsonov's armies, concentrating first against one of the Russian armies, then, after defeating it, moving against the remaining army and destroying it as well. The Cannae-like part of the upcoming operations would be the separate attacks against and destruction of the individual Russian armies, caught operating isolated, unsupported, and without proper reconnaissance in hostile territory. Groping wearily and blindly into an unknown situation, both flanks improperly guarded, and without a clue as to their German opponent's true dispositions and intentions, the soldiers of Samsonov's and Rennenkampf's forces pitched forward fitfully, albeit determinedly.

Another factor that helped Hoffman's plan succeed was the deep-seated animosity between Samsonov and Rennenkampf that dated back at least to the Russo-Japanese War. After the battle of Mukden (February–March 1905), in which both commanders had taken part, the two began accusing each other of failing to provide expected support. The argument grew so intense that they came to blows. Thus, neither was inclined to provide the other with much useful assistance. If the poor road and transportation network, the vast separating distances, and the absolutely abysmal Russian staff planning and coordination did not completely prevent the two armies from assisting each other, the personal animosity of the two commanders probably would.

Hoffman considered the threat posed by Samsonov's forces to be the greater. If successful in advancing west and north, Samsonov could then proceed to cut off most of East Prussia, possibly trapping most of the German Eighth Army in the process. Samsonov's Second Army also presented Hoffman with the greater chance of achieving an immediate and decisive victory, given its isolated position, weak supply system, weary troops, and lack of any meaningful reconnaissance. Hoffman's plan, therefore, called for the bulk of Eighth Army to move south and strike Samsonov's Second Army first, while only a thin screen of German troops would remain in front of Rennenkampf's First Army farther north. From intercepted Russian radio messages, Hoffman already knew that the First Army was not planning to move rapidly or aggressively forward and that Rennenkampf would probably not interfer with the planned movement south against Samsonov. By the time Hindenburg and Ludendorff arrived at Eighth Army headquarters in Marienburg on August 23, orders had already been issued for the German army corps to redeploy to the south, forming a rough half-moon shape in front of Samsonov's advancing troops, leaving only a weak screen in front of Rennenkampf's army. Hindenburg and Ludendorff approved Hoffman's plan.

Closing the Trap

Samsonov's troops, obedient to the frantic exhortations of higher command to press forward regardless of the consequences, were exhausted even before they entered German territory in East Prussia three days before Hindenburg and Ludendorff's arrival in Marienburg. Along the sandy tracks that passed for roads in the frontier region, amid the oppressive heat and humidity of the late summer, the weary Russian troops of the Second Army plodded onward, dragging their weapons, equipment, and pitifully few supply wagons. Making only about fifteen miles per day, the men were often forced to abandon some of the few supply wagons they did have in order to double-team the wagons carrying precious ammunition when those became bogged down in the deep sand of the miserable roads. Off-road movement was often more difficult, the marshy ground between the countless lakes making the passage of large bodies of men extremely time-consuming and even more exhausting. Any firm, passable ground between the lakes was very often dominated by the numerous small villages, which, abandoned by their inhabitants, had been turned into fortified strong points by the German army and stoutly defended. Samsonov's men desperately needed a day's halt to rest, refit, and sort themselves out.

Samsonov's pleas to his higher commander, General Jilinsky, commander of the Northwest Group of Russian Armies, that the Second Army be allowed to halt and reorganize were answered only by demands that he move his troops forward even faster. Jilinsky worried that Rennenkampf's First Army, now forward of Gumbinnen with no anchor on either flank, was vulnerable to a German counterattack. The situation seemed to the army group commander to warrant Samsonov's immediate and vigorous advance in order to maintain pressure on the German Eighth Army and keep it from turning on Rennenkampf. Jilinsky's appreciation of Samsonov's own position (which was becoming ever more dangerous with every mile he advanced into East Prussia) was limited at best. To assist Samsonov in applying more pressure on the Germans, Jilinsky attached the Russian I Corps to the Second Army on August 20 (this unit had earlier been removed from Rennenkampf's First Army and dispatched to Warsaw). This attachment, instead of strengthening Samsonov's forces, actually increased the control problem for the overburdened Second Army commander, further drained the chaotic supply system, and added to the confusion of the jammed command and control network. Samsonov's troops, exhausted and nearly starving, began plundering the countryside as they advanced, making the maintenance of military discipline extremely difficult, and further complicating command and control. Overhead, German airplanes and zeppelins freely roamed, observing in great detail the progress of the enemy and occasionally bombing the advancing Russians without interference. The Germans not only had nearly perfect intelligence concerning the positions of all the advancing Russian forces, they continued to eavesdrop on Russian radio transmissions, intercepting orders for future movements. Samsonov (and Rennenkampf), however, continued to fail to conduct even the most basic reconnaissance to find out the actual German dispositions, and instead groped blindly ahead.

Meanwhile German plans to crush the Russian invaders were continuing to develop smoothly and efficiently. In front of Samsonov, the German XX Corps, though heavily outnumbered, was only slowly giving ground, while forcing the Second Army to fight its way forward. The other German corps, less the weak units left in front of Rennenkampf's First Army, were being moved without interference and with legendary Prussian efficiency to their battle positions on the flanks of Samsonov's unwary army. General Hermann von François's German I Corps, moving the greatest distance of any of the German formations, was the first unit to move, leaving its position on Rennenkampf's right flank at the far northern point on the German line, and intending to detrain at the farthest southern point of the German line, on Samsonov's exposed left flank. General von Mackensen's XVII German Corps readied to about-face from its position in front of Rennenkampf and advance south toward Samsonov's equally exposed right flank. The German I Reserve Corps of

General von Below would fall in on Mackensen's right flank and prepare to join in the attack on Samsonov's unwary troops. Rennenkampf, feeling isolated, inadequately supported, and surrounded by a hostile populace in unfriendly country, made no attempt to move boldly forward or to determine what strength force was facing him. The Russian First Army commander behaved exactly as his German opponents wished, allowing them a freedom of movement he denied to himself and to his counterpart, Samsonov.

On August 23, Samsonov's center (three army corps) had made contact with the main forces of the German XX Corps which continued to give ground slowly and steadily. The Eighth Army's I Corps was still on the move, making its way to XX Corps' assistance. The haphazard Russian advance, however, had caused Samsonov's remaining two corps, operating on the Second Army's widely diverging flanks, to become further and further separated from the main body. As the center pressed forward, the divergence became more acute, and the resulting disposition of the Second Army became increasingly more vulnerable. By the evening of August 23, the Russian Second Army was spread out along a front of over sixty miles, with the right and left flank corps dangerously distant from the center units.

On August 25, Ludendorff (acting on Hoffman's daring, if sound, advice) ordered the two remaining German corps in front of Rennenkampf to about-face and move against Samsonov's exposed right flank. Ludendorff considered this removal of the last remaining substantial force in front of Rennenkampf extremely risky, since, if the Russian First Army moved southward in strength, the German Eighth Army could be caught in the same trap it was preparing to spring on the Russians. However, Hoffman, soon supported by more intercepted Russian clear text radio messages, convinced Ludendorff (and, of course, the actual army commander, Hindenburg) that failure to send the remaining corps against Samsonov would jeopardize the entire operation. If Samsonov was not surrounded and totally destroyed, the German situation in East Prussia would remain precarious. To completely restore German fortunes in the east, the Second Army must be annihilated. François's German I Corps was

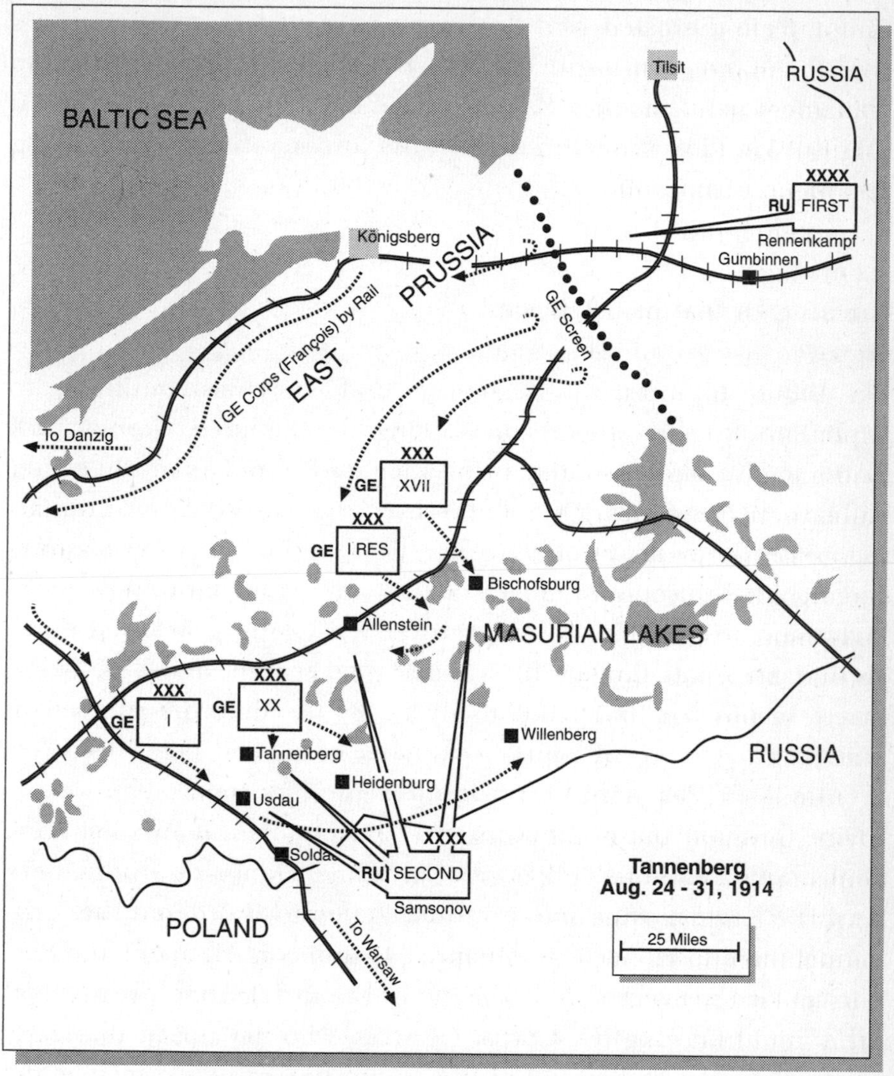
BALTIC SEA
Tilsit
RUSSIA
XXXX
RU FIRST
Rennenkampf
Gumbinnen
Königsberg
EAST PRUSSIA
I GE Corps (François) by Rail
GE Screen
To Danzig
XXX
GE XVII
XXX
GE I RES
Bischofsburg
Allenstein
MASURIAN LAKES
XXX
GE I
XXX
GE XX
Tannenberg
Willenberg
RUSSIA
Heidenburg
Usdau
Soldau
XXXX
RU SECOND
Samsonov
Tannenberg
Aug. 24 - 31, 1914
25 Miles
POLAND
To Warsaw

Tannenberg, August 24–31, 1914

already moving into position to strike Samsonov's equally exposed left wing while Ludendorff and Hoffman were debating the decision to complete the operation. An overpowering attack on Samsonov's right by Mackensen's and Von Below's corps would complete the enactment of a "modern Cannae." Ludendorff issued the order on August 25, and by the following day, the forces were poised to spring the trap on Samsonov.

Turning Defeat into Disaster

On August 26, 1914, the Russian Second Army was continuing to experience general success in forcing the battered German XX Corps to give more ground, as the weight of numbers in the center still favored Samsonov. Overall, however, the Second Army, now facing nearly the entire strength of the German Eighth Army, was outnumbered. Samsonov's 150 battalions, until that morning's dawn possessing a significant advantage over XX Corps, now faced up to 180 German battalions, with François, Mackensen, and Von Below nearly in position and ready to strike. By the time the sun set on that long day, both of Samsonov's flank corps had been decisively defeated—the left flank corps on the verge of a rout.

The German rout of the Russian I Corps on Samsonov's left flank almost failed to come off decisively. While François's troops were detraining and moving into position, Ludendorff ordered the independent-minded I Corps commander to immediately attack the Russian left wing in order to take some of the unrelenting pressure off the still-withdrawing XX Corps. François, who did not at that early hour on August 26 have all of his supporting artillery available, demurred, informing Ludendorff that he would attack later, when all his units were present and his dispositions were complete. Even a firm order from Eighth Army headquarters failed to get him to launch a premature attack. Instead, François made only a token assault against the Russian left wing while continuing to deploy his troops to the rear of Samsonov's army, turning his left flank in the process. By the evening of that day, François was prepared to finish off the Second Army's left wing by delivering a devastating blow.

Farther north that same day, on Samsonov's right flank, Macken-sen's XVII Corps, soon to be supported by Von Below's I Reserve Corps, crashed into the Russian VI Corps and sent it reeling back in defeat. The Russians lost half of their infantry and much of their artillery to Mackensen's determined and disciplined ground attacks, supported by overwhelming German artillery barrages. Incredibly, in its panic and haste to get away from the advancing German columns, the defeated Russian VI Corps failed to notify Samsonov or any other Russian unit of the disaster it had suffered. Samsonov went to bed on August 26 without realizing that his army had already been badly beaten. In fact, the Second Army commander and staff thought their corps were still handily beating the Germans, preparing and issuing their orders to the army based on that unbelievably bad appreciation of the actual state of affairs. The British military attaché in Samso-nov's headquarters reported that the Second Army commander was "content and satisfied" with his army's performance on the evening of August 26. This incredible ignorance would persist even into the next day.

At dawn on August 27, François launched the full force of his now completely assembled German I Corps against the ill-fed, uncompre-hending mass of Russian troops to his front. Striking the Russian I Corps in the vicinity of Usdau, François's massive artillery barrage stampeded the exhausted Russians into panicked retreat. Nearly thirty field artillery batteries thundered forth an overpowering rain of high explosives and splintered steel on an already demoralized Russian left wing that was ill-prepared to receive such a pounding. Most Russians were not even dug in properly and were pathetically unready to endure a barrage so violent and deadly. The great mass of Russian I Corps troops streamed rearward to the vicinity of Soldau. Although one sharp, Russian counterattack, well supported by artil-lery, briefly held up the lead brigade of one of François's divisions near Heinrichsdorf, this setback was localized and only temporary. Samsonov's entire left wing was irretrievably shattered, as his right wing had been the day before. On the evening of August 27, Sam-sonov prepared orders for his army that turned the crushing defeat it had just suffered into an unmitigated disaster: he ordered his center to attack.

Samsonov's orders to his center corps (XIII and XV still fighting opposite the German XX Corps) to attack into the middle of the German line near Tannenberg seems entirely bizarre. Even if the two units were successful in their attack, such success would only drive them deeper into the German trap and effectively eliminate any possibility of escape. By this time Samsonov knew that his right wing (VI Corps) had been soundly beaten and driven back, and even though he probably did not yet realize the extent of the disaster on his left wing, reports were filtering in that must surely have alerted him to the fact that his left was at least in serious trouble. Nevertheless, the attack orders were issued that night and XIII and XV Russian Corps began the ill-advised action the next morning, August 28.

By the time the attack was under way shortly after dawn, Samsonov must have finally realized the true nature of his army's situation. He quickly rode to XV Corps headquarters, announcing that he had arrived to take personal command of the attack. Despite some brief, local successes, the doomed and useless attack ground to a halt that afternoon. Plunged into despair, Samsonov at last ordered the general retreat that should have begun days earlier. The Second Army commander ordered the XIII and XV Corps to withdraw toward the key town of Neidenburg, which had to be kept open if any of the Russian units were to escape the swiftly closing German pincers. Even before Samsonov issued these instructions, however, Neidenburg had been captured by François's German I Corps troops. The only door to safety for the Russian Second Army had been slammed shut in their faces.

Encirclement

Once again, in this grand battle of encirclement, the key to the phenomenal success of the German Eighth Army was François's disobedience. Earlier on August 28, Ludendorff, becoming anxious about the intensity of Samsonov's suicidal attacks against the battered German XX Corps, had ordered François to turn his corps northward, away from its march around the Russian rear toward Neidenburg, and to shore up the XX Corps' threatened right flank. François saw that Ludendorff's order was certain to allow a great number of Russians to escape the nearly completed encirclement. Just as he had disobeyed Ludendorff's order to attack the Russian left wing prematurely on August 26, so now François disobeyed the equally wrongheaded order to give up his encirclement maneuver. Sending only a single division north to aid XX Corps, he continued his advance on Neidenburg, capturing the town that evening. Securing the vicinity against any possible breakthrough by the Russians, he pushed his units farther east another twenty miles, occupying Willenberg and establishing a thin cordon of troops all along the route to gather any Russians attempting to flee across the border.

Few Second Army troops had escaped the German trap. Only those from the Russian I Corps who had fled south from the debacle on August 27, and those from the shattered VI Corps who had streamed east after the crushing defeat on August 26, made it safely back to Russia. The vast majority of Second Army soldiers were firmly and hopelessly trapped within a German-controlled pocket, approximately twenty-five miles wide by ten miles deep. For most it was the first stop on the way to the prisoner-of-war cages—for many others it became their grave.

During the next few days, Russian troops caught in the German trap witnessed scenes of utter confusion. Command and control broke down, units became hopelessly intermixed, and columns or mobs of fleeing troops met deadly German machine-gun fire and overwhelming artillery barrages wherever they turned. Efforts by commanders and staff officers to sort out the mixed units and organize breakout attacks were inevitably stymied by German pressure, the broken and rugged terrain, and, ultimately, the near-total confusion in the Russian ranks. Throughout August 29 and 30, the slaughter continued as the Germans either killed the Russians who were attempting to break out or rounded them up as prisoners. An attempt to break the German line from the outside, near Neidenburg, by the survivors of the Russian I Corps who had escaped the trap on August 27 (by fleeing southward) was beaten back by François's troops. On August 31, General Jilinsky ordered the surviving Russian forces outside the German pocket to retire.

A Single Pistol Shot

At no time during the battle did Rennenkampf and the Russian First Army attempt to move vigorously southward to assist Samsonov's outmatched and outnumbered troops. Although the First Army commander had been moving west toward Königsberg at a reasonable speed (twenty miles per day over bad roads), the force was only six divisions—hardly strong enough to cause Ludendorff to call off the attack on Samsonov. When Jilinsky (who until the trap was fully sprung on Samsonov continued to pester the Second Army to move farther and faster into the interior of East Prussia) belatedly realized his subordinate's dire predicament, he telegraphed Rennenkampf to move his "left flank forward as far as possible" toward Samsonov. It was far too little and far too late. By August 27, when the telegram was sent, Samsonov had already lost the battle.

The Russian Second Army commander, trapped with his men within the circle of German steel, rode from unit to unit trying to rally his exhausted troops. Impotently witnessing the continuing death and destruction, he became more and more distraught. Realizing his own responsibility for the certain loss of nearly all of his 200,000 soldiers, Samsonov told his staff that he wanted to end his life. On the night of August 29, two days before the bitter end for his men, he made his lonely ride into the forest.

Aftermath

The German victory in this battle resulted in one of the most complete destructions of any enemy on any battlefield of any war. It truly was a modern Cannae, although in many ways this resemblance owes more to Samsonov's incredible ignorance and François's inspired disobedience than to Hoffman's or Ludendorff's plan. Hoffman's plan had not specifically envisioned the two pincers of the German attack actually being able to enclose Samsonov's entire Second Army. However, by placing the right forces in motion at the right time to arrive in just the right place to take advantage of Samsonov's mistakes, the plan created the conditions that resulted in the double envelopment.

When the final tally of Russian prisoners was completed, the Germans counted 92,000 unwounded captives and claimed that an additional 30,000 wounded Russians were picked up across the battlefield—a staggering 122,000 prisoners. The numbers of Russian dead went uncounted. Of equal consequence to the artillery-poor Russian army was the loss of several hundred hard-to-replace modern field artillery guns. The Germans announced their capture of 300 to 500 Russian guns. The Russians admitted to losing only 180 to 190. The czar could ill afford to lose either amount, as obtaining replacement weapons was nearly impossible. Total German losses, in comparison, were light—about 13,000 killed, wounded, and missing.

This stunning German victory only became known as the battle of Tannenberg when Ludendorff suggested it be used for propaganda purposes. Recalling the earlier battle of Tannenberg in 1410, where the combined forces of Poland and Lithuania had soundly trounced the Knights of the Teutonic Order, Ludendorff trumpeted the 1914 victory as long-awaited revenge for that defeat. The public announcement of the Eastern Front victory was also carefully timed to produce the maximum morale-boosting value, with the intention of diverting the German populace's mind from the disappointing loss at the Marne and filling it instead with visions of victory and glory.

But if the aim was to assuage German disappointment over the failure of the main attack in the west, this strategy ultimately served only to raise false hopes that the war might yet be one of weeks and months instead of years. The victory at Tannenberg destroyed the Russian Second Army and effectively ended the invasion of East Prussia. It did not win the war on the Eastern Front, however, nor did it decisively influence the overall course of the war in the west. The war in the east continued for three more years. The German victory at Tannenberg, as great an accomplishment as it was, was soon over-shadowed by the failure of the German opening offensive in the west, taking place at nearly the same time. A modern Cannae in the west might have been decisive and spared the world the horror of the next four years. The reenactment of this classic double envelopment in the east only served to encourage those who would manage the slaughter for those terrible years.

The Battle of Verdun

February 21–December 18, 1916

Exactly how many human beings—French and German—were killed, maimed, wounded, captured, or driven out of their minds in the hundred or so square miles of French soil that was the Verdun battleground is still somewhat open to debate. Estimates range from a low of 600,000 to a high of nearly 1 million. The conditions of that terrible battlefield and the immense scope of the brutal ten-month combat make it difficult to measure the true number of victims accurately. Corpses were frequently left to rot on the battlefield, and many others were entombed in their trenches or fighting positions. Countless soldiers simply disappeared as flesh and bone were blown to bits by the millions of high-explosive artillery rounds. Alistair Horne, one of the battle's most distinguished historians, reckons in *The Price of Glory: Verdun 1916* that the combined total of French and German casualties reached at least three quarters of a million. But Horne also points out that if the casualties in the Verdun area for the entire war are considered, the total is as high as 1,250,000.

Seldom is Verdun mentioned without reference to these staggering casualty rolls. The reason for this is that casualties were what the battle of Verdun, the war's single longest engagement, was all about.

The German general staff chief's stated purpose was to "bleed the French Army white"—not to achieve a stunning breakthrough or a strategic penetration that would win the war quickly or restore the lost mobility to the Western Front, but simply to kill Frenchmen, thereby killing the spirit of the French army. Its ranks depleted and its esprit de corps ruined, it would then surely collapse.

Verdun's impact on the psyche of the war's combatants was widespread and significant, for the interminable slaughter for no appreciable gains or larger purpose drained the morale of the armies of both sides. The French rotation system coupled with the sheer duration of the battle led to seventy of the total ninety-six divisions in the French army of 1916 serving at Verdun, while the Germans employed nearly fifty divisions. Liddell Hart, in his *History of the World War, 1914–1918,* observed that "a great part of the French Army was drawn through the 'mincing machine' " of Verdun in 1916; the psychological toll of this hellish experience contributed significantly to the mass mutinies of the following year. In the past eighty-odd years since Verdun, the pitiful remnants of human beings who perished in that battle have regularly been unearthed by farmers or workmen. Their remains are added to those of their comrades in the giant ossuary that serves as the final resting place for at least 150,000 French and German soldiers.

Falkenhayn's Plan for 1916

Field Marshal Erich von Falkenhayn, a quiet, introverted officer who had gained sufficient favor with Kaiser Wilhelm II during the prewar years to be named minister of war in 1906, was chosen to succeed the younger Moltke as chief of the German general staff following Moltke's failures in the fall of 1914. By the end of 1915, Falkenhayn presided over a strategic situation that was definitely not in Germany's favor. Germany and the Central Powers, having failed to decisively defeat either the Russians in the east or the French and British in the west, were caught in the German High Command's worst nightmare—a major war fought on two fronts. On the Eastern Front,

5 million Russian soldiers were arrayed against him, and the Romanov dynasty, though tottering, was not yet sufficiently weakened to promise a quick Austro-German victory without a massive offensive. The 2,800,000 Austro-Hungarian troops of the Central Powers were spread over the southern portion of the vast Eastern Front, and, in addition to the Russians, had to deal with the Serbs, Italians, and Romanians. Split between the east and west, the bulk of the 4,200,000 German troops faced 2,750,000 French and 1,340,000 British soldiers along the Western Front—a static, deadlocked trench system extending from the English Channel to the Swiss frontier. Outnumbered on both fronts, Germany needed a realistic strategy for 1916.

Falkenhayn's strategic choices for the coming year were basically between two types of warfare in two theaters of war. He could elect to conduct the main effort in the east *or* in the west—attempting major efforts in both theaters was simply not possible—and he could choose between fighting a chiefly defensive campaign or an offensive one. There were definite advantages to the former, and the machine gun, barbed wire, field fortifications, and overpowering artillery fire had demonstrated that the defense was, at this time, clearly the most effective form of warfare. But by waging purely defensive warfare, Germany could not obtain the quick, decisive victory it needed. Surrounded by enemies and forced to endure an ever-tightening naval blockade, the Central Powers were not in a position to survive the years of attrition warfare required to wear the Allies down; indeed, they were more likely to collapse first. Thus the length of time that waging a purely defensive war entailed, more than anything else, rendered this option unviable. Falkenhayn was forced to set Germany's armies on an offensive course for 1916.

What type of offensive and exactly where to strike was his next decision. With the limited number of fresh divisions Falkenhayn could muster for an offensive in 1916—he could raise only about twenty-six divisions by scraping together cadres, school troops, and theater reserves—the combined German and Austro-Hungarian armies in the east could inflict a sharp, but not necessarily fatal defeat on the huge Russian army. The czarist host was so large and the country so vast that even a massive defeat might not knock Russia out of the war. Therefore, the offensive of 1916 had to be delivered in the west, against the French and/or their British allies.

But twenty-six new divisions were not a large enough force to ensure a decisive breakthrough in the west either. Having failed—just—to obtain a potential war-winning rupture of the British lines in Flanders in 1915, Falkenhayn realized his 1916 offensive needed to be more clever and subtle in design. He reasoned that by forcing France to throw her precious manpower resources into the debilitating defense of an important objective—one that was also a national symbol, as Verdun was—the resulting slaughter might break that nation's will to carry on the war and lead to a public outcry for an armistice. Knowing full well that France resented the fact that her armies were bearing the brunt of the war in the west (Britain still had not adopted national conscription and was failing to fill her ranks through volunteers), Falkenhayn wanted to cause "the forces of France to bleed to death," forcing a break with Britain and leading to an end of the war on terms favorable to Germany and the Central Powers.

Operationally, Falkenhayn planned to accomplish this massive bloodletting with significantly fewer casualties to his own troops. Thus he focused his attack on a carefully chosen, narrow front, where his massive artillery firepower could make up for massive numbers of troops. A narrow front would also make it easy for Germany to handle the inevitable relieving attacks in other areas without having to draw troops away from the main offensive. In this way, Falkenhayn insisted, the German Command would be "perfectly free to accelerate or draw out her offensive, to intensify it or break it off from time to time, as suits her purpose." In other words, Germany would be able to manipulate the pace and scope of the offensive, inflicting the maximum number of casualties on the enemy while avoiding massive casualties on her own side—at least in theory.

For the setting of the offensive, Falkenhayn chose Verdun, the ancient French fortress on the Meuse River.

Fortress Verdun

The city was historically, if not just then strategically, important enough to demand the maximum defensive effort by the French army. Verdun traced its historical importance back to Roman times; and a treaty signed there in 849 A.D. divided Charlemagne's empire between his sons. Vauban fortified it in his classical manner during the reign of Louis XIV, and in 1870, it endured a heroic ten-week siege before succumbing to Prussian invaders. The defense of such a place was a matter of honor and national pride to the French army. Sitting just south of the center of the long trench line stretching from the Channel to Switzerland, the Verdun salient was a thirty-mile-wide bulge into the German lines. Serving as a counterweight to the nearby German fortress of Metz, Verdun, however, at the beginning of 1916, was not in the forefront of the war. Although it had witnessed much violent activity during the battles of the frontiers in 1914, the French High Command did not consider it to be in much danger as 1915 ended.

The modern reconstruction of "fortress Verdun" into one of the principal fortified zones shielding France from Germany had begun in 1874 and had produced a formidable fortress complex by 1914. Verdun initially had been heavily fortified with powerful underground positions, disappearing guns, heavy artillery, and a complex system of interlocking forts that made it appear to be nearly invulnerable to attack. Protected by a double ring of twenty-one smaller fortresses and over forty other works, the town sat in a bowl in the valley of the Meuse River. The outer ring contained four major forts (Douaumont, Vaux, Tavannes, and Noulainville) and the defenses of the inner ring were tied together by three principal forts (Belleville, St.-Michel, and Belrupt). The strongest fort in the complex was Douaumont. It was sited to dominate the northeastern approaches and sat on a 1,200-foot hill. Its nearly nine-foot thick concrete walls could withstand the heaviest artillery of the day. The larger inner fortress outwardly presented an imposing picture of strength, but its real defensive cornerstone rested on the interaction and mutual supporting fires of the outerworks. Thus the reality of "fortress Verdun" at the beginning of 1916 was altogether different from the picture of insurmountable strength it presented.

After the rapid German destruction of the other outwardly imposing forts like Liège, Namur, and Maubeuge in the opening weeks of the war, the importance of Verdun as a fortress was suspect and its role as a shield of France downplayed. Over the previous months, the powerful Verdun forts had been stripped of most of their heavy guns, and their large contingent of garrison troops were shipped off to more threatened portions of the front. General Joffre, French commander in chief, viewed the fortress as a liability, draining precious manpower and resources that could be better utilized elsewhere. The fact that Verdun was much stronger, significantly more powerful, and based on more modern and technologically superior designs than the Belgian forts was dismissed. By the time that Falkenhayn was ready to launch his 1916 offensive, Joffre's transfers of nearly all its garrison personnel and much of their artillery had significantly reduced the fortress's strength. Only 270 artillery pieces remained in the Verdun fortified zone.

This weakened state of the once seemingly inpregnable fortress was only too obvious, and a minor national scandal was caused when an officer (who also happened to be a politician) serving at Verdun brought the matter to the attention of the government. Embarrassing questions were asked, but Joffre, blustering and fuming that such reports "disturb[ed] profoundly the spirit of discipline in the Army," caused the questioning to be dropped.

By February 1916, therefore, most of the forts surrounding Verdun had been gutted of their primary means of defense. Although they still looked imposing to any attacker, they lacked the "teeth" necessary to fulfill their intended purpose. Instead of being protected by a stout ring of twenty-one powerful forts, each with its own strong garrison force and supporting artillery, the Verdun sector's defense now rested primarily on a single line of open trenches. Even this flimsy trench line lacked the strength found in other areas of the long Allied line. There were no communications trenches, no barbed-wire entanglements, and telephone lines were not even buried. Manning the entire Verdun fortified zone were just four divisions of varying reliability.

The Storm Breaks

Falkenhayn entrusted command of this battle to the Kaiser's son, Crown Prince Wilhelm. The latter's Fifth Army would launch the offensive, called Operation Gericht (Judgment), on February 12, 1916. Despite Falkenhayn's stated objective of conducting a drawn-out battle of attrition, the crown prince seems to have developed his operational and tactical plans on the assumption that the German general staff chief actually wanted the Fifth Army to capture Verdun—an unbelievable misappreciation. While the crown prince submitted a plan that called for attacking the French positions on both the east and west sides of the Meuse River (a sensible plan that, at that early stage in the battle, would likely have resulted in a German victory), Falkenhayn disapproved any German attacks west of the river. Furthermore, Falkenhayn apparently withheld the reserve forces the Fifth Army counted on to follow up its initial assault, despite the fact that the general staff chief had personally approved the Fifth Army plan. Nevertheless, Fifth Army preparations for the February 12 opening attack continued apace.

Only six German divisions were allocated for the initial assault—hardly an overpowering force, even against the weakened French forces known to be there. Of course, the primary reason for such a small German assault force was the assumption that overwhelming German firepower would completely pulverize the French defenders and their sheltering fieldworks. Some German officers confidently informed their men that instead of assaulting the French positions, they would merely be occupying the ground, since nothing could possibly endure such a devastating barrage as the Germans were preparing.

This barrage would truly be monumental. Delivered by a massive force of over 1,200 guns, the opening bombardment was to be the

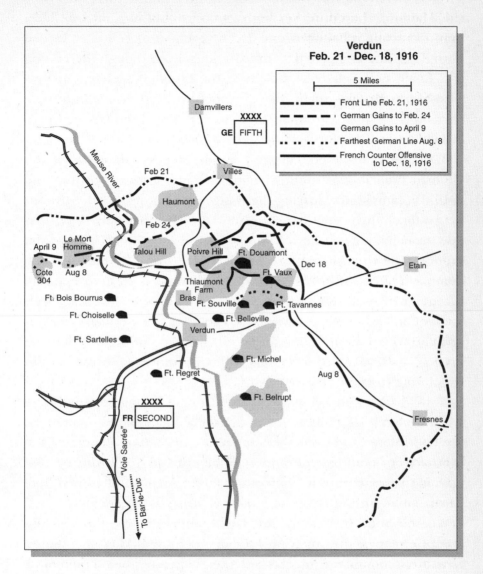

Verdun, February 21–December 18, 1916

greatest firestorm yet witnessed in the war. More than 2,500,000 shells were prepared, mostly high explosive, but also mixed with a new and deadly gas—phosgene. By the evening of February 11, the Fifth Army had completed its preparations. Even though the French had finally and belatedly awoken to the fact that their enemy was readying a massive assault, there seemed to be precious little time remaining for Joffre to do anything to counteract the German plan or even to prepare for it adequately.

That night, however, fate and nature stepped in to upset the German timetable: a storm of rain, ice, and snow broke over the entire Verdun sector, forcing the postponement of the offensive for twenty-four hours, then for nine full days. This probably saved Verdun from falling to the initial German assault, since it gave the French time to rush reinforcements to the area. By the time the weather cleared, two full French divisions were in position opposite the point of the initial assault, which, only days earlier, had been manned by only a single division. To counter the German attack of seventy-two battalions along an assault frontage of eight miles, the French now had twenty battalions, with an additional fourteen within supporting distance.

At 0715 hours on February 21, the German barrage opened. The 1,200 guns of all calibers firing 2,500,000 high-explosive and gas shells splintered trees, smashed bunkers, and shattered bodies. Each foot of front endured the impact of almost fifty shells during that opening barrage, utterly obliterating entire sections of trench line. The rumbling thunder of the guns was heard 100 miles away.

When, about five hours into the bombardment, the shelling abruptly ceased, the surviving French troops, thinking an infantry assault was imminent, quickly left the shelter of their bunkers or trenches and manned defensive positions. But just as abruptly as it had stopped, the bombardment began again—the midday lull had only been a German ruse to lure the survivors out of their protecting fortifications. The shelling continued for hours longer, reaching a crescendo at about 1600 hours. German air observers reported to Fifth Army headquarters that the devastation appeared complete, and that nothing living could have survived the massive shelling. At

1645 hours the barrage finally ceased, and the German infantry began to move forward.

Storm Troops and Flamethrowers

The initial strong patrol-sized formations taken from the seventy-two battalions of the six German assault divisions moved forward as soon as the final shells of the opening bombardment exploded over the French positions. Searching for the weak points in the French lines, the patrols moved through and around the surviving pockets of French defenders. Instead of immediately sending forward the well-dressed lines of advancing infantry, the German commanders along most of the eight-mile assault front held back until the patrols had scouted out the best routes of advance. Bypassing strong points, quickly overrunning weak centers of resistance, and probing the depth of French defenses, the patrols utilized a rudimentary precursor of the so-called Hutier Tactics (storm-trooper methods) later used with such excellent results in the March 1918 offensives. Although the patrols made good, if somewhat tentative, progress during this initial onslaught, they lacked sufficient size and strength to force a really significant breakthrough. Ironically, by holding back the massed lines of infantry in this particular battle, the German commanders failed to take early advantage of the rupture caused by the massive bombardment. The storm-trooper tactics of the opening German infantry actions at Verdun proved too tentative to complete the break of the French line begun by the artillery barrage, and the small pockets of surviving French infantry, which surely would have been quickly overcome by the massed attack of the main body of German infantry, presented stiff resistance. Only in the sector of the VII German Reserve Corps, whose commander (against orders) sent in his main body immediately after his patrols set out, was really significant progress made the first day. Occupying the entire section of the French main defensive line containing the Bois d'Haumont, the VII Reserve Corps achieved the only rupture in the French line.

The German attacks in the Verdun sector were assisted by an entirely new weapon developed especially for the purpose of eliminating resistance from well-fortified bunkers or strong points. February 21 saw the first use of the flamethrower (*Flammenwerfer* to its German inventors). Shooting forth a stream of flame several yards long, this portable, man-packed weapon gave the assault troops a new and terrible means of overcoming any stubborn defenders firing from concrete or earthen bunkers. They simply burned them out.

On February 22, the second day of the battle of Verdun, the main body of the German attack prepared to move forward after more artillery shelling had further softened up the French positions. Before the German main attack could begin, however, the French defenders launched a series of vigorous, if not particularly powerful or well-coordinated, counterattacks. But French spirit and morale could not hope to overcome the great disparity in numbers or the disruption caused by the massive bombardments. The counterattacks soon petered out, and then were swamped by the overwhelming numbers of the German main assault.

Despite the German numerical advantage in troops and guns, however, their attacks made surprisingly little progress on February 22 and 23. Even after suffering tremendous casualties, portions of French units continued to put up a stiff resistance to the German attackers, keeping the enemy advance to a minimum and extracting a terrible price in German flesh and blood. The French 72nd and 51st Divisions stubbornly fought for every inch of ground, yielding grudgingly to the slowly advancing German forces. By February 24, however, weight of numbers and steady pressure began to tell against the French defenders. Beginning the battle with over 26,000 men, the two divisions started the fighting on February 24 with only slightly more than 10,000 battered survivors. Such weakened resistance at the main point of the German attack should have resulted in a stunning breakthrough on February 24; but steadily mounting German casualties coupled with a cautiousness caused by the unexpectedly sharp French resistance led to another day of only mediocre progress.

February 25 represented a change in fortune for the slowly progressing German attack. Worn down by the tremendous barrage, the unrelenting German infantry attacks, and the subsequent dampening of their usually high morale, French forces at Verdun were very near their breaking point. Having already received permission from Joffre to withdraw from the most forward of the defensive positions and concentrate along the heights east and southeast of Verdun, French commanders were anticipating a relinquishment of the entire east bank of the Meuse River. With the situation looking increasingly bleak, another shattering blow fell on the French defenders: Fort Douaumont was captured.

Douaumont and Pétain

Largest and most imposing of all the many forts comprising the Verdun complex, Douaumont dominated the northeastern—and most threatened—portion of the entire battlefield. It was a key position on the twenty-fifth of February, since the withdrawal from the forward defenses the day before had caused the main line of French resistance to move to the outer ring of forts, of which Douaumont was the largest. The threatening image of the huge fort, however, belied its true state. Stripped of all its heavy guns and its entire garrison, Douaumont, on February 25, was defended only by its single 155mm medium turret gun manned by a small group of overage territorial gunners. Its approaches, designed to be guarded by several squads of infantry, stood open to any attacking force. During the afternoon, several small German patrols swarmed through the outerworks, which the Germans were surprised to find completely undefended. Crossing the lowered drawbridge into the fort's inner works, the German assault troops entered the nearly empty fort and surprised all twenty-three members of the turret gun crew. The largest and most famous of all the Verdun forts fell without a shot being fired.

The German capture of Douaumont stunned the French. The morale and propaganda value of this coup was incalculable, and the German press was exultant. Conveniently ignoring the fact that the position was taken with virtually no opposition, the kaiser decorated both the attacking division commander and the junior officer who was erroneously believed to have captured the fort with the Pour le Mérite—Germany's highest valor award. French soldiers and the remaining citizens in Verdun were on the verge of panic, and plans for the abandonment of the entire Verdun sector were being considered. If such a stronghold as Douaumont could be captured so easily, defenders wondered, what chance did the rest of the defense have? French morale had sunk to its lowest ebb.

That very night an event occurred that gave the sagging French morale a needed lift. At midnight, General Henri-Philippe Pétain arrived to take command of the Second Army and overall responsibility for the Verdun sector. An acknowledged master of defensive warfare in an army filled with disciples of the offensive, Pétain inspired the utmost confidence in superiors and subordinates alike. He was considerate of his soldiers' lives and needs and they trusted him implicitly.

Pétain's assignment to command the Verdun defense was suggested to Joffre by his chief of staff, De Castelnau, who had been sent to evaluate the situation in the sector the day before (February 24). Finding it to be near collapse, De Castelnau spent the day reorganizing the sector's defensive arrangements, issuing strict orders forbidding abandonment of the east bank of the Meuse, and directing the overall strengthening of the French lines. In the process, he reaffirmed the decision to bring Pétain to Verdun on the twenty-fifth and convinced Joffre to give the Second Army commander control of the entire Verdun area. In bringing Pétain to Verdun, De Castelnau and Joffre also assured that France would unwittingly comply with Falkenhayn's plan to turn the ancient fortress into a "mincing machine," for Pétain would ensure that the area was defended to the last Frenchman.

Pétain immediately set about reorganizing the defense of the entire area, paying particular attention to French artillery forces. Realizing that the overwhelming German superiority in guns and mortars would eventually be decisive if not counteracted, he turned the growing French artillery force around Verdun into one, increasingly efficient killing machine. As more and more French artillery pieces and mortars arrived in the sector, Pétain had the remaining forts and outerworks rearmed and reoccupied with strong garrisons. Well supplied with food and ammunition, these reinvigorated forts would not surrender as easily as the hapless Douaumont. Fresh infantry also began arriving, and Pétain reorganized the infantry defenses into four mutually supporting corps, including the veteran French XX Corps under General Balfourier.

Perhaps Pétain's most significant innovation during the final days of February 1916 was the establishment of Verdun's logistical lifeline. With the rail line into the town blasted by German long-range heavy guns, the sector's defense was in grave danger of withering away from lack of supplies and reinforcements. To ensure a steady flow of men and matériel into the city, Pétain turned the single road linking the city with the outside world into the "Voie Sacrée"—an indispensable artery for the entire sector. Assigning the equivalent of a division of territorial troops the full-time duty of repairing and maintaining the road, Pétain created a somewhat precarious, but still resilient, and absolutely essential link with the rest of France. Maintained by road crews that operated twenty-four hours a day, this all-important road became an umbilical cord, providing a steady flow of nourishment into the sector. Sometimes averaging one vehicle every five seconds, traffic on the Voie Sacrée made the continuing slaughter at Verdun possible.

Second Wind

By February 28, the opening German offensive had ground to a halt, its momentum expended in forcing the French main line of defense away from the outerworks and back into the strong line of forts and supporting positions. De Castelnau and Pétain's reorganizations of the French fighting forces and supporting arrangements had provided the necessary stiffening of the overall line to finish off the first attacks. Without reserve forces to reinforce it (the units that had been promised by Falkenhayn before the offensive began), the crown prince's Fifth Army could not hope to maintain the assault.

Exhausted by a week of constant attacking, increasingly battered by French artillery pieces—the number of French heavy guns had grown from about 150 to over 500—the German divisions slowed, then finally stopped.

During this first lull both sides frantically gathered reinforcements and sent them to the threatened area. Falkenhayn finally released three full corps to the crown prince along with twenty-one additional heavy-artillery batteries. Over the next week the Germans tried to gain their second wind while the French continued to move more troops and artillery into the zone. Additionally, the French used this hiatus to gather air assets to challenge German air superiority. Amassing almost 190 aircraft of all types—airplanes, observation balloons, and zeppelins—the Germans had dominated the skies of the Verdun sector, preventing free observation of their advancing forces while exercising nearly perfect surveillance of their enemy's movements. In early March, however, the French assembled about 120 aircraft, including a squadron of their aces. Their successful operations ended German air superiority and resulted in a marked improvement in French artillery observation. Its vision restored and its numbers increased, French artillery now assumed a dominant position on the battlefield and proved crucial in preventing a German breakthrough.

It was this French artillery success, as much as anything else, that determined the scope and nature of the renewed German offensive. French artillery positions on the west bank of the Meuse River, unmolested by German infantry attacks, hammered away at the exposed flanks of the German right wing on the east bank. Silencing these artillery positions was a key objective in the new German assault, directed at the dominant terrain feature west of the Meuse—a hill aptly named "le Mort Homme" (the Dead Man). The Fifth Army had originally planned to attack the west bank of the Meuse during the initial assault, but Falkenhayn had vetoed the idea. Now, however, he permitted it to attack in the west, just as he had changed his mind concerning the provision of the reserve units. Belatedly, the key elements of the Fifth Army offensive against Verdun were incorporated into the renewed attack.

On March 6, Fifth Army units launched the second phase of the battle of Verdun with an all-out bombardment similar to the first. Following the massive artillery shelling, German infantry units moved out in force toward le Mort Homme. But instead of being defended by one weak division (as it had been on February 21), the west-bank sector contained four full French divisions. Consequently, German progress against the French infantry and artillery was agonizingly slow. The French defense was assisted by relative German inactivity in other sections. The German attack of March 6 was originally intended to be supported by a simultaneous attack on the French positions on the east bank of the Meuse, in the vicinity of Fort Vaux, and against the Côte-de-Poivre heights. Due to the extreme difficulties of bringing up sufficient infantry and artillery assault forces, however, this attack was delayed. As a result, the French were able to concentrate their resources on slowing and stopping the German west-bank attacks without having to fight for the east bank at the same time.

The German attack to capture le Mort Homme continued throughout the month of March, and was characterized by frontal attacks, fierce bombardments, and French counterattacks. As the front line swept back and forth across the shell-cratered no-man's-land surrounding the hill, the farthest point of the German advance slowly crept up the battered slope. Artillery, no longer merely the instrument of opening barrages, became the principal killing machine. This pounding war of attrition was the characteristic form of combat of the next nine months of the battle. At the end of March, the total of the dead stood at 80,000 Frenchmen and nearly 90,000 Germans. By the time May finally ended, the German attackers had taken le Mort Homme and most of its immediate neighbor, Côte 304, and had secured the west bank of the Meuse. Verdun, however, remained in French hands.

Fort Vaux, the Somme, and the German High Tide

Falkenhayn's objective of bleeding the French army white was in full swing by the time June arrived and the main focus of the German effort had shifted back to the east bank of the Meuse River. But his plan to manipulate the ebb and flow of the battle and to substitute artillery firepower for precious manpower had gone tragically awry. Once Pétain overcame the overwhelming German superiority in fire-power and personnel by building up French forces, Falkenhayn's original idea had been replaced by the standard, uninspired Western Front slaughter, consuming German as well as French troops. After the horrors of March and April, the German general staff chief had queried his operational commander, the crown prince, as to whether or not the entire offensive should be continued. The prince was determined to finish off the French, and so the battle continued.

With the focus of attack now returned almost exclusively to the east bank of the Meuse, the renewed German offensive during the first week of June concentrated on Fort Vaux, southeast of Douaumont, and the Thiaumont Farm, west of the German-held fort. Fort Vaux, completely denuded of any artillery pieces, contained a full-strength garrison of 250 men, plus another 300 or so stragglers from other units who had sought shelter from the artillery fire. Commanded by Major Raynal, who was still crippled by wounds from previous battles, the fort's defenders stood off the concerted German attacks with machine guns and hand grenades.

For an entire week Fort Vaux withstood the intense German attacks, some of which penetrated into the interior of the fort itself. Fierce hand-to-hand fighting in the dark, smoke-and-gas-filled corridors of the stronghold alternated with German demolitions and flame-thrower assaults on its exterior. French attempts to relieve the battered garrison were consistently unsuccessful, and although Raynal and his men stoutly resisted each new German attack, the lack of water within the fort fatally weakened the Frenchmen. The defenders of Vaux lost a total of about 100 men during the week-long assault, but the attacking Germans suffered nearly 3,000 casualties.

On June 7, with many of his men collapsing or mad from thirst, Raynal reluctantly surrendered the fort and its garrison. His heroic defense of the important outer fort somewhat mitigated the loss, but the German capture of Vaux on June 7 and the Thiaumont Farm two days later placed the entire French defensive position on the east bank of the Meuse River in danger.

Pétain, promoted to army group command in May, conferred with his subordinate commanders, Generals Nivelle and Mangin, about the critical situation on the Verdun front. All agreed that unless the German pressure was relieved by Allied attacks in another area, the east bank positions, including Verdun itself, would likely be lost. Pétain petitioned Joffre to push for an early start to the planned Allied offensive on the Somme River in the British sector. The Somme offensive, intended to be the Allies' major effort in 1916, had been delayed because of Verdun. Now, however, the critical situation at the latter position, coupled with the Allied belief that the enemy was pushing so hard there, out of weariness, caused the high command to implement the Somme plan, moving the attack forward from August 1 to July 1.

Before the Somme offensive kicked off, however, the Germans continued to flail at French defenses east of Verdun. On June 20, German gunners blasted French artillery positions with shells containing deadly phosgene, which disrupted French artillery support and greatly facilitated the progress of a vigorous German attack on June 23. Sweeping nearly to the commanding heights directly east of the Meuse River, the German attack brushed aside the frantic French counterattacks and made good progress.

On June 24, however, the Somme erupted. The week-long bombardment preceding this (mostly) British offensive began on the morning of June 24, and had the effect of distracting German attention away from Verdun. Falkenhayn, fearing the new Allied offensive, diverted reinforcements from the Verdun sector to the Somme and redirected the flow of artillery ammunition to the northern sector of the front lines. This redirection of resources effectively ended the most threatening of the German assaults and essentially saved the city for France.

Despite this weakening of the German forces in the Verdun sector, however, the farthest line of advance by the crown prince's Fifth Army had not yet been reached. German forces surged forward once more, nearly cracking the French line on July 11. Pressing on even though the necessary resources of men and matériel were no longer flowing in, the crown prince's forces reached a high-tide mark on August 9. This farthest line of German penetration, however, still left the Fifth Army well short of capturing the inner ring of protecting forts in the Verdun complex, as well as leaving the French in possession of the east bank of the Meuse. The German failure to produce any positive results from its six months of attrition warfare also cost Falkenhayn his job as chief of the general staff. While Falkenhayn's scheme had indeed produced the predicted number of French corpses at Verdun, it had produced equal numbers of German ones.

Counteroffensive—Ground Regained

Falkenhayn's replacement as German general staff chief was the team of Generals Hindenburg and Ludendorff. Upon assuming command, the heroes of Tannenberg and the Eastern Front immediately suspended offensive operations in the Verdun sector, concentrating Germany's efforts on the Somme. From that point to the end of the battle in December, the roles of attacker and defender reversed: the French assumed the offensive and the German Fifth Army became the beleaguered defenders.

The primary French assault of the Verdun counteroffensive began on October 24 after another massive artillery barrage. For this bombardment, Pétain's subordinates, Nivelle and Mangin, had gathered together 650 artillery pieces, about half of them heavy guns, including two giant 400mm railway guns. Stockpiling of artillery ammunition continued throughout September and October, resulting in over 15,000 tons of shells. The tremendous bombardment began on

October 19 and pounded the German positions for several days. By the time the three French infantry divisions of the first wave set off on the initial assault, only 90 of the 158 German batteries remained in operation. Even massive Fort Douaumont suffered under the pounding of the super-heavy railway guns, and the 400mm shells penetrated into the interior of the stronghold, cracking its roof and killing many of the German garrison. Fires within Douaumont threatened the magazines, and the fort's commander ordered it abandoned. When the French attack started, only about twenty German soldiers defended the huge fort.

Backed by a second line of three divisions with an additional two divisions in close reserve, the three French divisions moved forward on October 24, progressing at a stately 100 yards every four minutes behind another innovation of the battle of Verdun, the "creeping barrage." Designed to eliminate the dead space following the ending of the assault barrage and the arrival of the attacking troops in the enemy's trenches, this maneuver required perfect coordination between the advancing infantry and its supporting artillery. Tried for one of the first times in the war during the French counterattack, the tactic proved successful.

Rapidly covering ground that had been so fiercely fought over for eight months, the advancing French forces captured huge sections of the German line. Disheartened by the constant attrition warfare, the German forces failed to show the stubbornness that had characterized their fighting during the previous months. Douaumont, which should have played a key role in holding up the French assault, fell on the first day of the attack, after only a token resistance by its two dozen German defenders. That same day French forces recaptured territory it had taken the Germans nearly five months to overrun.

The French success in the October counteroffensive was repeated to a lesser degree in December, when the final phase of the nearly year-long battle of Verdun occurred. The demoralization of the crown prince's forces was reflected in the fact that the French December counteroffensive managed to seize 11,000 German prisoners while pushing the main German line back from its hard-won ground.

By December 18, the French had regained a large portion of the Verdun sector lost to the Germans between February and August. In addition to reclaiming Douaumont, the French dramatically recaptured Fort Vaux. Although sporadic fighting continued to occur in the battered sector up to the end of the war, the great battle was over by mid-December 1916.

Aftermath

For the expenditure of a million casualties and untold amounts of national treasure, the tangible results of the battle of Verdun were negligible. After ten months of grueling combat, the front line separating German and French forces had been advanced an insignificant distance to the west. Although somewhat smaller than it had been in February 1916, the Verdun salient still thrust itself into the center of the German line, and it would continue to do so nearly to the end of the war. No appreciable tactical gains or strategic breakthroughs resulted from the struggle. There was no dramatic shift in the balance of forces.

But Falkenhayn's original plan was not supposed to produce any dramatic battlefield breakthrough. It was designed, rather, to cripple the French army. In that regard, the ten months of fighting were much more successful. The French suffered half a million casualties, and three quarters of its army contributed to them. Rotating the bulk of French forces through the Verdun sector during the battle spread the physical and, perhaps more important, the psychological horror of that battle through most of the French army of 1916. Possessed of a seemingly indomitable spirit at the beginning of the battle, French forces were bleating like sheep and stoning prime ministers by its conclusion. As we said, Verdun set the stage for the mutinies that took place in many French units in 1917.

The flaw in Falkenhayn's plan, however, was that the slaughter worked both ways, and about half a million German forces were lost. Attrition warfare seldom produces significantly fewer casualties on one side. The German Verdun offensive went a long way toward breaking the spirit of the French army, but it also served to break the spirit of the German army. By making battlefield attrition his single objective, the German general staff chief had, as it turned out, charted a course to an unobtainable goal.

The Meuse-Argonne Offensive

September 26–November 11, 1918

What turned out to be the final major offensive of World War I was fought in the French countryside along the banks of the Meuse River and in the tangled, rugged forests of the Argonne a dozen miles to the west. It began as an attempt to force the German armies to retreat back onto German soil, where the Allies, in a spring 1919 offensive, could launch a final assault and bring the four-year bloodbath to a conclusion. But the results of the Meuse-Argonne offensive, along with major complementary assaults farther north by British, Belgian, and French armies, far exceeded its planners hopes. Instead of merely pushing the German lines back into stronger positions within the borders of Germany, there to await the inevitable coup de grâce of a massive attack, the Allied offensives of August to November 1918 unexpectedly shattered Ludendorff's carefully prepared defensive lines, and sent the German armies into final retreat.

The key element to the success of Allied commander in chief Maréchal Foch's unprecedented general offensive all along the front in the late summer and fall of 1918 was the surprising performance of the inexperienced American army in the Meuse-Argonne. Eventually employing 1,250,000 troops, the American attack managed to capture the one German defensive sector that proved absolutely vital to Ludendorff's forces maintenance of a cohesive defensive line.

The Meuse-Argonne offensive ended the war, but the American armies of General John J. Pershing paid a stiff price for their triumphs. Fully 120,000 Americans became casualties, resulting in a total of 320,710 U.S. casualties for the war, during barely four months of wide-scale participation. This is far less than the numbers of British, French, Russian, Germans, and Austro-Hungarians who perished, were wounded, or were captured, but represented nearly 10 percent of the American troops who participated. This sacrifice ensured the success of an offensive that was expected to take much longer and was meant merely to set up the enemy for a final assault rather than knock him out completely. In this light, the Americans who gave up their lives helped save the lives of countless more Britons, Frenchmen, and Germans who might otherwise have perished in that final thrust.

No End in Sight

As the summer of 1918 progressed, the leaders on both sides of the long front line could foresee no rapid end to the terrible conflict. It was generally assumed that no end could reasonably be expected before the middle of 1919, at the earliest. By mid-1918, Germany could no longer entertain any hope of actually winning the war, but Hindenburg and Ludendorff still thought their forces were fully capable of conducting a skillful, cohesive defensive battle that would force the Allies to grant peace terms favorable to their country.

The Ludendorff offensives of the spring and summer had come dangerously close to breaching the Allied lines in several places, and forcing the Allies to the peace table. Employing seventy fresh German divisions freed from the Eastern Front by the Russian Revolution, Ludendorff's offensives hit the Allies with a series of powerful blows. Utilizing the imaginative Hutier tactics we referred to earlier, which emphasized surprise attacks by specially trained storm-troops infiltrating and bypassing strong points, and supported by carefully coordinated artillery barrages, the Kaiserschlacht offensives kicked off on March 21. Nearly accomplishing their purpose, the attacks were stopped before fatal ruptures of the Allied line could occur. Although they failed to win the war, the Ludendorff offensives left three huge salients protruding into the Allied side of the line.

Even as the great Ludendorff offensives of the spring and early summer of 1918 were grinding to a halt, Allied commander in chief Maréchal Foch was planning how he might finish off the Germans in France and Belgium during the latter half of that year, then break the enemy armies defending their own homeland with a powerful offensive against Germany in the spring of 1919. Having withstood the greatest German challenge since 1914 by turning back Ludendorff's recent attacks, Foch's Allied armies, now bolstered by the arrival of American troops, were poised to jump off on their own powerful offensive. The initial phase of Foch's plan involved eliminating the three great salients Ludendorff had created over the past few months—in the north near Amiens, east of Paris around the Marne, and at St.-Mihiel, south of Verdun. The clearing began in the second half of July.

On July 18, French, British, Italian, and American troops, supported by 300 tanks, began reducing the Marne salient. Progressing steadily against stiff German resistance, the Allied attack succeeded in eliminating the Marne salient by the end of the first week of August. With barely a breather, the Allied forces took on the Amiens salient in the north, jumping off on August 8 (later called, by Ludendorff, the "Black Day" for the German army). An Anglo-French effort, the offensive included seventeen British and ten French divisions, supported by 600 tanks, several thousand guns, and nearly 2,000 airplanes. By September, the Amiens salient was gone, as were another 100,000 German soldiers. The third salient, St.-Mihiel, was essentially an all-American show.

Pershing's newly formed U.S. First Army (officially activated on August 10) was assigned by Foch to attack and eliminate the thirty-two-mile St.-Mihiel salient, just south of Verdun. The sixteen big United States infantry divisions (about twice the size of any Allied or German division) were supported by troops of the French II Colonial Corps, 3,000 guns, and 2,000 aircraft. The operation was a solid success for the American army, although Ludendorff's rearranging of his forces at the start of the battle resulted in an easier go for the United States troops. Commencing on September 12, the American attack hit the St.-Mihiel salient three days after Ludendorff had decided to order its evacuation. By the eleventh, all of the German heavy guns had already been withdrawn, though most of the infantry was still in position. Within thirty-six hours, the salient would be cleared of all German troops, and U.S. forces would capture 15,000 of the enemy and 250 of his guns. Continuing to advance, Pershing was forced to halt his troops on Foch's order forty-eight hours after the attack began. Suffering only about 7,000 casualties, Pershing thought his troops could have continued on and captured the German fortress city of Metz if Foch had not stopped them. By September 14, the last of the German salients was eliminated. Phase two of Foch's grand scheme was ready.

Foch's Plan

The successes of the Allied attacks in reducing the three salients gave Maréchal Foch increasing confidence that the Germans could, at least, be thrown out of France during the remainder of 1918 (and he was also beginning to suspect there might be an outside chance to end the war early in 1919). For the next phase of the Allied offensives, he planned to execute a series of major thrusts at several critical portions of the German lines north of Verdun and south of Flanders. Foch chose to threaten the critical German rail arteries in four important sectors of the front. The rail links were absolutely essential to providing the logistical base for maintaining any form of cohesive defensive line, and their capture would prevent the Germans from continuing operations of any intensity in their present positions.

By mid-September 1918, Foch had amassed 220 Allied divisions, including 42 of the large American divisions. He decided to put 160 divisions in the line and keep the remaining 60 in reserve to exploit any breakthroughs that might occur. In attacking in four separate locations, set to begin at different times in different locations, and thereby throwing the German defenders off balance, Foch hoped to exhaust the already depleted German reserves and force Ludendorff to spread his thin forces across the width and breadth of the battle-field.

Opposing the Allies were, on paper at least, 197 German divisions. There were 113 divisions occupying positions in the line backed up by 84 in reserve. In reality, the Germans mustered no more than 50 divisions capable of fighting effectively. Nevertheless, the Germans were still capable of conducting a skillful and determined defense. They had not yet reached the point of complete exhaustion, and any withdrawal to rearward positions need not yet be a panicked rout. Ludendorff still hoped to continue a cohesive defensive line behind which the German forces could, when finally forced by the pressure of the Allied drives, retire in good order. In anticipation of the in-evitable Allied drives, Ludendorff had directed the preparation of strong defensive sectors behind the German front lines. Taking their names from German legend and history, these sectors included Sieg-fried, Hundung, Brunhild, Kriemhilde, and Michel. Ludendorff hoped the strong defenses of these sectors would allow his outnum-bered forces to keep the Allies off German territory until the spring of 1919. If so, the possibility of a negotiated peace with terms favor-able to Germany was still feasible. To make this scheme work, how-ever, the Argonne Forest region—a key part of the overall German defensive arrangement—was expected to hold against any Allied as-sault. If the Argonne fell, the German line would likely collapse de-spite Ludendorff's troops best efforts.

Foch assigned the mission of clearing the Argonne Forest to the eager American troops of Pershing's First Army. Assisted by the French Fourth Army, the American First Army (later divided into the First and Second American Armies under Pershing's overall army group command) were to crack the strong German defenses be-tween the heights overlooking the Meuse River and the imposing positions within the Argonne Forest. The French Fourth Army would follow, in echelon, along the Americans' left flank, advancing when the Argonne had been cleared. Moving forward only after the Amer-icans had provided them with a protected flank, the French would allow the U.S. formations to handle the bulk of the heavy fighting.

The Franco-American attack in the Meuse-Argonne would be the leadoff assault for the entire Allied offensive. Scheduled to begin on September 26, it would be followed in rapid succession by the other three offensives in other sectors of the line. On September 27, the British First and Third Armies would launch an attack toward the Canal du Nord, east of Amiens. The next day, the Belgian army and the British Second Army at the north end of the Allied line would launch an attack eastward to seize Brugge and Brussels. Finally, on September 29, the British Fourth and French First Armies would kick off an offensive near the center of the line, just north of the Meuse-Argonne sector. If all went well, and especially if the Americans could seize the defensive positions in their key sector, Ludendorff's strong defenses would be cracked once and for all.

The Argonne Forest—Tactical Nightmare

The sector assigned to Pershing and the Americans was a difficult one for several reasons. Just getting there and maintaining a large force was no mean accomplishment. Before the beginning of the battle, 600,000 U.S. troops had to be moved in secrecy, at night, to replace the 220,000 French troops already in place. The U.S. zone included the Verdun battlefield—what little of it remained. The American First Army staff had to deal with the innumerable problems created by the vast, widespread devastation in the entire sector resulting from the fighting of 1916, while simultaneously overcoming their own lack of experience in controlling mass forces. With the transportation network in the Verdun area virtually destroyed, the movement of troops, supplies, and equipment was extremely difficult, even for experienced units and staffs. There were only two militarily usable roads in the U.S. zone, one on the extreme end of each flank. Both roads were continually exposed to German artillery interdiction.

Once the American divisions were situated in their assigned sector, the Argonne Forest itself became a principal enemy. Virtually unmolested for the previous four years of war, the Argonne region contained a carefully prepared German defensive system of thousands of interlocking fighting positions. The forest region is spread over the hills, ridges, and sharp gullies of the Aire and Aisne River areas. With sharp slopes up to 750 feet high, it is a rugged, forbidding place to fight a major battle. To worsen an already bad situation, the preliminary Allied bombardment turned a barely passable region into a nearly impassable mass of shattered trees, broken terrain, and thick underbrush. The Germans contributed to the chaotic situation on the ground by covering the entire area with barbed wire and netting. Any attempted advance through this tangle of natural and man-made obstructions would be a soldier's nightmare.

The twelve-mile sector between the forest and the heights above the Meuse River was also difficult to advance across, not because of its terrain but because of its German defenders. The Germans had decided to use a "scorched earth" strategy to delay any Allied advance in this sector, and systematically destroyed the infrastructure of the entire area. They burned all villages and destroyed every road and railway bridge, large or small. They blew up railway and road embankments and cuttings and poisoned or polluted wells and water supplies. Finally, they laid booby traps throughout the sector, forcing any advancing troops to proceed with extreme caution. Any American success in this forbidding zone would be costly.

The First U.S. Army Attacks

For the initial assault on September 26, General Pershing gathered fifteen infantry divisions and one cavalry division. Nine infantry divisions were arrayed in the front line to lead off the assault, with three infantry divisions in immediate reserve. The remaining units were initially kept in army reserve. The total frontage for the American attack, including the Argonne Forest area, was twenty-two miles, across which the first 300,000 U.S. troops would operate. At 0230 hours on September 26, the 2,700 artillery pieces of the Allied barrage began a three-hour bombardment of the German lines opposite the waiting American divisions. At 0530 hours the U.S. troops moved out.

The first phase of the American attack went relatively well. In the sector between the Meuse River and the Argonne Forest, the troops advanced seven miles in just two days. In the center of the sector, the formidable defenses of Montfaucon were expected to delay their advance for quite some time (at one point before the beginning of the offensive, Foch doubted the Americans could take Montfaucon before the beginning of 1919), but to everyone's surprise, the city was surrounded on the first day of the attack, then taken by storm by the 79th Infantry Division on the second day. By the end of September 28, Bullard's III Corps on the right flank and Cameron's V Corps in the center had pushed the front forward about seven miles from the Meuse River to the edge of the Argonne. During the next eleven days, however, the troops were able to progress only an additional two miles. Although much of the slowness of the American advance can be attributed to stiff German resistance—Ludendorff moved German reserves into the area and eventually had forty divisions opposing the Americans—acute problems in moving supplies to the forward troops accounted for much of it.

Pershing's hopes that his units might be spared the agony of fighting within the treacherous forest were dashed early on in the battle by the persistent and accurate flanking fire coming from well-sited German guns in the forest. Instead of being able to bypass the Argonne, Pershing's troops would have to clear the region, especially if the French Fourth Army were to take part in the fight—without a protected right flank, they could not move forward. The American units of General Hunter Liggett's I Corps moved into the nightmare terrain of the Argonne, where the fighting would literally be from tree to tree.

The restricted terrain, already a challenge, was blasted into near impassibility by the Allied barrage and German counterfire. Orderly advances were impossible through the precipitous slopes, deep ravines, and tangled underbrush, and units found it increasingly difficult to maintain contact with each other. The German barbed wire, much of it laid four years earlier, was now concealed by dense un-

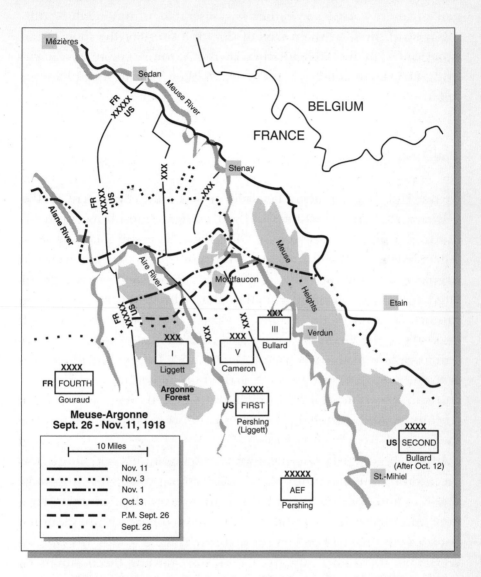

Meuse-Argonne, September 26–November 11, 1918

dergrowth, trapping troops and further slowing their progress. To make matters worse, the weather was miserable, with rain falling during forty of the forty-seven days of the offensive. For the men of the American 77th and 28th Infantry Divisions, the Argonne Forest was living hell. By the end of September 28, they had advanced barely a mile.

The Lost Battalion

At the end of September, Pershing ordered a general halt to the offensive in order to reorganize the American lines, bring up fresh units, and prepare to continue the attack. The stiff German resistance, bolstered by fresh reserves, the agonizingly slow going in the Argonne, and the difficulty of bringing up supplies over the devastated rear area convinced Pershing that a brief halt was critical to success. In front of the III and V Corps, the Americans faced the outskirts of the German Hindenburg Line, the third and strongest defensive line in the Meuse-Argonne sector. The line included several strong terrain features, such as the Bois de Forêt, Cunel Heights, and the Romagne Heights, which the Germans had, as was their custom, skillfully fortified. The American forces prepared to resume the general offensive on October 4.

In the Argonne Forest, meanwhile, slow progress had continued even during the halt. On October 2, Pershing reluctantly informed the 77th and 28th Infantry Divisions to give up all attempts to conduct an orderly advance while maintaining contact with flank units. Such an advance had proven futile in the rugged woods. Instead, all units were to advance straight ahead, disregarding the positions of any units on their flanks, and attempt to capture as much ground as possible. Once a position was captured under this procedure, it would be stoutly defended against any German counterattack. These strong points would, presumably, so occupy the German defenders that they would not be able to interfere with the advancing American forces to the east of the woods or the French forces to the west. One force from the 77th Infantry Division which followed Pershing's instructions to the letter, became known as the "Lost Battalion." The unit's experience highlights the difficulties of the fighting in the Argonne Forest.

Under the command of Major Charles Whittlesey, the so-called Lost Battalion was neither lost nor a battalion. The force Whittlesey commanded consisted of about 550 men from portions of three battalions of the 77th Infantry Division. Whittlesey, with six companies of the 308th Infantry Regiment, was joined by a company of the 307th Infantry Regiment as well as men from two companies of the 306th Machine Gun Battalion in a forward position Whittlesey's men had captured just south of Charlevaux Mill on October 2. Occupying the position in compliance with Pershing's directive not to worry about flank communications, Whittlesey's men were cut off by a strong German counterattack at dawn on October 3. Bringing up barbed-wire barricades and numerous machine guns, the Germans blocked any possible retreat. Ringing Whittlesey's men with artillery and mortars, they began a deadly bombardment. Without proper equipment to prepare trenches and earthworks, the Americans were nearly powerless.

The 77th Division knew the approximate location of Whittlesey's men, but was unable to reach him through the strong German defenses. Expedients, including a primitive airdrop, were tried in the hope of getting relief supplies to the men, but all attempts failed. Several planes were shot down by German ground fire as they skimmed the woods searching for Whittlesey's unit, and nine of the trapped men were killed or captured as they made a desperate dash to retrieve air-dropped supplies that had fallen just beyond their perimeter. Runners sent out by the trapped unit to reach the 77th's lines were all killed. Not knowing the Lost Battalion's precise location, the 77th's supporting artillery inadvertently fired friendly artillery rounds into the unit's perimeter, adding to the casualty count. The unit's last carrier pigeon, wounded but still flying, miraculously made it back to 77th Division headquarters and got the artillery fire lifted. Finally, Private Krotoshinsky made it through German lines, then guided the relieving force back to save the survivors of Whittlesey's force. On the evening of October 7, five days after being cut off, the Lost Battalion was rescued by advancing units of the 77th Division. Only 194 men were left.

Constant Pressure

By October 10, over 1 million American troops were involved in the Meuse-Argonne offensive battle area, and on that day Pershing formed the Second U.S. Army, under command of Major General Robert Bullard (moving up from his command of III Corps). Lieutenant General Hunter Liggett gave up command of the I Corps and assumed command of the First Army. Through these unit reorganizations and command changes, Pershing moved up to the equivalent of army group command. Progress of his newly reorganized American forces, however, continued to be difficult as Ludendorff stiffened German defenses in the sector.

Bullard's command was expanded to include the east bank of the Meuse in order to clear the heights on that side and so end German interdiction of the American advance. The combined U.S. and French forces operating here, including the U.S. 29th and 33rd Infantry Divisions, successfully cleared the heights and facilitated the advance of the units on the west bank. With the American advance in the center moving beyond the Argonne, and the flank attack on the forest threatening the remaining German defenders, Ludendorff ordered the woods evacuated on October 9. By the end of October 10, the forest had been cleared, and the front line moved beyond its edges.

On October 12, the attacks all along the American line quieted down to allow supplies and ammunition to catch up with the advance. When the offensive resumed once more on October 14, the Americans faced the strong Kriemhilde Line defenses. The lineup of U.S. divisions had changed since the offensive began eighteen days earlier. From right to left the units were: 4th, 3rd, and 5th Infantry Divisions of the III Corps; 32nd and 42nd Infantry Divisions of the V Corps; and the 82nd and 77th Infantry Divisions of the I Corps. Despite slow going, the Kriemhilde Line was breached three days later. Pershing directed another strong general offensive on October 21, to keep the pressure on the German defenders and prevent them from stabilizing their defensive lines.

Ludendorff's situation was becoming increasingly desperate. With the loss of the key defensive positions in the Meuse-Argonne region, the entire German defense was unhinged. The British forces farther north had broken through near Cambrai and were moving into the open country beyond. The resumption of the Franco-American offensive would complete the giant pincer maneuver, forcing the Germans all the way back beyond the Belgian border, effectively evacuating France for the first time since 1914. Keeping up a constant pressure all along the line, the Allied forces continued to gain ground and push the Germans back until, by the final day of October 1918, the Americans faced relatively open country, and the last, final push could begin.

The end to organized German resistance began with this Allied push along the line on November 1. After a heavy, but short barrage, the Allies surged forward, encountering ever-weakening German resistance. By November 3, the left wing of Pershing's forces had advanced another ten miles and was prepared to sweep north and eastward to close up on the Meuse. On November 7, I Corps units were prepared to enter the important city of Sedan, scene of the French humiliation in 1870. The U.S. forces were stopped at the gates of Sedan, however, so that French units could be given the honor of entering the city and so removing some of the bitterness of the 1870 debacle. (This sop to French honor, it seems, became an American habit, continuing through World War II, where it was continually invoked by French leaders trying to regain some pride after losing yet another war to the Germans.) After closing up on the Meuse River, the American First Army was pointed toward Longwy, and the Second Army prepared to attack in the direction of Briey. At 1100 hours on November 11, however, the armistice ending the fighting stopped both drives.

Aftermath

Abandoned by its Central Powers allies and faced with starvation, revolution, and chaos, Germany sued for peace. The final Allied offensive had severely beaten Germany's forces in the field, and they were too weak to continue fighting. But the armistice saved the German military forces from the final humiliation of abject surrender on the battlefield, allowing a later generation of German leaders to create the myth of "Germany's stab in the back" while it still possessed the means of achieving victory. Such nonsense was as actively promoted by such men as Ludendorff, who had a stake in the fiction, as it was lapped up by a demoralized population. If Germany was stabbed anywhere, it was in the chest, not the back—and the knife was wielded primarily (but certainly not solely) by an American.

The Meuse-Argonne offensive showed that the forces of the United States, barely off the transatlantic boat, were capable of accomplishing astonishing feats of organization, command and control, and combat. An army that numbered only thousands at its country's entry into the war in 1917, had become a combat-proven force numbering in the millions a short eighteen months later. Possessing no formation larger than a regiment only a few months before the beginning of the war, the American Expeditionary Force comprised two field armies containing dozens of divisions by its completion. Creating, virtually from scratch, the First American Army in August 1918, Pershing led the unit into the largest American military operation to that point in the nation's history a month later.

Of course, the American Command and the exuberant but inexperienced American troops made many mistakes during the final months of the Great War. More experienced, seasoned staffs and troops would probably have planned better and suffered fewer casualties than did Pershing's forces in the Meuse-Argonne. It is almost certain, however, that more cautious, deliberate leaders and soldiers would not have enjoyed the unexpected successes of Pershing's men. The American advances in the Meuse-Argonne showed the mistakes of inexperience—especially in maintaining the flow of logistical support—but their progress throughout the offensive was steady and reliable. The young, aggressive Americans marched through a long series of defensive strongholds skillfully held by determined German defenders. The U.S. attack, continually pressed against the German lines, prevented the enemy from strengthening his successive lines of resistance and reorganizing his defenses in a manner that would have allowed him to slow or stop the Allied attacks. Without the American success in the Meuse-Argonne region, the war would likely have dragged on for another six months, well into 1919. The United States had done much better than anyone on the Allied side expected, and surprised friends and foes alike.

CHAPTER FIVE

The Second World War

• 1939–1945 •

STALINGRAD,
BATTLE OF THE BULGE, OKINAWA

Mass Grave, Last Gamble, and Imperial Sunset

Three of the most horrific battles in human history occurred during
the greatest tragedy of the twentieth century—the Second World
War. These three struggles took place at different times and on different fronts, but each marked a significant turning point or established a terrible landmark in the global conflagration. In the brutal
Russian winter of 1942–43, the rubble that was once the city of Stalingrad became a mass grave for the German Sixth Army as the battered Red Army regrouped itself and took the offensive to shatter
Hitler's dream of an eastern empire. Two years after this German
disaster on the Eastern Front, the Nazi dictator attempted a final
offensive, a last gamble to stop the relentless Allied advance in the
west. The German Ardennes offensive, known as the Battle of the
Bulge, was and remains the greatest land battle ever fought by the
United States Army. By winning this monumental struggle, the Western Allies destroyed Hitler's last remaining mobile reserves and
opened the way for the final invasion of Germany. The last and
greatest land battle of the Pacific War was the struggle for Okinawa,
fought on that rugged island from April to July of 1945. The Japa-

nese imperial sun had finally set by the end of this battle, and Japan surrendered unconditionally six weeks later. The bloody cost of this last major battle of World War II was 50,000 American casualties and nearly 120,000 Japanese, mostly killed. Perhaps more important, the fanatical Japanese resistance and willingness to launch countless suicide attacks during this battle was a large factor in convincing American leaders that an invasion of Japan would be too costly. Their alternative solution was dropped on Hiroshima on August 6, 1945.

Stalingrad, Russia, October 20, 1942: *Sergeant Jacob Pavlov, a squat, stocky, Russian peasant commanding a motley force of men from all parts of the Soviet Union had been defending a battered, red-brick house standing a scant 200 yards from the Volga River for nearly a month. Despite repeated attacks on his stronghold, by then known throughout the ranks of the Russian defenders as "Pavlov's House," the enemy had been unable to dislodge Pavlov. With their backs to the river, however, and German assaults constantly hammering on the outnumbered defenders, holding on to this strong point in the crumbling city was rapidly becoming problematic. Suddenly four panzers approached the house from behind the rubble of the German positions, accompanying infantry scurrying between the armored monsters. Pavlov instantly reacted to the threat, ordering half his men into the cellar, the other half upstairs to the fourth floor. Moments later, when the Nazi tanks began to blast away at Pavlov's House, their close proximity to the building permitted them to fire only into the now unoccupied first, second, and third floors. From their fourth floor vantage point, Pavlov and his antitank gunner sprayed the German infantry with deadly fire. The Germans gave up the assault and retreated to safety. Sergeant Pavlov and his beleaguered soldiers would continue this life-and-death struggle for the crumbling, shattered shell of a house for fifty-eight terrible days.*

Hundreds of miles away and two years later, other German armies were attempting a last, desperate gamble to stop the nearly irresistible advance of the Western Allies. As his target for what would be Germany's greatest offensive on the Western Front, Hitler chose the rugged, isolated, Ardennes region of Belgium and Luxembourg— the most thinly defended sector of the entire Allied line.

Baugnez Crossroads, near Malmédy, Belgium, December 17, 1944: *Tech Sergeant Eugene Garrett of Battery B, 285th Field Artillery Observation Battalion, jumped out of the back of the two-and-a-half ton truck that was carrying his unit southward to reinforce the outnumbered defenders of the threatened sector of the Allied line on what was then the second day of the massive German Ardennes offensive. Garrett's*

*unit, part of the 7th Armored Division, had started its journey from Holland early
that morning and had experienced nothing but stop-and-go travel, and numerous
delays. To Garrett and most of his comrades, this particular stop seemed so routine
that they did not even bother to take their weapons when they left the trucks. But as
soon as the men got out of the trucks, they were confronted by Nazi troops backed up
by an armored convoy. Without a shot being fired, the 100 men of Garrett's unit
were rounded up and captured by a powerful Nazi combat unit, elements of SS
Colonel Jochen Peiper's 1st SS Panzer Regiment.*

*Garrett immediately recognized the danger he was in, since most American soldiers
were very familiar with the stories of the brutality of Hitler's SS. A few minutes after
his capture, while the Americans were being herded into ragged ranks by their captors,
one of Garrett's officers protested that the Nazis were stealing his men's watches and
personal effects. An SS man casually put his pistol to the officer's forehead and pulled
the trigger, murdering the man. Within a few minutes all the captured Americans
were marched into an open field near the crossroads. After standing in the field a
brief time, a German half-track pulled up. An SS officer stood up in the back of the
vehicle, took out his pistol, and shot a captured medic in the front row of prisoners.
Soon machine guns, placed into position to cover the helpless men, opened up on the
remaining Americans, cutting them down where they stood. The most notorious incident of the Battle of the Bulge—the Malmédy Massacre—had begun.*

Two months after Hitler's Ardennes offensive was crushed in Western Europe, the last great land battle of the Pacific Theater began.
Although no major action occurring on any island or archipelago in
the Pacific Ocean can be solely a land battle, the terrific struggle to
defeat the Japanese 32nd Army on the 800-square-mile island of Okinawa was, in scope and intensity, the largest single land-combat
phase of any campaign in that watery theater.

Near the Southern Tip of Okinawa, June 18, 1945: *U.S. Army and Marine Corps
units had pushed the remnants of the battered Japanese 32nd Army into a rapidly
closing box on the southernmost tip of Okinawa after nearly three months of savage
fighting. Now they were moving in for the kill, and their commanding officer, the
Tenth Army's Lieutenant General Simon B. Buckner, wanted a closer look. Early
that morning Buckner made his way to the command post of the 3rd Battalion, 8th
Marine Regiment of the 1st Marine Division, whose troops were maneuvering
through the still-lethal Japanese fire in these final days of organized resistance. Despite
warnings that Japanese snipers and shellfire made it extremely dangerous to get too
close to the advancing elements, Buckner pushed on to a small observation post
nestled in the coral rock where he could overlook the marine advance. Peering through
a narrow slit in the coral, he could observe the brutal fighting and tank-infantry-
artillery-team tactics necessary to blast the suicidal Japanese defenders from their
concealed positions in every cave, spider hole, and bunker in their way.*

The Japanese commanders had decreed that they and their men would turn back the Americans or die in the attempt. By this point in the war, defeating an American attack was no longer a possibility. Only an honorable death in battle or ritual suicide were acceptable, and Japanese soldiers intended to take as many Americans with them as they could. Suddenly, as Buckner was observing the marines' progress against this fanatical resistance, a well hidden Japanese antitank gun opened up and began pumping 47mm rounds into the cramped space of his observation post. Four, then five, and finally six rounds exploded in and around his position, spraying shell fragments and equally deadly pieces of rock-hard coral in every direction. As the smoke and dust cleared, aides spotted Buckner lying on the ground with a gaping wound in his chest. A few moments later the commander of all American forces on Okinawa lay dead. General Buckner was one of 6,319 Americans killed during this last great land battle of World War II. One hundred thousand Japanese troops died there defending the emperor's honor in a tragic and futile continuation of the war Japan had lost years earlier.

These three great land battles of the Second World War were indeed terrible, but they were far from unique. This global war's gifts to posterity include blitzkrieg, genocide, carpet bombing, kamikaze suicide attacks, mass murder, man-made firestorms, and, ultimately, the atomic holocaust. The world had not seen six such years of horror, cruelty, and abomination, and even now, it has not yet fully recovered from them.

In the Europe of 1919–39, France and Great Britain presided over a vastly changed map with a significantly different cast of characters from the one that existed prior to the war. Newly created countries, anxious to promote their own interests, were not content to be obedient pawns in the machinations of their more powerful neighbors. Germany, the most important prewar economic and military power of central Europe, was struggling with the Weimar Republic democracy the Allies had imposed upon it at the end of the war as well as suffering under an economy crippled by war reparations. Most European leaders realized that Germany should be allowed to become a major European power again, but how and when that delicate transformation should be accomplished was another matter. Some of the Allies, notably France, wanted Germany to abide strictly by the provisions of the Treaty of Versailles, including the payment of all reparations and the prohibition against rearmament. Other Allies, led by Britain, were willing to allow the country more leeway. They assumed that when it did regain its former position, Germany would responsibly and constructively exercise its power as a member of the family of nations. Within this context of international tension and domestic turmoil arose a political predator who was quite capable of turning the situation to his own advantage. The German electorate, disheartened by the years of despair and anxiety, responded to this charismatic leader's strident demands for a new order. By September 1930, German voters had made Adolf Hitler's Nazi Party the second strongest political organization in the Reichstag.

Britain and France, distracted by their own domestic problems and saddled with the increasing burden (and steadily dwindling benefits) of maintaining global empires, proved unable to control events as they would have liked. Russia, which under the old balance of power had served as an effective counterweight to any overly ambitious power in central or Eastern Europe, had been converted into a pariah nation by the West's fear of international Bolshevism. Indeed, the industrialized nations of Western Europe regarded Stalin and the Soviet Union as more dangerous than Hitler. France and England assumed, apparently, that Herr Hitler would abide by the generally accepted diplomatic practices of the day, responding as any rational politician would to good-faith negotiations and reasonable concessions. But, as the world soon found out, Hitler operated from a significantly different set of assumptions. In this tragic error lay the roots of "appeasement."

In the Orient, meanwhile, a dynamic, industrious, and swiftly modernizing Japan was emerging as the dominant power. After its crushing defeat of Imperial Russia in the Russo-Japanese War of 1904–05, Japan strengthened its position in East Asia by siding with the Allies in the Great War. At virtually no cost to itself, Japan—simply by being the primary victorious belligerent in the Orient—acquired a Pacific empire when it assumed mandates over the former German possessions scattered through the central and western Pacific. The Western nations, forced by circumstances to recognize the island nation's "legitimate interests" in mainland Asia, did little to stop the Japanese from expanding their sphere of influence westward to Korea and Manchuria and southward to Mongolia and China—provided, of course, that this did not interfere with their own spheres of influence, carved out of China and East Asia.

Japan, having seized Manchuria in 1931, continued to pressure a weaker China into granting concessions, until, finally, Japanese armies crossed the border into China proper in July 1937. The new order in Asia, it seemed, would be pursued behind Japanese bullets and bayonets.

Once again, the League of Nations proved itself an inadequate intercessor. The United States, which had so feared foreign entanglements that it turned down membership in the league, thereby fatally crippling it, was now concerned lest its own commercial interests in Asia be threatened by Japanese expansion. But by the time Japan invaded China, it was already allied with Nazi Germany and fascist Italy. Britain and France had their hands full in Europe, while the Soviet Union, the only other Eurasian power that might have been persuaded to oppose Japanese expansion, remained a pariah. The United States could do little by itself to dissuade Japan from pursuing its course of conquest. It was only a matter of time before Japan's ambitions in the Far East led to outright war.

Weapons and Tactics

The array of weapons of destruction available to the ground combat commanders of World War II was staggering. Such weapons, mass-produced in the millions by industrialized societies waging total war upon each other, made the 1939–45 war the deadliest in history. The dominant weapon of the war was the tank, which had been used late in World War I. Now, however, it burst upon the battlefield like a lightning bolt, changing the nature of war and the face of battle forever. In the hands of the new masters of armored warfare, like Germany's General Heinz Guderian, the tank became the central weapon of the new tactic of blitzkrieg, and ensured that the mechanized war of maneuver would dominate the battlefields of World War II. Combined with the destructive power of mobile artillery, the maneuverability of motorized infantry, and the awesome reach of tactical air support, tank forces could be nearly unstoppable. It was largely the tank, and the innovative use of armored and mechanized forces, that determined that the Second World War would not be bogged down in the frustrating, nightmarish, trench warfare of the first.

The tanks developed and deployed during the Second World War by Germany, Russia, Japan, and the United States were a mixed bag. Germany consistently produced the most technologically sophisticated ones, the Panzerkampfwagen (Pzkw) V "Panther" and the Pzkw VI "Tiger" and "King Tiger." The forty-three-ton Panther, with 120mm of front armor and a high muzzle-velocity 75mm cannon was clearly superior to the most ubiquitous Allied tank on the Western Front—the American-designed-and-manufactured M4 "Sherman" (thirty-three tons; 81mm of front armor; low muzzle-velocity 75mm cannon). But the American "Arsenal of Democracy" turned out the Sherman in huge numbers, producing some 50,000 during the war. With strength in numbers, Allied tanks could eventually surround and destroy the superior German tanks, and replace their losses from an ever-growing assembly-line production.

German tank superiority on the Eastern Front in the first two years after the invasion of Russia was overcome once Soviet tank design and mass production swung into high gear by 1943–44. In fact, the German development of the excellent Panther and Tiger tanks was largely in response to the Russian fielding of two sturdy, well-designed tanks. The powerful KV heavy tank and the outstanding T34/76 medium tank—the all-around best mass-produced tank of the war—helped change the course of the fighting on the Eastern Front by their potency in tank-to-tank combat and their ever-increasing numbers. Russia produced over 80,000 tanks during the war, while Germany struggled to turn out barely 25,000 from 1939–44. The Soviet tanks, initially mounting 76mm guns, were later improved by the addition of 85mm cannon (and even larger guns on the massive "Josef Stalin" heavy tank produced near the end of the war). German armor may have been qualitatively the best, but American and Russian tank production was able to overcome this technology gap.

In the Pacific Theater, the technologically crude Japanese machines posed no threat to the M4 Sherman, and Japanese industry proved ineffective in designing, producing, or fielding new models. The American use of limited numbers of tanks to root out the stubborn Japanese defenders, dug into caves, tunnels, and fortified bunkers on the Pacific islands, proved to be an important tactic—especially when flamethrower-mounted tanks could be maneuvered close enough to burn out the enemy. Nevertheless, the role of the tank was much more decisive in the European Theater.

As in the First World War, artillery played a crucial role, though now the tank had joined the infantry-artillery team to make a new, deadlier trio. The massed fires of field artillery howitzers and cannon were integral parts of virtually every World War II battle, whether blasting a gap for attacking infantry and armored forces to exploit, or laying down a protective barrage for defending troops. Usually, objectives to be seized, such as a town or high ground, were subjected to an artillery "preparation" before initating attack—that is, hundreds or even thousands of rounds were fired on the target to soften it up and prepare the way for the troops. In a similar manner, forward observers assigned to the infantry or armored maneuver units would call in the fires of supporting batteries to break up or destroy the attacking enemy formations before they could close on the defending friendly unit. Typically, the combatants used light (75mm, 85mm, 100mm, or 105mm) or medium (122mm, 155mm) field guns to provide close support to their maneuver forces. Excellent fire-control procedures and abundant radio communications made the Allied artillery, especially American, the most feared and respected weapons system on the Western Front. On the Eastern Front the sheer number of Russian artillery weapons—32,000 were massed for the Soviet crossing of the Vistula in January 1945, for example—made Stalin's legions doubly dreaded by their German opponents.

In the Pacific, lightweight construction, primitive design, and substandard manufacture made Japanese artillery inferior to Allied. Japanese land forces relied heavily on light artillery, and especially mortars, as primary fire support in jungle and island fighting. As in Europe, artillery support was crucial to the battlefield tactics of both sides in the Pacific, but the Allies usually had the upper hand, with an uninterrupted, steady supply of weapons and ammunition. When augmented, as it often was, by naval gunfire from the massive Allied invasion fleets, steaming unchallenged in the nearby water, Allied fire support could be overwhelming.

The defining tactic of World War II, and its most famous "maneuver," was the blitzkrieg. Named for the lightning speed (compared with the experience of World War I) at which the attacking forces tore through the defender's positions, the blitzkrieg was a rapid, highly mobile, war of maneuver, emphasizing speed, flexibility, and the coordination of tanks, infantry, artillery, and tactical airpower. First unleashed on Poland (September 1939), then France (May 1940), German blitzkrieg tactics defeated numerically superior forces possessing a static-warfare mind-set through the initial Russian campaign (June–December 1941), and for much of Rommel's desert warfare operations in North Africa (March 1941–August 1942).

But beginning about 1943, the deterioration of German forces, fighting on at least three fronts, precluded its continued use. The American-led campaign to regain France in the summer of 1944 resembled, in many ways, a "blitzkrieg in reverse," but achieved its stunning success against a much-weakened opponent. Likewise, the successful Russian offensives of 1944–45 against the steadily deteriorating German Eastern Front forces relied more on the Red Army's overwhelming numbers of personnel, tanks, artillery, and other matériel than on the blitzkrieg's coordinated tactics of mobile maneuver. Despite the fame of this tactic, it was not used in the majority of World War II battles.

Much of the fighting of World War II resembled the standard "two up, one back," fire-and-maneuver operations taught at virtually all postwar service schools around the world. Higher commanders usually mixed attacking forces with infantry, armor, and artillery. They seldom utilized pure infantry or pure tank forces, since each type of force had inherent weaknesses that could be overcome only by employing the two together. Adequate fire support in the form of artillery and tactical airpower was allocated to an attacking or defending force consistent with the mission to be accomplished and the amount of fire support available.

In the Pacific Theater, especially during the desperate struggles for rock-bound islands that characterized the final two years, the style of warfare resembled the worst of the European city fighting. Typically, the outnumbered Japanese forces, having lost the battle for control of the sea and the air, forced the attacking Americans to blast them out of their fortified caves and bunkers, sometimes sallying forth in maniacal "Banzai!" charges of massed troops, seeking to kill as many Americans as possible before dying themselves. In both theaters, however, superior resources usually prevailed.

The Battle of Stalingrad

August 23, 1942–February 2, 1943

"Every Seven Seconds . . . "

At the height of the war's most decisive battle on the Eastern Front, the state-controlled Soviet radio repeatedly broadcast in German this chilling message: "Every seven seconds a German soldier dies in Russia . . . tick . . . tick . . . tick . . . tick . . . tick . . . tick . . . tick . . . Stalingrad—Mass Grave!" By the battle's end, that horrible message proved to be more than just Soviet propaganda. The German Sixth Army, which in August 1942 had nearly 330,000 men, was virtually destroyed. On February 2, 1943, its fewer than 100,000 survivors led by their defeated commander, newly promoted Field Marshal Friedrich Paulus, staggered ignominiously across the frozen steppes of the Russian winter into a humiliating captivity. Perhaps 5,000 of these men eventually returned to Germany, some as late as ten years after the war's end. Behind them, in the rubble of the city, lay the bodies of 150,000 comrades, as dead as Hitler's dream of an eastern empire.

The German defeat in the battle of Stalingrad was the major turning point of the Russo-German war in the east, and Hitler's needless sacrifice of an entire German field army with all its equipment and supporting forces (including such precious assets as 500 Luftwaffe transport planes) effectively transferred the initiative on the vast Eastern Front to Stalin's ever-growing military might. Except for isolated actions, never again would the German army possess the resources in men and matériel to conduct the lightning-fast, sweeping maneuvers of massed forces to surround and capture entire Russian armies of hundreds of thousands like it did in the summer and fall of 1941. The Soviet victory at Stalingrad—followed closely by the German disaster in the huge tank battles around Kursk five months later—changed everything on the Eastern Front, causing the overextended German forces to begin a seemingly endless series of delaying actions and defensive operations that only postponed their defeat, while draining the country's remaining reserves of manpower and equipment.

But the "mass grave" of Stalingrad was not filled with only German corpses. The Soviets lost as many as ten times the number of men in the horrific fighting for the town and surrounding area. Stalin later admitted to 300,000 losses, but such figures, like everything in Stalin's "paranoid" empire, have always been viewed with skepticism. Recently declassified documents in the archives of the former Soviet Union reveal that an astonishing 1 million Soviets were killed at Stalingrad, including 13,500 soldiers executed for "cowardice" by Stalin's special squads of NKVD secret police units, which operated just behind the front lines. Both Hitler and Stalin were prepared to sacrifice staggering numbers of lives and equipment to claim possession of a city reduced to rubble by nearly 200 days of constant fighting—the longest sustained battle of the war. Both dictators were determined to exploit the very real military advantages and the equally important propaganda coup of capturing and holding the city named after the Soviet leader. In the end, Stalin's seemingly endless supply of the raw materials—cold steel for cannon and warm bodies for cannon fodder—gave victory to the Red Army, but before it was over, the vaunted Russian capacity for enduring massive suffering was stretched to the breaking point.

Forward to Stalingrad?—Hitler's Russian Campaign of 1942

Once fighting began in earnest in September 1939, Hitler's strategy seems to have been to knock France and Britain out of the war early, then turn on Russia, capturing the resource-laden western region along with the oil fields of the Transcaucasus. With the Soviet Union destroyed (or at least driven beyond the Archangel–Volga line), Germany could freely exploit the natural resources of the area without fear of retaliation from the air. Hitler, however, kept getting distracted. His initial offensive against France and Britain was stunningly successful, yet he broke it off before delivering the knockout blow to Britain—a crucial error. Turning on Stalin before completely securing his back in the west meant that not all of Germany's limited resources could be applied to destroying the Soviet Union in the critical opening campaign in the east. Additionally, Hitler further weakened his forces—and postponed the beginning of the attack by a critical six weeks—by diverting German forces to Greece and Yugoslavia to rescue the embattled Mussolini. Similarly, his dispatch of Rommel and the Afrika Korps to prevent an Italian disaster in North Africa wasted more critical resources and accomplished little. Despite Rommel's smashing victories in the desert, the African adventure ended up draining badly needed troops and equipment.

By the time Hitler's armies forced their way into Stalingrad at the end of summer 1942, Germany had missed its opportunity to knock Russia out of the war. Then, instead of allowing his commanders in the east to withdraw to where they could at least conduct a successful mobile defense against the ever-increasing power of the Red Army, Hitler adopted a "no retreat" strategy that doomed his aims on that front.

Despite the failure of his 1941 invasion to capture Moscow and Leningrad and decisively defeat the Red Army, Hitler remained optimistic as the campaign season of 1942 approached. The Nazi dictator still hoped to destroy Stalin's war-making ability and utilize a newly won eastern empire to fuel Germany's own war machine in its struggle against the Western Allies. The fact that the United States was now an active participant in the war against him didn't seem to seriously concern Hitler or to influence his immediate plans. Turning his back on his western enemies, Hitler once again prepared to throw his armies against Stalin.

The German army in Russia had lost heavily during the vigorous Soviet offensives of the winter of 1941–42, and was finding it increasingly difficult to hold a front of over 1,000 miles while continuing to prosecute a deadly siege against Leningrad at the front's northern end. Most German infantry divisions were at only about 50-percent strength, and panzer divisions could barely muster three quarters of their authorized vehicles. In an attempt to make up for this lack of troops, Hitler turned to his Axis allies to supply him with fresh cannon fodder. The Romanians, Italians, Hungarians, Slovaks, and Spanish provided a total of fifty-two divisions to bolster Hitler's combat power in the east. Most of these "allied" units were lightly equipped, poorly led, and of dubious value to the German cause. Hitler's subordinate commanders, therefore, would find themselves sorely pressed to conduct the kind of sweeping offensive operations the Führer had in mind.

Hitler's plan for offensive operations in Russia for 1942 was to hold firm in the center and north while pushing south to seize the rich oil fields of the Caucasus. Sandwiched between the Black and Caspian seas, this rugged region could theoretically supply Germany with the oil reserves it so desperately needed. Its seizure could also open the door to a German bridgehead in the Middle East, possibly leading the way to even greater war-making resources. Accomplishing this, however, would not be easy. Hitler's plan had four phases. First, the city of Voronezh on the central Don River must be seized to protect against counterattack from the north. Second, an advance down the Don would link up with a corresponding thrust from Kharkov to secure operational areas between the Don and the Donets rivers. Third, two columns advancing toward each other along the banks of the Don would clear the area in the bend of that river and seize bridgeheads. Fourth, units would move toward Stalingrad and occupy that important city on the Volga while the main German forces thrust southward into the Caucasus region.

The plan was ambitious, and concentrating the combat power necessary to punch through Russian lines into the Caucasus would stretch the already strapped German forces dangerously thin. However, the basic strategic and operational goals of the campaign were sound enough to permit the German armies in the south to accomplish them, provided the units conducting the operation were consistently given the necessary support, and the plan was adhered to with a minimum of meddling by Hitler. As it turned out, neither of these conditions was met, with disastrous results. The greater of these two errors, certainly, was Hitler's meddling. In his postwar interviews with senior German commanders, *The Other Side of the Hill*, B. H. Liddell Hart quotes Field Marshal von Manteuffel's succinct summary of Hitler's shortcomings as a tactician: "He had a real flair for strategy and tactics, especially for surprise moves, but he lacked a sufficient foundation of technical knowledge to apply it properly. Moreover, he had a tendency to intoxicate himself with figures and quantities." Hitler's constant shuffling of units around the area of operations and his shifting of objectives disrupted the flow and momentum of the German attack, thereby hindering the success of the campaign. But Hitler's distractions, on their own, did not lead to the German disaster at Stalingrad. More important was the fierce determination of the Red Army.

The Resurrection of the Red Army

The German military's all-out effort in the summer and fall of 1941 had crippled, but not fatally wounded, the Soviet forces along the wide Eastern Front. Despite the Red Army's horrendous losses—over 3 million Russian soldiers were captured between June and December 1941 alone—it had rallied sufficiently by winter to stop the Germans at the gates of Moscow and keep them from capturing Leningrad. After the initial shock of the early German successes,

Stalin emerged from self-imposed isolation to rally his shaken forces and regroup the defense of the nation. Calling up reserves of troops from the Soviet Far East (Japan's attack on Pearl Harbor in early December convinced him that that country's efforts were directed elsewhere) and turning to capable leaders such as General Georgy Zhukov, the Soviet dictator took the first steps toward turning back the Nazi tide.

Marshal Timoshenko, tasked with rebuilding the army's officer corps after the debacles of the Russo-Finnish War of 1939–40 exposed the disastrous effects of Stalin's brutal purges of ranking officers, had begun replacing ineffective commanders with more capable men, but had not made sufficient progress at the time of the surprise German attack in June 1941. Poor leadership, coupled with the Red Army's disastrous attempts to cope with the German mobile war of maneuver by standing fast, led to the terrible losses of the first year's campaigning. Forced by circumstances and the necessity of combat to adjust to the new parameters of warfare, however, Stalin's forces regained their confidence and began turning back the Germans from Moscow and holding them at Leningrad.

Stalin's newfound confidence was so high, in fact, that he prematurely committed his reinforced units to a general offensive across the entire front in January 1942. Although advised by his best field commanders, including Zhukov, to concentrate their assets and strike the Germans only in their now vulnerable center, Stalin insisted on attacking all across the 1,000-mile front. This overly ambitious effort was never powerful enough to achieve widespread success, and the offensive's inability to gain a significant breakthrough meant that Hitler's forces remained in a position to strike another massive blow at the Soviet lines that summer. The result was Hitler's plan to push southward into the Caucasus, and to protect that drive with the capture of Stalingrad.

On the Soviet side, an offensive launched in May 1942 to recapture Kharkov ended in disaster when three Russian field armies ran smack into a German offensive and were annihilated. Prevented by Stalin and the Soviet High Command—STAVKA—from a timely withdrawal, Timoshenko's forces were surrounded and destroyed. Without these twenty-nine divisions, Timoshenko was unable to mount stiff resistance to the German southern thrust when it was launched in earnest in June. All he could do was continue to withdraw in front of the advancing German columns, avoiding at all costs another costly encirclement. Despite the growing skill and confidence of Russian soldiers and leaders, they were forced to pull back as the Germans pushed forward. To Hitler and his commanders, this only seemed to confirm their opinion that "the Russian is finished." As things turned out, however, the Red Army, tempered by the fierce combat of the previous year and now receiving the tools of war from the industrial complex in the Urals, was only beginning to realize its potential. Soon, the withdrawals would cease.

The Sixth Army's Road to Stalingrad

Hitler's Army Group South (to be redesignated Army Groups A and B, July 7–9) began the offensive that led to the battle of Stalingrad on June 28, 1942. Rapidly advancing against weak Russian resistance, the seven field armies composing the two army groups achieved some striking successes. Driving the Russians back everywhere, Army Group A was making good progress in its push to capture Rostov, a key position on the eastern terminus of the Sea of Azov, while Army Group B moved to clear the west bank of the Don River. This early success, however, led Hitler to make one of his many operational interventions, one that had a fatal impact on the ensuing battle. On July 13, seemingly convinced that the Russians in front of Army Group B were on their last legs, he ordered the Fourth Panzer Army, which was advancing to help the Sixth Army take Stalingrad, to switch to a southerly route in order to assist the First Panzer Army's attack on Rostov. The result was a twofold disaster for Paulus's Sixth Army. First, Hitler's meddling delayed the capture of the city, since the Sixth and Fourth Armies would surely have quickly taken the town if the Fourth had not been diverted. Unassisted, the Sixth Army struggled toward Stalingrad during the next few critical weeks, and was unable to reach the northwestern outskirts of Stalingrad until

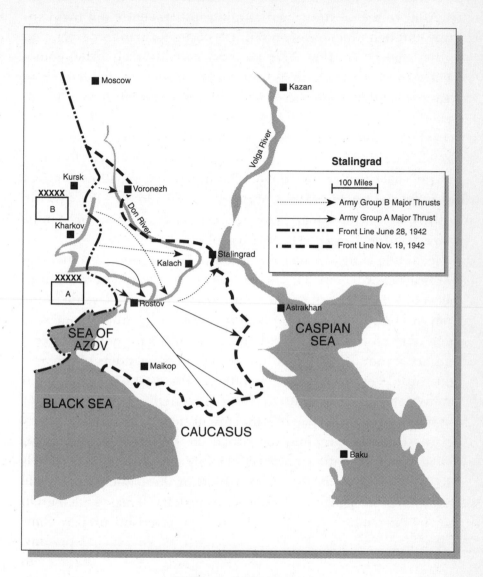

Moscow

Kazan

Volga River

Kursk

XXXXX
B

Voronezh

Don River

Kharkov

Stalingrad

100 Miles
·····▷ Army Group B Major Thrusts
──▶ Army Group A Major Thrust
─··─··─ Front Line June 28, 1942
▄ ▄ ▄ Front Line Nov. 19, 1942

Kalach

Stalingrad

XXXXX
A

Rostov

Astrakhan

SEA OF
AZOV

CASPIAN
SEA

Maikop

BLACK SEA

CAUCASUS

Baku

Stalingrad Campaign

August 23—six weeks later. Second, the diversion of the Fourth Panzer Army to the south opened a wide gap between it and the Sixth Army, through which nearly two thirds of the Russian forces trapped in the bend of the Don River escaped, carrying their heavy equipment with them. These units were sorely needed in the defense of Stalingrad and later proved critical to the Russian effort to hold the city.

Paulus's troops moved laboriously toward their fateful destination, impeded by more than just stiffening Russian resistance. Running short of vital supplies, including ammunition, since the Russians had destroyed the single rail line running eastward toward the city, the Sixth Army sat immobilized for ten critical days while fuel for its panzers and motorized vehicles was collected.

Meanwhile Hitler once again added to his operational commanders' headaches by diverting more units from the southern front at the end of July. This time he removed most of the Eleventh Army from Army Group A, along with all the heavy siege artillery, and sent them to reinforce the siege of Leningrad on the far northern front. This action not only deprived his southern commanders of the only unit capable of acting as an operational reserve force, it hindered Paulus's attempts to capture Stalingrad by denying him the use of the heavy siege artillery. While the absent siege artillery significantly delayed Paulus's entry into the city at the beginning of the battle, the lack of an operational reserve seriously affected the Sixth Army's efforts to escape from the encircled city at the battle's end. While Hitler was prolonging the already too long delay in taking Stalingrad, the city's defenders were using this time to feverishly prepare their defenses.

The City on the Volga

The city that bore Stalin's name stretches for miles along the bluffs of the Volga River's west bank. Stalingrad is long but quite narrow; thus, any point along its western outskirts is close to the mile-wide Volga. Its central sector is dominated by Mamaev Hill, a 350-foot mound that affords nearly perfect observation of the southern half of the city and both banks of the river. Forward observers placed on the slopes of this hill can direct devastating artillery fire or call in air strikes with deadly accuracy on any Volga crossing point within miles.

In 1942, Stalingrad had a population of about 500,000, most of them workers in factories or industrial plants. Major industrial complexes, most located just to the north of Mamaev Hill and the city's downtown and residential sector, included the Lazur Chemical Plant, the Red October Plant, the Barrikady Gun Factory, and the Dzerhezinsky Tractor Works. Each was extremely large, particularly the Tractor Works, a Soviet industrial showplace that extended for over a mile in a north-south axis along the river. The city also had many grain elevators, railroad yards, and commercial stores and businesses as well as workers' houses and apartment buildings. At the center of the "downtown" sector was the western terminal of the only usable ferryboat. Bisecting the city like giant scars were two huge gullies—the Tsaritsa Gorge in the southern quarter and the Krutoy Gully in the downtown residential area. The bombs and shells of invaders and defenders would soon turn Stalin's "Model Communist Industrial Community" into a nightmarish landscape of horror and death.

Battle for the City—Part I: The Sixth Army Fights Its Way In

Much delayed by Hitler's whims, an overextended supply system, and increasing resistance from the Red Army, Paulus and the soldiers of the Sixth Army finally fought their way to the bluffs overlooking the west bank of the Volga on August 23, 1942. Assisted by attacks to the south of Stalingrad by Hoth's Fourth Panzer Army (which Hitler belatedly returned to the Stalingrad attack after diverting it to Rostov), the Sixth Army forces held a narrow strip along the river on the northern outskirts of the city and were preparing to advance into Stalingrad, hoping to capture it rapidly. Opposing them within the city were the heavily outnumbered forces of the Soviet 62nd

Army, part of Colonel General Andrei Yeremenko's newly formed Southeastern Front.

On that same day, Hitler ordered an action that was intended to terrorize the inhabitants of the city into a quick surrender, but ended up slowing the German advance. Late that afternoon, much as they had done at Warsaw and Rotterdam, the Nazis sent wave after wave of aircraft in a frenzy of terror bombing that resulted in the deaths of 40,000 civilians. Six hundred planes of Luftwaffe general Freiherr von Richthofen's Luftflotte IV flew the equivalent of 2,000 bombing sorties, leaving the city in flames that night. Although this saturation bombing had little direct impact on Yeremenko's Red Army units who were defending the city, it began the process of pounding Stalingrad into a patternless rubble—which, ironically, provided the hard-pressed Russians with excellent defensive positions.

Effectively blocking streets, rail lines, and other avenues of approach, the widespread destruction hindered the movement of Paulus's panzers and hobbled the German army's superior mobility. The battle became a grim, brutal, hand-to-hand combat between German and Russian infantrymen, fighting desperately over each cellar, bombed-out shell of a building, and pile of bricks and mortar. It became a *ratzenkrieg*—rats' war—where men fought each other like animals against the surreal landscape of the doomed city. Progress was measured in mere meters of territory gained, usually at the cost of dozens of lives, and sometimes taking weeks to accomplish. This was the kind of fighting Sergeant Pavlov and his squad conducted in their fifty-eight-day defense of Pavlov's House, scrambling from cellar to attic, and from room to room to fend off the constant German panzer and infantry attacks. It was a war of attack and counterattack, waged by small groups of soldiers armed with rifles and grenades, for the control of useless bits and pieces of property. Above all, it was a battlefield whose weapons were the sniper's rifle and the hand grenade, not the armored panzer and Stuka dive-bomber. Masters of the mobile war of maneuver, Hitlers's forces found themselves drawn into a static fight in which the outnumbered Russians could face them on a nearly equal footing.

Stalin did not intend to lose his namesake city. He issued "hold

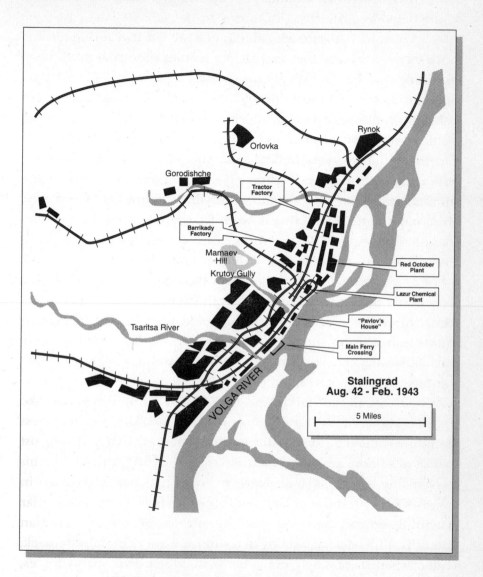

Stalingrad, August 1942–February 1943

at all costs" orders to Yeremenko, and the Red Army was expected to die defending the city: withdrawal to the safety of the east bank of the Volga was prohibited. Additionally, Stalin had forbidden the evacuation of the factories and their precious industrial machinery, reasoning that his Russian soldiers would fight harder for a "live" city than they would for a "dead" one. Although the evacuation of noncombatant civilians was authorized shortly after the Germans arrived, all able-bodied men and boys over fifteen years of age were impressed into workers' militia and integrated into the city's defenses. Despite the overwhelming German edge in numbers and equipment, Stalingrad's defenders retained some key advantages. Most important, the Germans were incapable of completely surrounding the city and sealing it off from outside assistance, and Yeremenko and his commanders would continue throughout the battle to use the Volga to ferry supplies from the safety of the Russian-held east—fresh personnel, ammunition, and replacements for lost and damaged equipment. The Germans could interdict these resupply efforts with artillery and air bombardment, but they could not stop them. Crossing the Volga under intense fire was a nightmare, but the Russian defenders endured it.

Another significant advantage of the Red Army forces resulted from the dangerously thin dispersion of the attacking German units along the southern front. With the push of Army Group A into the Caucasus region and the resulting spread of the already overextended line, the 1,000-mile Eastern Front had nearly doubled in length. Concentrations of German forces, such as those taking place around Stalingrad, were separated by vast distances, thinly manned, and difficult to defend against determined Soviet counteroffensives. Hitler relied increasingly upon his weak allied divisions to fill the gaps, gambling that they could stand up to Red Army attacks. As Paulus concentrated his Sixth Army units in the outskirts of Stalingrad and prepared to push them into the city, both vulnerable flanks of the German salient around the city were guarded by weaker units of Hitler's allies. To the south, the Romanian Fourth Army provided the main security against any Soviet force advancing across the broad Kalmyk Steppe, while Paulus's long, exposed northern flank was protected by the Romanian Third Army (whose left flank was, in turn, protected by two other allied units—the Italian Eighth Army and the Hungarian Second Army). Paulus's troops, fighting to capture the battered city, were dangerously exposed to the risk of being cut off and encircled.

Meanwhile, Sixth Army soldiers inching their way into Stalingrad proper were having a tough time against Red Army troops bolstered by workers' militia. The early optimism of German commanders, who expected the city to fall to them by August 24, had degenerated into sullen resignation before the likelihood of months of fighting. A rapid attack to capture the industrial northern sector of the city was beaten back by stiff Soviet resistance, and the Germans had to give up trying to enter the town from the north. Ironically, the German decision to concentrate their massive air bombings on the city instead of on the Red Army units aided these Russian units in beating back this attack.

Launched on the morning of August 25, the main German assault to capture the town began in the western outskirts and pressed forward a few meters at a time. Through tenacious fighting and sharp counterattacks, Yeremenko kept the German advance to a crawl. Hoth's Fourth Panzer Army, whose belated attack toward Stalingrad from the south had helped the Sixth Army gain its toehold on the Volga, was still struggling against the Soviet 64th Army to close up on the city's southern outskirts. The brunt of the effort to seize Stalingrad would have to be borne by Paulus's troops. Each day's air bombardments and steady shelling increasingly reduced the city to a pile of rubble. While this took a toll on the Russian defenders, it made any maneuver on the attacker's part increasingly difficult.

During the first week of September, front commander Yeremenko moved his headquarters from the command bunker in the Tsaritsa Gorge across the Volga to a less threatened location outside of the city. This allowed him to exercise better control over the forces supporting Stalingrad, but left the 62nd Army to conduct the building-by-building defensive struggle by itself. Although suffering terrible casualties in the process, the Soviet troops stubbornly continued to deny Paulus's forces complete control of the city. One reason for their perseverance was the new commander of the 62nd Army, General Vasily Chuikov. Highly regarded as a combat leader, Chuikov took over command of the Stalingrad garrison when Stalin relieved the 62nd Army's previous commander for attempting to pull his troops out of the city.

By the end of the first month, the Germans had advanced only as far as the center of the downtown business district. Although Chuikov had been pushed to the very bnks of the Volga (in some places the Germans were only a few yards from the river), key positions, such as Mamaev Hill, the ferry landing, and the industrial factories, remained in Russian hands. An all-out German assault on the northern factory district in October nearly caused Chuikov's defense to collapse, but the 62nd Army refused to give up control of the town. By November, Chuikov's forces had been split into four separate bridgeheads, clinging to key defensive points, but still receiving re-supply and reinforcements from the east bank of the Volga. While Chuikov kept Paulus's troops focused on the capture of Stalingrad—a goal that continually eluded them—the vulnerable flanks of the German Stalingrad salient remained an inviting target for a Soviet counteroffensive. Such a target did not escape the notice of Stalin or his ablest troubleshooter, General Zhukov.

Battle for the City—Part II: The Soviet Counteroffensive

While the 62nd Army was preventing the Germans from capturing Stalingrad, Zhukov was reorganizing the entire southern portion of the Russian front and carefully assembling the forces he would need to launch a devastating, unexpected counteroffensive. Targetting the weak allied armies protecting Paulus's overexposed flanks, the plan was to surround the Sixth Army (as well as any part of Hoth's Fourth Panzer Army it could bag) and enclose the Germans in a steel trap. If successful, it would spell disaster for Hitler's ambitions in the east.

From the Caspian Sea in the south to well past Voronezh north of the Stalingrad area, Zhukov reorganized the now reinforced Soviet forces into four mutually supporting fronts. Yeremenko continued to command the front area containing Stalingrad and its immediate environs, now designated the Stalingrad Front, and expanded southward to include the entire Kalmyk Steppe and the shores of the north Caspian Sea. Immediately to the north of Stalingrad, General Rokossovsky's Don Front stretched for 100 miles along that river. On Rokossovsky's right flank was the newly activated Southwest Front commanded by General Vatutin. Farther north, centered on the Don city of Voronezh, was General Golikov's Voronezh Front. Poised to conduct the massive Soviet counteroffensive were over 1 million Red Army soldiers, backed up by 1,500 tanks and 18,000 artillery pieces and mortars.

At 0720 hours on November 19, 1942, a one-hour artillery barrage blasted the Romanian Third Army all along the northern flank west of Stalingrad. At its end, Rokossovsky and Vatutin's tanks and infantry rolled over the dazed Romanians, quickly precluding any cohesive defense, and rapidly driving toward the key bridge over the Don at Kalach. The following day, Yeremenko's troops of the Stalingrad Front south of the city began an all-out assault to form the southern pincer around the German forces. Yeremenko's forces routed the weak Romanian Fourth Army, then sliced through Hoth's Fourth Panzer Army, driving part of those German armored forces into the Stalingrad trap (although the bulk of Hoth's force was pushed to safety in the west and south).

On November 21, the northern Soviet pincer reached the key objective of Kalach on the Don, as did Yeremenko's southern pincer a day later. By the end of November 23, powerful Red Army forces had trapped Paulus's Sixth Army in a steel ring less than forty miles wide and half as deep. This detailed and near-flawlessly executed counteroffensive came as a surprise to Stalin's enemy on the Eastern Front, and Hitler was slow to see that it ushered in a new phase in this brutal theater.

Hitler's failure in this regard as well as his continued obsession with holding Stalingrad caused him to reject suggestions that Paulus's encircled forces be permitted to break out of the Stalingrad pocket while they could still do so. Hitler refused to allow Paulus to withdraw from the city, promising to resupply the cutoff Sixth Army by air. Reichsmarschal Hermann Göring rashly promised him that the Luftwaffe could deliver enough tonnage by air to meet Sixth Army's needs (estimated at between 500 to 700 tons a day). During the first two days of Göring's vaunted airlift, a pitiful seventy-five tons of supplies reached the three operational airfields within the Stalingrad perimeter. The best that the overworked Luftwaffe pilots could manage in the face of massed Soviet antiaircraft fire and the horrible weather conditions of the Russian winter was 100 tons—and this seldom. As a result, each passing day saw the 270,000 trapped German soldiers becoming progressively weaker. And with the Volga frozen solid, Russian forces within the city were able to receive larger and larger amounts of supplies, becoming progressively stronger. Chuikov's stubborn defense within the city coupled with the success of the massive Soviet counteroffensive completely changed the military situation. Although the *ratzenkrieg* continued from day to dreary day within the ruined city, the outcome of the battle of Stalingrad was assured. Stalin, not Hitler, would win.

Battle for the City—Part III: German Rescue Efforts Fail

In an attempt to deal with the fallout from the unexpectedly powerful Soviet counteroffensive, and with hopes of recapturing the initiative on his now reeling southern front, Hitler once again reorganized his forces in the south. Creating Army Group Don from the Fourth Panzer Army, the Sixth Army, and the Third and Fourth Romanian Armies, he appointed the brilliant proponent of blitzkrieg, Field Marshal Erich von Manstein, as the new army group commander. Ordered to recapture all of the areas formerly held by German forces, Manstein arrived at his new command on November 26. The situation did not look promising. Although the Russians remained primarily focused on destroying the German forces in and around Stalingrad, Manstein found that he had very few forces to pit against them. The Romanians were virtually useless, and Paulus's Sixth Army had its hands full trying to cling to Stalingrad. With the Luftwaffe flying in only an average of seventy tons of supplies each

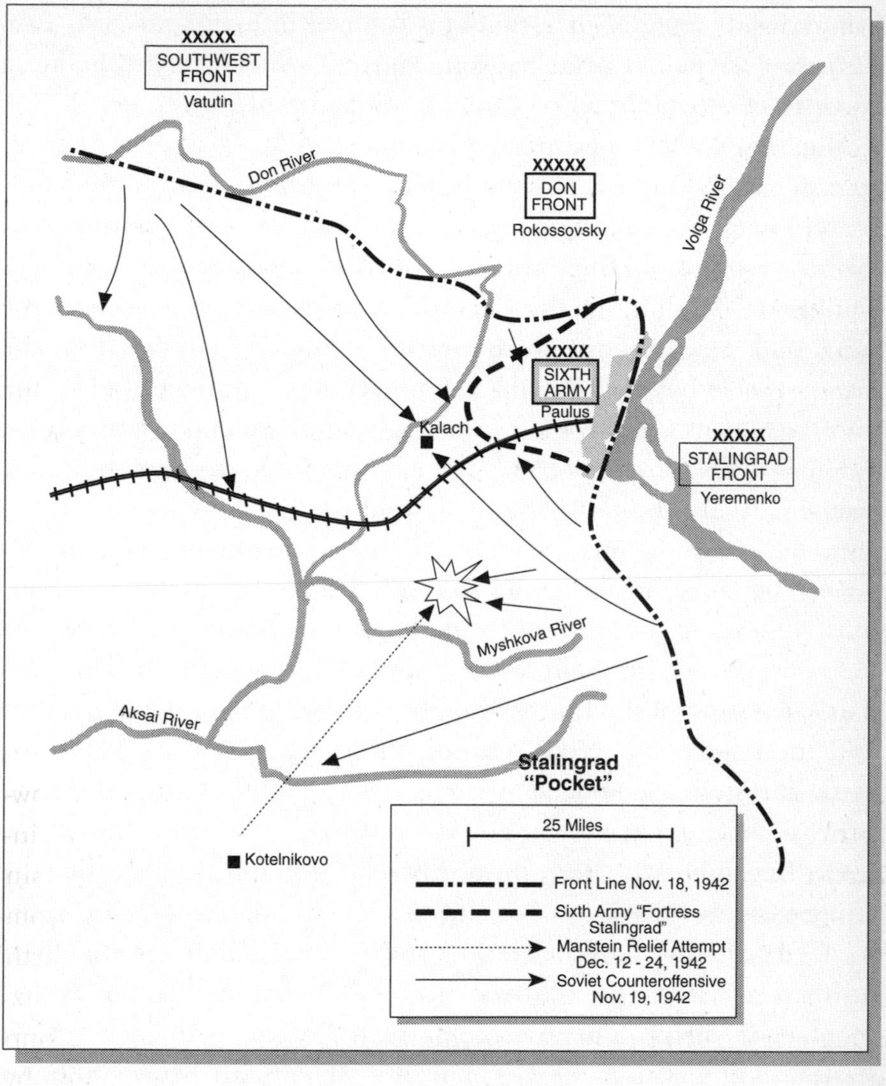
XXXXX
SOUTHWEST FRONT
Vatutin
XXXXX
DON FRONT
Rokossovsky
XXXX
SIXTH ARMY
Paulus
XXXXX
STALINGRAD FRONT
Yeremenko
Don River
Volga River
Kalach
Myshkova River
Aksai River
Stalingrad "Pocket"
Kotelnikovo
25 Miles
Front Line Nov. 18, 1942
Sixth Army "Fortress Stalingrad"
Manstein Relief Attempt Dec. 12 - 24, 1942
Soviet Counteroffensive Nov. 19, 1942

Stalingrad "Pocket"

day, Paulus's troops were, as we said, getting steadily weaker. Hoth's Fourth Panzer Army, weakened by several months of constant fighting and with some of its formations trapped in Stalingrad with Paulus, was Manstein's principal fighting unit—not an overwhelming force to effect the relief of Paulus's trapped army.

Manstein's attack began on December 12, 1942, after a delay of several days brought on by the bitter weather, the intermittent flow of replacements and supplies, and the ever-more-stiff Soviet resistance. Starting from the town of Kotelnikovo about seventy-five miles southwest of Stalingrad, the Germans made steady progress over the next week, reaching the Myshkova River line thirty miles from the city on December 18. The attack, however, was running out of steam, and the Soviets were rushing in strong reinforcements. Manstein decided that his only option was for Paulus's forces to launch a complementary attack out of the Stalingrad pocket in order to link up with the relieving force. Paulus, however, demurred. Despite his worsening situation, he would not defy Hitler and attempt a breakout. He answered Manstein's request with a shower of excuses: he was short of fuel; his ammunition supplies were insufficient; his men had eaten most of the horses, thereby destroying the army's mobility; and the inadequate aerial resupply effort had left his soldiers too weak. Manstein tried once more to convince Hitler to order the Sixth Army to mount a breakout, but was refused.

On December 22, Hoth threw his relief columns against the stiffening Russian resistance in one final effort to open a corridor to the trapped city. When this failed, Manstein's relief action was effectively finished as well. The renewed Soviet offensive on December 24 slammed into Hoth's exposed columns and drove them back to their starting points within the German lines. The Sixth Army's fate was sealed.

The Bitter End of "Fortress Stalingrad"

That Paulus's weakened and demoralized forces held out in the ruined city against increasingly powerful Russian assaults for more than another month seems incredible. The Stalingrad pocket, battered by Russian tank and infantry forces all around its ever-shrinking perimeter, continued to avoid complete collapse, but it was clearly a lost cause. During December alone, the Sixth Army lost over 80,000 men to wounds, sickness, and hunger. As this went on, the Russians were preparing to launch a final assault.

On January 8, 1943, a Russian delegation presented Paulus with a demand for an "honorable surrender" of the remaining forces but the German commander rejected it. Two days later, elements of seven Soviet armies ringing the Stalingrad perimeter launched the massive final assault. The meager supplies being flown in by a dwindling number of Luftwaffe transport planes finally dried up altogether when the advancing Soviet forces overran the airfields, one by one. On January 16, the last major airfield was captured, cutting off Paulus's last link to the outside.

Strong formations of Russian tanks and infantry hammered at the tottering German units, splitting the Stalingrad perimeter into smaller pockets of ever-weakening resistance that controlled less than half the area they had held the previous week. By January 24, only two major pockets of resistance remained—one in the central part of the city near Paulus's headquarters, in the basement of the Univermag department store, and one farther north in the ruins of the tractor factory. Through radio contact, Hitler continued to forbid Paulus to negotiate a surrender, ordering Fortress Stalingrad to fight to the last man and the last round. Intermittently, he raved about mounting a final effort to relieve the trapped Sixth Army, now surrounded by seven powerful Soviet armies, with a single battalion of the newly produced Pzkw V Panther tanks—one of his many "wonder weapons" that would save the Reich. In Stalingrad, the death agony of Paulus's army continued.

On January 30, Russian forces located Sixth Army headquarters and began shelling it and the surrounding buildings in preparation for storming Paulus's command post. Later in the day Hitler sent a radio signal promoting Paulus to the rank of field marshal. At a few minutes past 0600 hours on January 31, officers from Paulus's headquarters contacted Russian officers in the attacking force and offered to begin surrender negotiations. Still later Paulus was taken to the 64th Army headquarters, where he surrendered to the army's commander, General Shumilov. Field Marshal Paulus entered Soviet captivity shortly thereafter.

While the German field marshal's humiliation was playing itself out, farther to the north, in the ruins of the tractor factory, the final pocket of German resistance was still holding. Under command of General Strecker, this pitiful remnant held their final positions amid the destruction of the industrial complex for two more days. On February 2, 1943, they gave up, and the battle ended.

Aftermath

By the time Paulus surrendered what was left of the Sixth Army, his army of 330,000 men with all their equipment had been reduced to barely 91,000 freezing, starving survivors. Newsreels recording the aftermath of the surrender show endless lines of ragged, hopeless German captives trudging across a bleak, windswept steppe, as if marching toward a frozen oblivion. A decade later the 5,000 or so who survived in Stalin's gulags finally returned to Germany.

Included in the final tally of captives were twenty-four general officers and 2,500 officers of lesser rank. Shortly after the end of the battle Russia announced that in addition to the staggering number of prisoners, the Germans lost over 1,500 tanks, 8,000 mortars and artillery pieces, 750 aircraft, and an astonishing 61,000 trucks. When the figures for the entire campaign are included, the German army and its allies saw at least thirty-two divisions destroyed; another sixteen divisions suffered casualties of up to 50 percent. A total Axis casualty figure of about 1,500,000 (killed, wounded, missing, and captured) is not an unreasonable estimate. Add to this the certainly higher Soviet casualty figures (including the recently disclosed figure of 1 million Russian dead) and the total human cost of this man-made inferno is nearly incomprehensible.

That the battle of Stalingrad was the turning point on the Eastern Front goes without saying. Prior to it, Hitler and his eastern armies held the upper hand throughout the area. Despite the Soviet Union's larger population, Germany was consistently able to meet Soviet forces on the Eastern Front either with a local numerical advantage or at least a general parity. Before Stalingrad, German tactical, technical, and operational superiority was unchallenged. The crushing defeat on the Volga, however, changed everything.

Hitler was never again able to dominate his Soviet opponent, nor were German forces ever again to achieve even rough parity with their Russian enemies. Soviet manpower and technically sound Russian equipment started to flow westward, drowning the weaker German forces. The huge German casualty lists forever altered the balance of power in the east, and resulted in Hitler's stripping his western defenses to the bare minimum in order to keep the "Russian hordes" at bay. This ultimately facilitated the Western Allies' victory in France and Germany, shortening the war and no doubt saving countless Allied lives. Hitler claimed that the battle of Stalingrad was fought to save Western civilization. He was undoubtedly right.

The Battle of the Bulge

December 16, 1944–January 28, 1945

Greatest American Victory

The greatest single land battle ever fought by the United States began at 0530 hours on December 16, 1944, when the powerful vanguard of what would eventually be nearly a half-million German troops crashed into the weakly held Ardennes sector of the American lines. An overwhelming force of 200,000 infantry and panzer troops, supported by 1,900 pieces of heavy artillery and about 1,000 tanks, struck suddenly and with complete surprise the thin lines manned by about 80,000 American soldiers. Outnumbered and outgunned, U.S. soldiers, nevertheless, fought a stubborn and heroic delaying action that eventually bought the time necessary for General Dwight D. Eisenhower and the Allied Command to regain control of the battle and turn back the tide of German armor and foot soldiers. By the conclusion of the Battle of the Bulge, over a month later, the American army had won its greatest single victory.

In order to do so, American forces eventually used 600,000 U.S. troops, backed up by about 55,000 British soldiers, making it the largest effort of its kind on the Western Front and rivaling the enormous Russo-German encounters on the vast Eastern Front, Stalingrad (ended February 1943) and Kursk (July 1943). The American army engaged six mechanized cavalry groups, three separate regiments, and twenty-nine divisions—fully one third of all army divisions that were activated during the entire war. This effort dwarfs all other American battles, including Yorktown (1781; 8,800 American allied with 7,800 French), New Orleans (1815; 5,000), Chapultepec

(1847; 7,200), Gettysburg (1863; 150,000 total Union and Confederate), and even Desert Storm (1991; about 500,000). But the price of victory was high.

American casualties during the Battle of the Bulge were nearly 80,000 to all causes. This represents about 10 percent of the total losses suffered by all U.S. forces in all of World War II (294,000 killed and 671,000 wounded). General Omar Bradley's 12th Army Group, whose forces bore the brunt of the attack, estimate they lost 50,000 soldiers the first week of the Ardennes offensive—40,000 of those were infantrymen. British forces, much less heavily engaged in a battle occurring mostly in the American sector of the Allied line, lost 1,400. German casualty figures remain in dispute, but the attacking forces lost at least 100,000—probably much more. The confusion and devastation that swept Germany at the end of the war caused the loss of many records and archives, and the true figure for German losses in the Ardennes will likely never be known. Partial Nazi railroad records that survived the war indicate the evacuation of 70,000 wounded during the month of December 1944 alone. When killed, missing, captured, and additional wounded for January are added, the German total must be staggering.

The Battle of the Bulge had far-reaching effects. Eisenhower's decision to give British Field Marshall Montgomery command of all U.S. forces on the north side of the "bulge" at the height of the battle precipitated the final showdown between Ike and Monty over the issue of an overall Allied ground commander—a question that had been festering since the D-Day landings. Eisenhower won. In addition, the concentration of Allied forces in the Ardennes region at the conclusion of the battle helped shape the nature of the Allies' final assault into Germany. American and British Armies would continue to advance into the heart of the dying Third Reich along multiple axes, thus ending Montgomery's hopes of leading a "single thrust" to Berlin. And despite Hitler's fervent hope that his Ardennes offensive would somehow save his crumbling empire, it merely consumed Germany's last reserves of mobile forces in the west. Not only did the Führer fail to delay Germany's collapse, his powerful, but ill-conceived offensive ironically succeeded in speeding it up.

Hitler's Last Gamble—WACHT AM RHEIN AND HERBSTNEBEL

Allied strategy up to December 1944 had been quite straightforward: "Undertake operations aimed at the heart of Germany and the destruction of her armed forces," Supreme Allied Commander Eisenhower was told by the Anglo-American combined chiefs of staff. He was given no other objectives, no specific instructions about how to achieve his mission, and a "negotiated peace" was not authorized. For the Allies, it was a war to the death, the complete destruction of Germany the only acceptable outcome. When Hitler made the desperate decision to go on the offensive in the Ardennes in December 1944, he was attempting to gain a political settlement to which the Western Allies would never agree. Just as his flawed strategy of "no retreat" had doomed the German army in the east at Stalingrad two years earlier, so did his ill-conceived Ardennes offensive waste Germany's remaining mobile reserves in the west.

Hitler's last gamble was meant to hit the most thinly held sector of the Allied line with a strength and fury that no one on the Allied side would believe possible at such a late stage in the European war. Expecting that Hitler's field commanders would be husbanding their remaining mobile forces for use against the inevitable Allied invasion of Germany, Allied leaders failed to realize that the German leader had taken absolute control of the war's prosecution. The Führer's commander in the west, Feldmarschal von Rundstedt, was merely a figurehead, disguising the Nazi leader's complete control of all operations. In October 1944, Hitler presented his plan for an Ardennes counterstroke to Rundstedt and began planning the attack in the strictest of secrecy.

Deceptively code-named WACHT AM RHEIN (Watch on the Rhine), the offensive was meant to repeat the success of the brilliant Ardennes attack against the French and British in May 1940, and used the same basic pattern. Devised to split the Allied line at its weakest point, the offensive's objective was to isolate the British forces in the north from the American forces in the south. Hitler optimistically hoped his scheme would allow his forces to annihilate the British army or, failing that, at least put Germany in a good position to sign separate peace agreements with the Allies, avoiding the humiliation of unconditional surrender.

The two principal German commanders charged with realizing this plan were Sepp Dietrich (SS general and Hitler's crony from his old Munich days) and Hasso von Manteuffel (later called the "Panzer General" for his successes with armored formations). The actual assault, code-named HERBSTNEBEL, would be carried out along a forty-mile section of the Ardennes Forest by the major combat units of Army Group B. Dietrich's 6th Panzer Armee on the right (north) was to lead the main attack, striking northeast for the Meuse River crossings, then driving on to seize the huge Allied base at Antwerp. Manteuffel's 5th Panzer Armee, directly to Dietrich's left, was to sweep through the Ardennes toward the Meuse, covering Dietrich's flank as it went. Anchoring the offensive on the left (south) flank were the infantry forces of General Eric Brandenberger's 7th Armee. None of the German commanders cared much for the plan or seriously believed in Hitler's goal of capturing Antwerp. However, they were sworn by their leader to carry out the plan to the best of their abilities, and they were too professional not to comply. It would be the last time in the war that the German army was on the attack.

In addition to providing the principal combat units, Army Group B also planned to employ a parachute drop behind Allied lines in an attempt to pave the way for the advancing panzer and grenadier units. Furthermore, Colonel Otto Skorzeny, the daring commando who had rescued Mussolini, would lead a force of English-speaking Germans in GI uniforms and gear (designated Panzer Brigade 150) in a daring venture to infiltrate Allied lines and sow confusion. By 0530 hours on December 16, 1944, the German assault units were in position. At that moment the eastern horizon erupted in a flash of light as the 1,900 German artillery pieces and rocket launchers began one of the biggest bombardments yet seen on the Western Front.

Nursery and Old Folks' Home—The Ardennes Front

Nearly the full brunt of the surprise offensive was borne by Major General Troy Middleton's understrength, overextended VIII Corps. Composed of slightly more than three divisions, the VIII Corps held a frontage that was five times wider than that of a "normal" corps elsewhere along the extensive Allied front. Each U.S. division was expected to defend a sector of about twenty-six miles, such a distance making any effort to conduct a cohesive defense virtually impossible. The length of the line and the thinness of his defenses forced Middleton to forgo any thought of maintaining a mobile reserve to plug gaps in an emergency. Once Middleton's beleaguered troops were attacked, any help would have to come from outside the Ardennes.

Complicating Middleton's task was the condition of the major combat units manning his weak front. Two of the VIII Corps divisions, Major General Dutch Cota's 28th Infantry Division and Major General Raymond Barton's 4th Infantry Division, were still recovering from the bloody Hürtgen Forest fighting of the previous three months. Neither of these battered, veteran units was at a peak of combat efficiency. Anchoring Middleton's shaky line on the left (north) flank was the brand-new 106th Infantry Division, commanded by the inexperienced Major General Alan Jones. This unit had arrived in the Ardennes just four days before Dietrich's 6th Panzer Armee, the main attack of Hitler's offensive, slammed into its sector. The men of the 106th had not yet heard a shot fired in anger. Middleton's last remaining unit was the 9th Armored Division, also new to combat. However, the VIII Corps commander had only two of the 9th's three combat commands available to help with the defense. One of these was on loan to the V Corps to support the First U.S. Army attack on the strategic Roer River dams north of the Ardennes. To make matters worse, the length of the Ardennes front forced Middleton to use one of the remaining combat commands to plug a gap in the VIII Corps front between the 28th and 4th Divisions. Neither of the 9th Armored's tactical combat commands, therefore, was available to the corps commander for use in a counterattack. Historian and Battle of the Bulge veteran Charles B. MacDonald aptly described the Ardennes sector of the American lines as "the nursery and old folks' home of the American command."

Dietrich's main effort was designed to advance along the so-called Losheim Gap, the classic Ardennes invasion route. This section of the Ardennes was located on Middleton's extreme left and was lightly defended by the 14th Cavalry Group. Complicating matters in the Losheim Gap area was the fact that the VIII Corps–V Corps boundary ran along it—unit boundaries habitually being weak points in any defense. To the north of the Losheim Gap was the higher ground of the Elsenborn Ridge, key defensive terrain from which a defender could interdict free passage of the gap with artillery fire and counterattacks. The Elsenborn Ridge, in Major General Leonard Gerow's V Corps area, was situated directly behind (west of) the 2nd and 99th Infantry Divisions, the units that had launched the U.S. attack on the Roer River dams only days before the German assault. If Dietrich's leading units struck these divisions at the same time as they hit Middleton's forces, and if they subsequently forced the V Corps units up onto the key terrain of the Elsenborn Ridge, the going would not be easy.

German Attack and American Response

The hour-long German barrage provided a rude awakening to the American soldiers guarding what had been, up to that point, the quietest sector in the line. The shells, some as large as sixteen inches, blasted their positions, cutting nearly all telephone lines from frontline units to their higher headquarters and destroying many of the troops' carefully prepared defensive positions. Shortly after the shelling stopped, advance elements of the first sixteen German assault divisions began to surge through the eerie mists of the Ardennes Forest toward the shaken Americans.

Bad weather, primarily the ubiquitous winter fog of northern Europe, turned into a principal German ally by grounding the Allied air forces and neutralizing the Allies' tremendous advantage of air superiority. The heavy mist and freezing fog also assisted the German advance by cloaking the Nazi units while making rapid vehicular movements on the limited road network of the region extremely treacherous and so impeding the American response. The U.S. defenders were in danger of being quickly overrun by the German assault units that suddenly materialized out of the mists. Hitler had gained complete surprise with the launching of this massive offensive, and his Panzer Armee commanders were doing their best to exploit it.

Almost as soon as the attack got under way, however, the German units began running into unexpected difficulties. Much of the trouble was a result of the extremely poor roads in the Ardennes region, which was considered "impassable" to large formations of mechanized units, lacking, as it did, the system of durable, hard-surfaced roads necessary to the rapid movement of modern units. The few good roads in the Ardennes tend to cluster around a limited number of choke points, such as St.-Vith near Losheim, and Bastogne, farther south. Off-road movement, especially at this time of the year, is extremely difficult. Further complicating the advance was the German Command's decision to use principally infantry forces to force the initial breakthrough, saving the bulk of the panzer units to exploit the rupture. The slow going of the leadoff foot soldiers clogged the few good roads, resulting in miles-long traffic jams. German assault units were pressing forward, but the lightning-quick progress of 1940 was conspicuously absent. Bad roads, however, were not the sole reason for the German's slowness. The American defenders, many individually or in small groups, were putting up an unexpectedly strong resistance.

The full force of the German attack fell on the veteran 28th Infantry Division in the center of VIII Corps' line in front of the key road junction of Bastogne, and on the untried 106th Infantry Division, near the Losheim Gap at St.-Vith, another key traffic grid. Not surprisingly, the Germans were once again using the classic invasion route through the Ardennes as the axis for their main attack. Over the course of the next few days, both of these U.S. infantry divisions

Antwerp
Brussels
Second BR
XXXX
Ninth US
Roer River
XXXX
NINTH
Simpson
Hürgten
Forest
Liege
Ninth
XXXX
First
Meuse River
XXXX
FIRST
Hodges
Elsenborn
Ridge
XXXX
6
PZ
Dietrich
Losheim
XXX
XXX
BR
Horrocks
St. Vith
Schnee Eifel Plateau
XXXX
5
PZ
Manteuffel
20 Dec 44
Boundary
Change
21 (Montgomery)
XXXXX
12 (Bradley)
Bastpgne
Our River
XXXX
7
INF
Brandenberger
XXXX
THIRD
Patton
Luxemburg
Hunsruck
Ardennes Region
25 Miles
Limit of German Advance,
26 Dec 44
Verdun

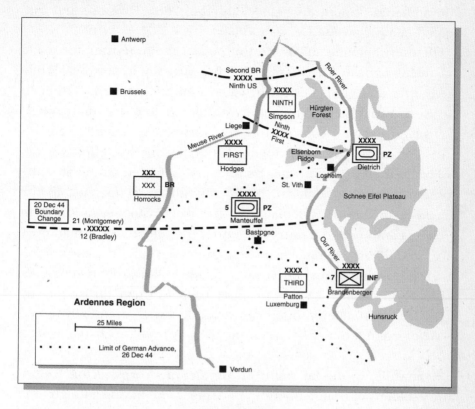

Ardennes Region

were destroyed as effective fighting forces, but the stiff resistance the outnumbered Americans, especially the 28th Division, put up, helped fatally slow the German attack.

The overwhelming attack and thinness of the American line made the maintenance of a cohesive defense virtually impossible. While the panzer and grenadier spearheads attempted to push farther to the west, VIII Corps commander Middleton found it increasingly difficult to exercise control over his northernmost units from his corps command post in Bastogne. Ultimately, he lost effective control of the 106th Division and the units trying to defend the St.-Vith–Losheim Gap area, and had his hands full trying to react to the attacks on his units immediately in front of Bastogne. As the 28th Division continued to disintegrate under the relentless German pressure, Middleton exercised personal command over the disposition of each precious unit, ordering individual tank-infantry-engineer teams to threatened sectors to parry each German thrust. Grudgingly, the outnumbered American defenders were eventually forced to yield ground, but the German attack was losing its battle against time.

Meanwhile, in the far south of Middleton's corps sector, the infantry soldiers of Brandenberg's 7th Armee were having a tough time against the 4th Infantry Division and Combat Command A, 9th Armored. Lacking an armored punch to assist the infantry attacks, Brandenberger's troops were in danger of failing to position themselves to protect the main German attack farther north from an Allied counterattack from the south. If Brandenberger could not advance far enough to block an Allied counterattack from the south, the entire plan could be doomed. It was not lost on the Germans that their most feared Allied commander, General George S. Patton, commanded the powerful Third U.S. Army, immediately south of their Ardennes assault. If this aggressive, dynamic leader was turned loose against the exposed, unprotected flank of their attack, real disaster was possible.

Elsenborn Ridge and the North Shoulder

While Middleton had his hands full trying to rally his shattered units and patch together some semblance of a defense in the VIII Corps area, immediately to his left flank V Corps units were also getting smacked by the 6th Panzer Armee's main effort. Major General Walter Robertson's veteran 2nd Infantry Division and Major General Walter Lauer's inexperienced 99th Infantry Division were being hammered by the same onslaught that was hitting Middleton's northernmost units—the weak 14th Cavalry Group in the Losheim Gap and the brand-new 106th Infantry Division in front of St.-Vith. But while the 14th Cavalry was being swept aside by the powerful German attacks and the 106th's major combat units were quickly in danger of being surrounded and cut off, Robertson and Lauer's divisions were having better luck.

Though nearly as green as the 106th Division just to its south in front of St.-Vith, the 99th Division nevertheless fought stubbornly and tenaciously to fend off the assaults of Dietrich's advance units. Slowly forced back onto the higher ground and key terrain of the Elsenborn Ridge, the determined defense mounted by company and battalion-size units of the 99th prevented the Germans from quickly grabbing dominating positions on the high ground. The fight for the twin villages of Krinkelt and Rocherath, a nasty, confused, brutal affair that involved desperate attacks and counterattacks from both sides over a period of several days, was instrumental in permitting the Americans to maintain control of the Elsenborn Ridge. Backed by units of the 2nd Division, men of the 99th managed to prevent the villages from falling into German hands. Failing to capture this key position and frustrated in their attempts to occupy the high ground along the extensive ridge, German commanders began to reroute their advancing units farther to the south—thereby adding to the traffic jams around St.-Vith and Losheim.

Between December 17 and 19, once the German attempts to seize the dominating terrain on the "bulge's" northern shoulder were turned back, the American commanders began to push reinforcing units onto and around the ridge, solidifying their hold on the ground. Most of all, the rushing of large numbers of American artillery battalions to the Elsenborn Ridge area turned that sector of the line into a giant fire-support platform, from which massive amounts of lethal firepower could be rained down upon the German 6th Panzer Armee units attempting to advance westward along the good roads in the shadow of the ridge. Historian Hugh Cole, in the official history of the battle, ascribes great importance to the U.S. artillery firing from the north shoulder, saying that these guns "stopped the German attack cold" in this sector. Dietrich's hopes for a rapid run to seize crossings over the Meuse River were dashed by the Americans' stubborn defense of the Elsenborn area, and his main attack was choked to death by the dominating American guns on the north shoulder.

With the 4th Infantry Division and elements of the 9th Armored leading the successful defense in the south, and the key northern terrain dominated by V Corps units backed up by massive artillery fire, the shoulders of the German penetration of the American lines were holding firm. Lacking the ability to widen their attack base, German commanders realized that their Ardennes offensive was seriously disrupted. In the soft center of the American lines, however, in front of the key road centers at St.-Vith and Bastogne, Manteuffel's 5th Panzer Armee was achieving better results.

Defense of St.-Vith—Disaster and Triumph

Alan Jones's 106th Infantry Division sector was probably the most difficult sector to defend along the thin American lines in the Ardennes. Impossibly wide, Jones's front meandered for some twenty-two miles along the broken terrain of the German-Belgian border. Although his right (south) flank rested in a somewhat defensible area of many streams and rugged hills near the 28th Infantry Division's section of the line, Jones's left (north) flank abruptly ended at the edge of the Losheim Gap. To his front, Jones was constrained

Elsenborn
V Corps (99th Div)
XXX
VIII Corps (106 Div)
Loshiem
XXXX
6
PZ
Dietrich
III
14
XX
HQ
106
Jones
14 CAV
III
422 INF
Our River
St.-Vith
Schönberg
III
422
EIFEL PLATEAU
422 INF
III
423 INF
XXXX
5
PZ
Manteuffel
III
423
SCHNEE
US/GE Front Line 15 Dec 44
423 INF
III
424 INF
St.-Vith
1 Mile
Major GE Attack
Unit Boundary
US/GE Front Line, 15 Dec 44
106 Div
XX
2BDiv
III
424

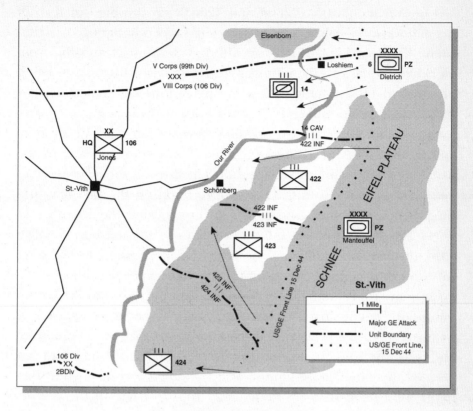

St.-Vith, Belgium

by higher command to place the bulk of his division's combat power, two full regiments (the 422nd and 423rd), on the high plateau of the Schnee Eifel—alone and exposed in a recently captured section of the Siegfried Line. Unable to withdraw without permission from higher headquarters, these units were extremely vulnerable to being surrounded by the natural flow of any serious German attack. At 0530 hours on December 16, Jones's worst nightmare came true.

Despite the fact that the opening German barrage cut all communications lines to his forward units, Jones knew by early in the day that he was facing a major assault. The division's meager reserves had been committed to the line before noon on the first day, and shortly thereafter Jones was forced to begin using the 106th's supporting engineer units as infantry reserves to the hard-pressed forward regiments. He did not, however, ask permission to withdraw his two exposed regiments from their Schnee Eifel positions.

On Jones's left flank in the Losheim Gap, the 14th Cavalry Group was quickly falling apart. Middleton, Jones's immediate boss, tried to help his subordinate when it became obvious that the German assault was a serious threat, but the VIII Corps commander had few reserves to spare. Those limited assets Middleton controlled at Bastogne were needed to his immediate front to back up the disintegrating defense of the 28th Division. Middleton did, however, release a large portion of his precious armored reserve at about 1120 hours that morning when he was able to regain control of Combat Command B, 9th Armored Division, from V Corps and assign it to go to Jones's aid. But the unit was still at Faymonville in the V Corps sector to the north, and would take several hours to reach St.-Vith. Of greater assistance to Jones and his beleaguered 106th Division was a decision Eisenhower made that day at supreme headquarters.

Several hours after the beginning of the German attack, Eisenhower's G2, Major General Kenneth Strong, informed the supreme commander of the events occurring in the Ardennes. Ike, who was then meeting with his principal subordinate and commander of the 12th Army Group, Omar Bradley, to discuss the continuing problem of obtaining infantry replacements, immediately sensed that this was much more than a German spoiling attack to disrupt the First Army's drive to capture the Roer River dams. Despite Bradley's skepticism of the scope of the enemy assault, Eisenhower ordered that the 7th Armored Division in the Ninth Army area to the north of the Ardennes and the 10th Armored Division in the Third Army, south of the Ardennes, be dispatched at once to Middleton's assistance. That same day Eisenhower also ordered the only two divisions the supreme command held as a strategic reserve, the 82nd and 101st Airborne Divisions, to begin preparations for deployment to the VIII Corps area. Additionally, he directed the staff to begin planning to reorganize the entire front, with the main objective of counterattacking the German Ardennes offensive and cutting it off. These crucial decisions saved Bastogne, made the week-long defense at St.-Vith possible, and ultimately decided the outcome of the battle. At Jones's beleaguered headquarters, meanwhile, disaster loomed.

Jones's most urgent question on the evening of December 16 was whether or not to pull back his two regiments on the Schnee Eifel plateau before they became surrounded and while he still could. Middleton had informed him that the 7th Armored Division was being sent to back him up, and that it should arrive the next morning, December 17. Jones received scant help in making his momentous decision from the combat-experienced Middleton, who told him the decision was his as the commander on the spot. During a confusing and controversial phone conversation late on the evening of December 16, each man completely misunderstood the other—Middleton thought Jones was pulling the units back, but Jones understood his corps commander to approve his decision to leave them in place. By leaving them there, Jones (abetted by Middleton's failure to order him to pull the units back) destroyed his division, creating the conditions for the largest surrender of U.S. troops in the European war—8,000 men.

While this disaster was taking shape in front of St.-Vith, the man who would rescue the crumbling defense of the important road center was racing along icy roads from Holland toward Middleton's headquarters in Bastogne. Brigadier General Bruce C. Clarke had been informed by his division commander, Brigadier General Bob Hasbrouck of the 7th Armored, to report immediately to the VIII

Corps commander and his combat command would be sent south after him. After a several-hour drive over the treacherous roads, Clarke reported to Middleton at Bastogne and requested further instructions. The VIII Corps commander told him, "Alan Jones is having some trouble at St.-Vith. Get some sleep and some breakfast then go to him. If he needs help, give it to him."

By 1000 hours the next morning, December 17, Clarke, his operations officer, and their driver, had forced their way through roads jammed with U.S. vehicles fleeing westward from the onrushing Germans to reach Jones's headquarters in St.-Vith. What they found there was confusion and despair. Jones's 106th Division staff was rapidly packing up their gear and preparing to evacuate the town, while their division commander fretted about the two surrounded regiments on the high ground to the east, one of which contained the general's son, a junior staff officer. When Jones demanded to know how soon Clarke could attack eastward with his armored combat command and rescue his trapped units, Clarke had to tell him his troops were still on the road from Holland, their arrival time unknown. Clarke asked Jones what plans his staff had prepared for the counterattack and requested to be put into radio contact with the overall commander of the trapped regiments. Jones and his inexperienced, overwhelmed staff could comply with none of these requests. Furthermore, the near panic Clarke had witnessed on the clogged roads leading to St.-Vith convinced him that Jones and his staff could not even assure the timely arrival of Clarke's following combat command, since they were incapable of even keeping the roads open to eastbound traffic. During the time Clarke and Jones waited for the arrival of the armored column, no staff officer was observed to report to Jones for orders or instructions, nor did Jones call for anyone. Finally, at about 1500 hours, the two men went to the roof of the headquarters building to observe the cause of some close-in firing they had heard coming from the outskirts of town. When they saw what they took to be German infantry closing in on the town, Jones turned to Clarke and said, "Clarke, you take command. I'll give you all I have." The defense of St.-Vith now belonged to Clarke and the 7th Armored Division.

The situation confronting Clarke at 1500 hours on December 17, the second day of the all-out German attack, was discouraging. His combat command was still trying to force its way over traffic-jammed roads to reach the St.-Vith area, and there were few combat units in the immediate vicinity. To his left, the 14th Cavalry Group was being scattered by overpowering panzer and grenadier assaults, and on his right, the 106th's remaining combat regiment, the 424th, supported now by Brigadier General Bill Hoge's Combat Command B, 9th Armored Division, was barely holding its own against fierce German attacks. In front of St.-Vith, the bulk of the 106th Division's combat power, the 422nd and 423rd Regiments, were completely surrounded on the Schnee Eifel plateau with little prospect of a successful breakout. Protecting the immediate approaches to St.-Vith was Lieutenant Colonel Tom Riggs's pathetically small force of combat engineers, division bandsmen, and support troops. It seemed unlikely that the hard-pressed engineer officer could keep the Germans out of town much longer. The only bright spot for Clarke that afternoon was the appearance of Lieutenant Colonel Roy Clay and his 275th Armored Field Artillery Battalion. Clay's gunners had been firing in support of the now scattered 14th Cavalry Group, and when that unit was swept away, Clay sought out Clarke in St.-Vith and offered to throw his guns into the fight for the town. The offer was gratefully accepted, and Clay's gunners began firing in support of Riggs's tiny force east of town.

Finally, at about 1630 hours, advance elements of Clarke's combat command began to arrive at St.-Vith. Troop B, 87th Cavalry Reconnaissance Squadron, was the first 7th Armored unit to arrive, and Clarke immediately sent it into action. Gradually, the remainder of Combat Command B, 7th Armored, arrived in town and joined the defense. For the next week Clarke's troopers and the other units in the vicinity of St.-Vith conducted a skillful delaying action that, as much as any other of the desperate fights in the entire Ardennes offensive, bought the Allies the time they needed to regain control of the battle and ultimately defeat the German assault.

Using the same tank-infantry-artillery teams over and over again to meet each successive German attack, Clarke convinced the enemy

commander, Manteuffel, that the German forces were facing an entire American armored corps. Clarke's defenders, supported by the
division's other combat commands along with the remainder of Hasbrouck's 7th Armored Division, kept Manteuffel's panzers out of St.-
Vith until December 21, then controlled the surrounding road
network until ordered to withdraw from the salient on December 23.
Instead of grabbing St.-Vith and its important road system on the
first day of the attack, the German assault had been delayed for an
entire week—a delay fatal to German success. While this epic stand
was taking place in the north, the Germans were having even worse
luck at another crucial road junction farther south.

Defense of Bastogne—Besieged and Rescued

While Jones and Clarke were desperately trying to create a viable
defense in the north around St.-Vith, Middleton, the VIII Corps commander, had his hands full trying to patch together a defense of the
shredded 28th Division lines in front of Bastogne. By the time Clarke
took over the defense of St. Vith from Jones, Middleton was able to
exercise little effective control over the flow of events on his left
flank. He lost even nominal control over his northern units on December 20, when Eisenhower, seriously concerned about Bradley's
ability to properly supervise and command the units in the north
half of the bulge, placed all units north of Bastogne under command
of Field Marshal Montgomery. Events, therefore, rapidly conspired
to cause VIII Corps' defensive efforts to be concentrated on the 28th
Division's sector immediately in front of Bastogne.

Colonel Hurley Fuller's regiment of the 28th, the 110th Infantry
Regiment, spread out along the impossibly wide Skyline Drive high
ground above the Our River, received the worst battering from the
5th Panzer Armee's attack. As Fuller's overwhelmingly outnumbered
units were slowly yielding ground, Middleton tried to organize the
best defense he could from his meager reserves. While Fuller's front
collapsed, the VIII Corps commander grabbed his only armored reserve, Combat Command R, 9th Armored, and sent mobile teams to

Bastogne
(Dec 16 - 20)
1 Mile
To St.-Vith
Our River
424
106 Div
XX
28 Div
112
Houffalize
XXX
HQ
VIII
Middleton
XX
101
HQ
McAuliffe
X
10
B
Roberts
X
9
R
Noville
112 INF
110 INF
Heinerscheid
HQ
110
Fuller
XXXX
5
PZ
Manteuffel
Clervaux
Marnach
Longvilly
Bastogne
Hosingen
XX
HQ
28
Cota
Wiltz
Weiler
110 INF
109 INF

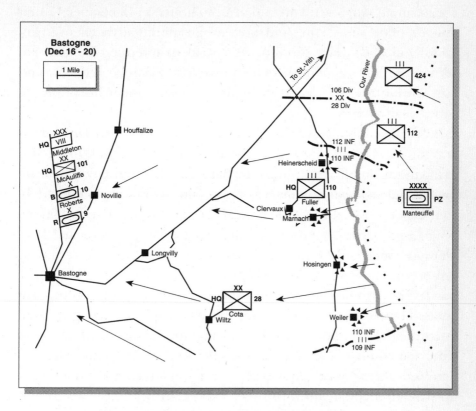

Bastogne, December 16–20, 1944

critical road junctions to try to delay the advancing German columns. For example, when word arrived at 2130 hours on December 17 that Fuller's regimental command post at Clervaux had been overrun, Middleton had a task force on the road to interdict the German advance within ten minutes. This procedure was repeated over and over during the first few days of the offensive and before outside help began arriving.

When Eisenhower decided to send the 7th Armored Division to St.-Vith, he also sent the 10th Armored Division from Patton's Third Army in the south of the bulge to Bastogne. Late on December 18, the leading combat command of the 10th, Combat Command B, commanded by Colonel William Roberts, began to arrive at Middleton's headquarters. Almost immediately, however, Roberts and Middleton clashed on the best use for the armored force. As a tanker, Roberts naturally wanted to fight his force as a single unit. Armored warfare doctrine, seemingly proven in the hugely successful dash across France the previous summer, called for maximizing the full weight and shock power of the tank-infantry-artillery team by operating the combat command as a single unit. To delay the German drive as long as possible, however, Middleton was compelled to break up Roberts's command into small tank-infantry-artillery teams and battalion-sized task forces scattered across the VIII Corps front at critical locations. Luckily for Bastogne, Middleton won the argument. Roberts's assets proved a key element in delaying the Germans until the 101st Airborne could arrive, and in holding the town thereafter.

Middleton supplemented the meager forces defending the approaches to Bastogne with his last small reserve forces, the combat engineer battalions that had been working in the area just prior to the attack. These soldiers joined the headquarters troops and the remnants of the 28th Division straggled in from the east and helped stiffen defenses until outside help arrived. On December 19, that much-needed help began to roll into Bastogne as the paratroopers of the 101st Airborne, joined by Roberts's armored combat command, survivors of the 28th Infantry Division, several VIII Corps artillery battalions, and other bits and pieces of shattered American units held the town against repeated German assaults. Their desperate defense had turned the siege of Bastogne into the most famous fight of the Ardennes offensive, and one of the most heroic events in U.S. military history. The 101st's acting commander during the battle, Brigadier General Anthony McAuliffe's terse rejection of a German surrender demand at the height of the siege, made the word "Nuts!" the most famous utterance of the campaign. Finally, on December 26, the 4th Armored Division of Patton's Third Army broke through the German defenses and dramatically lifted the siege.

Allied Command Reaction—Defeating the Attack

The arrival of the 4th Armored Division the day after Christmas 1944 was no accident, nor was it solely due to Patton's celebrated genius for armored combat. The lifting of the siege of Bastogne, along with the rapid dispatch of the 7th and 10th Armored Divisions to the Ardennes, and the swift deployment of the 101st and 82nd Airborne Divisions and the many other combat units sent to VIII Corps' aid in the first hours and days of the Battle of the Bulge, were the direct result of Eisenhower and the Allied Command's decisions. Ike's instantaneous recognition of the offensive for what it was, and his firm response to counter the German move, decisively stopped Hitler from disrupting the Allied Command and splitting the coalition. Throughout the early phases of the Ardennes fighting, Eisenhower not only reacted appropriately to German moves, he set the tone for successful Allied reaction to the threat. Above all, Eisenhower's battle leadership rose above petty jealousy and national pride, a fact demonstrated best by his giving Montgomery command of all Bradley's forces in the northern half of the bulge for the good of the Allied cause. More than any other commander, Eisenhower's inspired leadership won the battle.

In the first few days of the attack, the Allied Command began to reorganize the extensive front and send combat units to the threatened sector. Units were dispatched from Patton's Third Army, directly to the south of the Ardennes, and from Lieutenant General

William H. Simpson's Ninth Army, north of the bulge. Simpson dispatched seven divisions and twenty-eight nondivisional combat units to the threatened First Army area, while Patton was preparing his famous attack into the southern flank of the Nazi salient. After Eisenhower placed Montgomery in command of all U.S. units north of Bastogne, the field marshal moved the British XXX Corps into a blocking position on the west bank of the Meuse River to destroy any German unit that managed to force a crossing. Even while Dietrich and Manteuffel's assault troops were driving westward, Eisenhower and the Allied Command had set in motion the countermove that would stop them.

On December 19, Eisenhower met with his senior American commanders to coordinate their efforts and present his views on the "golden opportunity" presented by the German sortie from their defensive positions in the Siegfried Line. Ike wanted only "cheerful faces" on his commanders and clearly intended to use the German offensive to defeat the enemy's last remaining mobile reserves in the west. How soon, Ike asked, could Patton counterattack? To the astonishment of the other commanders, Patton replied that he could mount a corps-sized attack toward Bastogne "in three days, with three divisions." No one else seemed to realize that Patton, one of the few American commanders who had foreseen the Ardennes attack, had secretly had his Third Army staff prepare contingency plans for just such a counterattack. Now Patton would demonstrate his brilliance as a combat leader by successfully executing this dramatic and difficult maneuver, culminating in the lifting of the Bastogne siege on December 26. Unfortunately, a stunning counterattack would not occur with commensurate speed on the northern half of the bulge.

The early success of the German assault threatened to cut in two the U.S. First Army, commanded by Lieutenant General Courtney Hodges, and this caused Eisenhower to seriously doubt the ability of Bradley to exercise personal control over the American defense. Stubbornly refusing to move his headquarters in Luxembourg City on the far right flank of the bulge, Bradley maintained telephone and radio contact with Hodges's headquarters on the bulge's left flank, but made no effort to visit Hodges or any of the units in the north. Ike, who correctly saw the opportunity to cut off the German forces in the Ardennes by strong counterattacks from the north and south, felt Bradley was incapable of coordinating this effort if he remained far to the south. Accordingly, Eisenhower ordered the transfer of command of all of Bradley's units north of Bastogne to Field Marshal Montgomery on December 20. This controversial decision, which Bradley bitterly resented, helped the Allies regain control of the battle, but it engendered bad feelings among the senior Americans for the remainder of the war. Ironically, the command change actually thwarted Ike's hopes for an early counterattack to trap the bulk of German forces in the Ardennes. The overcautious Monty, thinking more about his upcoming attack into northern Germany than about bagging the Germans in the bulge, delayed the northern counterattack and moved his focus away from the base of the salient. Instead of coordinating his movements with Patton's to cut off the Germans, Monty delivered his counterattack against the nose of the penetration days later. Ike was bitterly disappointed, and this missed opportunity was the Allies' biggest mistake of the battle.

On December 26 the Ardennes offensive passed its critical point. Patton's relief column entered besieged Bastogne, and farther north, Major General Ernie Harmon's 2nd Armored Division thwarted the 2nd Panzer Division's last effort to reach the Meuse River. Despite the obvious failure of the German attack, Hitler refused to allow his commanders to begin withdrawing back into the Siegfried Line— Westwall—defensive positions. Instead, German units were ordered to continue to attack westward.

Finally, on January 8, with Montgomery's northern counterattack at last under way, and Patton's forces continuing to advance in the south, Hitler permitted his commanders to begin a fighting withdrawal. It required nearly another month of hard fighting before the Allies returned the front line in the Ardennes to its original position of December 16. A great victory had been won in the forests and hills of the rugged Ardennes region, but at a high price. The fighting was brutal, savage, and of an intensity seldom matched during the war. One incident has stood out over the years as an example of unusual horror and savagery. It occurred on the second day of the battle.

The Bodies in the Snow—The Malmédy Massacre

One of General Simpson's Ninth Army units, hurrying south to help the beleaguered defenders of St.-Vith, was Sergeant Eugene Garrett's artillery observation unit. Traveling as part of the 7th Armored's Division Artillery convoy, Battery B, 285th Field Artillery Observation Battalion passed through the American-held town of Malmédy on the afternoon of December 17 and proceeded up the steep hill to the tiny crossroads of Baugnez, on the plateau above the town. As the convoy arrived at the crossroads, it unexpectedly ran into the lead elements of SS Lieutenant Colonel Jochen Peiper's armored battle group (*Kampfgruppe*). Overpowering the lightly defended American soldiers, Peiper's panzer troops, backed up by armored vehicles and heavily armed combat formations, captured about 100 men. Marching them into a nearby field, the SS men opened fire with machine guns and small arms. Throughout the afternoon, passing SS units fired into the mounds of wounded and dead Americans. At nightfall, the dozen or so captives who had feigned death bolted for the woods or the presumed safety of a nearby café. Those men who reached the woods, among them Garrett, eventually worked their way back down the hill to Malmédy, where they rejoined the American forces. The ones who tried to hide in the café were murdered when the Germans set fire to the building, shooting the men as they ran out.

It is estimated that Peiper's men murdered at least four hundred people along their advance, including defenseless Belgian men, women, and children who had the bad luck to get in their way. At the Nuremberg Trials, Peiper and many of his men were convicted of murder and sentenced to death, but through the efforts of some American sympathizers (including Senator Joe McCarthy), all were eventually released. Peiper, apparently, was himself murdered at his home in France thirty years after his atrocities.

Aftermath

Eisenhower's forces won a great victory in the Ardennes, foiling Hitler's last attempt to prop up his crumbling Third Reich and destroying Germany's remaining mobile reserves of tanks and personnel. By the conclusion of the battle, the rapid crossing of the Rhine and the subsequent speedy occupation of the now defeated Germany were assured. On March 7, the still-standing Ludendorff Bridge across the Rhine at Remagen was seized by the U.S. 9th Armored Division, giving the First Army a toehold on the river's east bank. Just over two weeks later Montgomery's 21 Army Group (including Simpson's Ninth U.S. Army) crossed the river in the north, while Patton crossed in the south. In the first two days of April, the U.S. Ninth and First Armies encircled the Ruhr industrial area, trapping the last remaining German operational forces, the remnants of Army Group B. By mid-April, Simpson's forces had reached the Elbe River, the agreed-upon U.S.-Soviet demarcation line. When Soviet forces completed capturing Berlin at the beginning of May, surviving German commanders surrendered.

But the Battle of the Bulge was not all good news for Eisenhower and the Allied Command. Despite the later claims of some intelligence analysts, no one predicted the location, scope, or intensity of the attack. The Allied commanders were badly fooled by the German offensive, and the greatest share of the blame belongs to Eisenhower, for it was his insistence upon maintaining a general offensive all along the Allied front that led to the weak positions in the Ardennes region in the first place. And despite the excellence of Ike's leadership, his failure to force the cautious Montgomery to launch an early counterattack led to the escape of the bulk of German forces in the Ardennes.

Nonetheless, the Battle of the Bulge proved to be an American Stalingrad, a U.S. El Alamein. As the Russians proved their army's leadership and fighting qualities in the rubble of Stalingrad, and as Montgomery showed the mettle of British commanders and soldiers in the sands of El Alamein, so did American leaders and troops prove their worth in the forests and snows of the Ardennes. The Ardennes showed that American soldiers could fight, and that American commanders could lead.

The Battle of Okinawa

April 1–June 30, 1945

Last *"Banzai!"*

The greatest land-sea-air battle in history took place on and around the 800-square mile island of Okinawa, strategically situated only 350 nautical miles south of Kyushu—Japan proper. The culmination of over three years of hard fighting on the rocky islands, sweltering seas, and steamy jungles of the vast Pacific Theater, this last major battle of the Second World War marked the end of Japan's quest for empire. Despite the fact that Allied victory was virtually assured by this late stage of the war, the Japanese 32nd Army mounted a stubborn and determined defense against the overwhelming firepower and nearly unlimited resources of the American invasion force. Outnumbered two to one in personnel, and outgunned ten to one in fire support, they forced the struggle for the island to continue for eighty-two horrific days, then fought on as individual soldiers for days longer during "mop-up" operations. Over 6,300 Americans lost their lives (4,900 U.S. sailors also died during the naval phase) and probably 100,000 Japanese. When Okinawan civilian dead from the ground fighting and air and naval bombardment are added, total Japanese dead could be as much as 130,000. Neither of the opposing commanders survived the battle. The U.S. leader, Tenth Army commander Lieutenant General Simon B. Buckner, was killed by Japanese shellfire on June 18. His opposite number, Japanese 32nd Army commander Lieutenant General Ushijima Mitsuru, committed seppuku, ritual suicide, three days later.

During the nearly three-month-long campaign, Ushijima capably executed a defense in depth that maximized the effects of "fire-swept zones." Created by the interlocking fires of hundreds of fortified caves, bunkers, and pillboxes, these zones formed a no-man's-land of concentrated firepower reminiscent of the awful landscapes of World War I. More than in any other of the many Pacific battles, attacking American army troops and marines on Okinawa were forced to rely heavily on supporting tanks to overcome the stubborn Japanese defense. The intensity of this resistance is reflected in the fact that the Americans lost 153 tanks during the campaign.

Despite the odds against them, the Japanese defenders were successful in buying time for the construction and improvement of defenses on the Japanese home islands in preparation for the Allied invasion that was certain to follow—in a sense, they were too successful. Their determined and fanatical fighting and suicidal kamikaze attacks on U.S. ships helped convince Allied planners that the upcoming invasion of Japan could cost as many as 1 million Allied casualties. An alternative solution, even one that ushered in the atomic age, seemed preferable.

An Underground Empire

The very vastness of the Pacific perimeter caused Japan to disperse its military forces over too wide an area, and within months of Pearl Harbor, the Allies were able to strike back. By maintaining a line of communications to Australia, America and Britain were able to turn that country into a huge base of operations from which to begin taking the Pacific back from Japan. In June 1942, the American victory at the battle of Midway started to turn the tide against Japan, which lost naval and air superiority in the region. After Midway, the Allies held the upper hand.

With the capture of Guadalcanal in the Solomon Islands (August–November 1942) Allied forces began pushing back the Japanese from their defensive perimeter. Allied units in the southwest Pacific under General Douglas MacArthur and in the central Pacific under Admiral Chester Nimitz relentlessly pursued an "island hopping" campaign of amphibious operations that the Japanese could not resist. Bypassing and cutting off Japanese strong points, like the crucial bases at Rabaul on New Britain and Truk in the Carolines, American and Allied forces drove inexorably toward the heart of the Japanese empire. After capturing New Guinea (September 1942–November 1944), New Britain (January 1944), the Gilbert Islands (November 1943), Kwajalein (January 1944), Saipan and Guam (July 1944), and the Palau Islands (September 1944), American and Allied forces mounted a successful campaign to regain the Philippines at Leyte Gulf in October 1944.

After Leyte Gulf, the largest naval engagement in history, American ground forces established lodgements on Leyte and began operations against the 60,000 Japanese troops of General Yamashita. Winning here guaranteed the reconquest of the Philippines. By December 1944, MacArthur's troops had subdued Leyte and begun recapturing Luzon. After the costly U.S. victory on Iwo Jima (February 1945), only Okinawa remained to be taken.

The dogged Japanese defense of Okinawa owed more to the pick and shovel than to the rifle and antitank gun. The 32nd-Army worked for a year to improve the already existing caves and to construct bunkers, tunnels, and other underground structures, digging over sixty miles of usable space by the time the Americans landed on April 1, 1945. This prodigious effort produced enough subsurface space to house all of the 100,000 combat and support troops of the 32nd Army—a virtual underground empire. Capitalizing on the rugged terrain, characterized by ridges, hills, ravines, gullies, and innumerable terraces, the Japanese defenders created hundreds of underground machine-gun and artillery pillboxes in order to control the narrow and restricted avenues of approach. By siting a great number of these pillboxes on the reverse slopes of the hills and ridges, they could saturate the opposite hillside with fire while remaining impervious to counterfires. Safe from the preinvasion Allied bombardment and air attacks in their underground fortified zone, Ushijima's force could husband its strength and wait to unleash it when the Americans moved into the carefully sited "kill zones."

The most elaborate subterranean position of all was the 32nd Army's headquarters cave, situated 50 to 160 feet below Shuri Castle, seat of power of the ancient Okinawan kings. This "improved" cave complex stretched over 1,280 feet north to south and included several side tunnels, chambers, and shafts where more than 1,000 personnel lived and worked. The cave was essentially self-sufficient, containing its own food stores, kitchens, electricity, and sleeping quarters in addition to office areas and, near the surface, fighting positions. Other underground positions were not as finely constructed or as large, but proved just as impervious to American shellfire. Pillbox positions, containing a single machine gun or artillery piece, varied somewhat in size, shape, and construction, since the individual battalions or companies that would fight from them were responsible for their design and building, but in principal, they were all alike. A series of cleverly concealed entry shafts and narrow connecting tunnels, excavated to varying depths, depending on the terrain, led to a fighting position, usually about five-by-five feet, which typically had only one small firing port, only eight inches high by eighteen inches wide, tapering outward to a concealed, three-foot-wide opening. Nearly invisible, the resulting pillbox was immune from indirect fire.

In addition to headquarters caves and pillbox fighting positions, Ushijima's soldiers prepared large underground storage bunkers for ammunition and other supplies, and they also constructed subterranean barracks to house and protect infantry. The latter could thus fight on the surface, but would be able to withdraw to the barracks during American bombardment and shelling. Overall, Ushijima's extensive underground fortified area resembled the massive entrenchments of World War I, but with the added protection of dirt-and-rock overhead cover, which was vital for survival on the airpower-dominated World War II battlefield. Also like the soldiers occupying the earthen redoubts of that earlier war, the 32nd Army sacrificed virtually all of its tactical and operational mobility. Once Ushijima's defenders withdrew into the protection of the caves and pillboxes, they were unable to conduct a war of maneuver against the advancing American forces. They could, however, die in place, taking as many Americans with them as possible.

The Japanese defenders' troglodyte existence was safe but unpleasant. The caves and pillboxes were hot, stifling, and psychologically numbing. The temperature in the Shuri headquarters cave was over ninety degrees with 100 percent humidity, and everything was wet and damp. The stale, stuffy air caused continual physical discomfort that led to rashes and other infirmities, and the single, large ventilator fan set up in one of the access shafts was generally ineffective. Ushijima's staff worked in a world of darkness, illuminated only by the harsh glare of electric lights. Movement on the surface—communication activities, for example, between Ushijima's subordinate units—was possible only at night, when the ubiquitous American airpower could not observe them. Ushijima's shafts and tunnels allowed him to mount the most effective and sustained Japanese defense against the Allies in the entire Pacific war, but he paid a high price in terms of his staff and troops' morale and efficiency.

Beachhead Battle or Defense in Depth

The 32nd Army's stout defense of Okinawa departed from the time-honored tactics and operational procedures of the Japanese army. The desperate situation facing General Ushijima and his staff in the year leading up to the American landings forced his chief of staff, Lieutenant General Cho Isamu, and his senior operations officer, Colonel Yahara Hiromichi, to devise innovative and unconventional means to deal with the overwhelming American superiority in airpower and every category of firepower.

The Japanese army had proven itself to be a superb light infantry force, exceptionally skilled at such tactics as infiltration, close-in maneuver, and sudden, fearless attacks. In close combat, the tough, disciplined Japanese soldier had few equals. Lightly equipped to execute this style of war fighting, Japanese forces had been extremely successful against the Chinese, colonial forces, and other adversaries whose firepower was roughly equivalent to their own. The situation facing them in the final three years of the Pacific, however, was dramatically changed. Since late 1942, American and Allied warplanes had begun to sweep Japanese aircraft from the skies and gain air superiority, compelling Japanese ground forces to operate in an unaccustomed, and lethal, atmosphere. On the restricted terrain of far-flung Pacific islands, against massive and overwhelming firepower, their light infantry maneuver tactics were inappropriate and ineffective. The fearsome Banzai charge, which had shattered lightly armed Chinese resistance countless times, merely provided the heavily armed and richly supported Americans with a "target rich" environment for their superior fire support.

Japanese imperial general headquarters (IGHQ) was painfully aware of the importance of airpower in the Pacific and realized that attaining local air superiority was crucial to victory in any battle. In fact, IGHQ intended to conduct the fight for Okinawa in the skies over the island, not on the ground. IGHQ perceived the island, with its several airfields, as a giant aircraft carrier, an unsinkable flight deck from which to launch the planes that would destroy the American and Allied invasion fleet, and the 32nd Army's role as that of a supporting arm to Japanese airpower. Ushijima's troops were to construct and maintain the airfields, and provide whatever service support was necessary to keep them functioning. If American ground forces assaulted the island, IGHQ expected Ushijima's troops to mount a counterattack based on the Japanese army's standard light-infantry maneuver tactics.

By this late stage of the Pacific war, however, such a plan was simply not feasible. Acute shortages of planes, fuel, munitions, and, especially, trained, combat-experienced pilots meant that IGHQ could not possibly hope to gain even air parity, let alone air superiority. Thousands of planes from airfields on Formosa, Japan proper, and China could yet be launched against the invasion fleets, but maintaining Okinawa as a forward operational base for aircraft in the face of overwhelming Allied air, sea, and ground power was out of the question. Ushijima knew that IGHQ's promise to support his defense by sending 300 planes to Okinawa would never be carried out. Additionally, when, in November 1944, IGHQ took Ushijima's best combat unit, the 9th Division, and redeployed it to Formosa, the 32nd Army staff had to conclude that it no longer possessed sufficient combat power to mount anything like a successful defense at the beaches using standard maneuver tactics. They would have to devise another type of defense.

Chief of staff General Cho and operations officer Colonel Yahara convinced Ushijima to fight a war of attrition from a defense in depth, constructing underground fortifications only in the strategically important southern third of Okinawa where the rugged, broken terrain, pockmarked by numerous caves, could be utilized to delay the Americans as long as possible. Ushijima and his staff realized, even if IGHQ failed to acknowledge it, that the best the 32nd Army could hope to accomplish was to buy time for the forces in Japan proper, who would use it to prepare the best possible defense of the home islands.

Operation ICEBERG

At the outset, American and Allied planners were not certain that they wanted to invade and capture Okinawa. Initial plans focused Allied efforts on the island of Formosa—which, in an earlier conflict between MacArthur and Nimitz, had been bypassed in favor of the Philippines—followed by landings on the Japanese-held mainland of China. But some planners and many of the Pacific commanders had grave misgivings about the severe drain on resources a Formosan campaign would entail. The island is huge, and the Japanese had amassed a large number of combat forces there in expectation of an American invasion. The investment of tremendous amounts of personnel and war matériel required to conquer Formosa would be difficult to produce for a theater of war that was officially recognized as second in importance to Europe. MacArthur was already using a significant amount of scarce logistical support (especially shipping) to conduct the Pacific war, and little additional supply and service support could be expected before the end of the war in Europe. In a meeting with the joint chiefs of staff in early October 1944, therefore, Admiral Ernest J. King, the crusty chief of naval operations, recommended that once MacArthur's forces were firmly established on Luzon in the Philippines, the Allies should seize Iwo Jima, then invade Okinawa rather than Formosa.

Named Operation ICEBERG, the Okinawa campaign was scheduled to begin the month after the landing on Iwo Jima, about March 1, 1945. However, since ICEBERG would require much of the same naval and air-support assets used in the Luzon and Iwo Jima invasions, the date of the Okinawa invasion remained dependent upon the progress of those two operations. Finally, after some delay (due in no small part to the unexpectedly difficult fighting on Iwo Jima), ICEBERG planners received the go-ahead for an April 1, 1945, invasion—designated L-Day.

The fleet and landing force gathered for this invasion was awesome, rivalling the naval, air, and ground forces of Operation OVERLORD—the Allied invasion of France—the previous June. In support of the 180,000 assault troops were about 300 combat vessels and over 1,000 auxiliary ships of the various task forces taken from Admiral Spruance's massive Fifth Fleet. Before the campaign was over, nearly 550,000 soldiers, sailors, airmen, and marines would be involved. The Joint Expeditionary Amphibious Force, designated Task Force 51, was under the overall command of Vice Admiral Richmond Kelly Turner. Turner's ground commander in charge of the expeditionary troops and Tenth U.S. Army was Lieutenant General Simon B. Buckner, veteran of the American victory in the Aleutian Islands in 1943.

Buckner's two major subordinate ground combat units were the army's XXIV Corps, commanded by Major General John R. Hodge, and the Marine III Amphibious Corps, commanded by Major General Roy S. Geiger. Hodge's corps initially comprised the 7th U.S. Infantry Division (Major General Archibald V. Arnold commanding) and the 96th U.S. Infantry Division (Major General James L. Bradley). Geiger's force contained the 1st Marine Division (Major General Pedro A. del Valle) and the 6th Marine Division (Major General Lemuel C. Shepherd). Other major ground combat units available to Buckner were Major General Andrew D. Bruce's 77th U.S. Infantry Division, Major General George W. Griner's 27th U.S. Infantry Division, and the 2nd Marine Division under Major General Thomas E. Watson. In addition to carrier-based naval and marine aviation units, Buckner's troops were to be supported by the land-based Marine Tactical Air Force, Tenth Army, once they seized usable airfields on Okinawa. Army–air force bomber and fighter units were added to the air support effort during the campaign.

The ICEBERG plan called for Turner to land Buckner's ground forces on the good beaches of Okinawa's west coast, north and south of the city of Hagushi, located on the southern half of the island, midway between the airfields of Kadena and Yontan. The early capture of the two airfields would provide Buckner's ground forces with the tactical advantage of ground-based air support for the remainder of the campaign. On March 26, prior to the main landings on L-Day, the 77th Infantry Division captured the small Kerama Islands located about twenty miles from Okinawa's southwest coast, then on March 31, it seized the Keise Islands, which were within long-range artillery fire of Okinawa. With the capture of these two island groups in the face of only minor opposition, mine-sweeping and bombardment operations (the heaviest air-sea shelling of the Pacific war) began, and the stage was set for the main invasion. The ground battle of Okinawa was about to begin.

Happy Easter—April Fool

Turner's amphibious craft began landing Buckner's ground troops on the beaches of Hagushi Bay at 0800 hours on Easter Sunday. Several hours earlier the 2nd Marine Division had skillfully conducted a feint landing off the southeastern coast of Okinawa near Minatoga—exactly where Ushijima suspected the actual landings would take place. Since the 2nd Marine Division's demonstration coincided perfectly with his expectations, the Japanese commander expended the few air resources he had at his disposal on the mock landings. In the actual invasion area, only weakly defended by the 32nd Army forces, Buckner's soldiers and marines walked ashore to almost no opposition. By the evening of that Easter Sunday, Buckner had landed over 60,000 troops, including all of his divisional artillery and a good portion of his armor. The four divisions, landing simultaneously abreast, had secured a beachhead 15,000 yards wide and 5,000 yards deep. So far, it had been deceptively easy.

But that particular Easter Sunday was also April 1, April Fools' Day, and the invading force, wading ashore and moving inland with relative ease, would soon be confronting the 32nd Army's defense in depth. Nevertheless, the XXIV Corps on the right (south) flank and the III Amphib Corps on the left (north) flank, rapidly moved through only token resistance on April 2, cutting the island in half by reaching the east coast at the end of the day. On April 3, Buckner prepared to swing the XXIV Corps to the right in order to clear the southern part of the island, and wheel the III Amphib Corps to the left in order to sweep the island to the north. Since Ushijima had left the northern two thirds of Okinawa virtually undefended (except for the Motobu Peninsula), the marines of the III Amphib Corps made rapid progress, reaching the designated L+15 days lines on April 4. Reacting to the weak Japanese resistance, Buckner removed all restrictions to the advance of the III Amphib Corps, and gave Geiger free rein to move up the northern half of Okinawa as fast as the situation allowed. Utilizing tanks on the coastal roads and infantry along the narrow central spine, the 6th Marine Division rapidly moved northward to occupy the northern two thirds of Okinawa over the next few days. By April 13, the northernmost point on the island, Hedo Misaki (cape), had been captured by the fast-moving marines. The only stiff resistance Geiger's troops encountered was from the Kunigami Detachment, consisting of most of the 2nd Infantry Unit (Regiment) of the 44th Independent Mixed Brigade, commanded by Colonel Udo Takehiko. Udo's force of about 2,000 troops was dug in along the ridges and commanding heights (some 1,500 feet high) of the Motobu Peninsula on Okinawa's northwest coast. It took the 6th Marine Division until April 20 to secure the peninsula, at a cost of nearly 1,000 dead and wounded marines. Virtually all of Udo's force was killed.

While the 6th Marine Division was subduing Udo's forces on Okinawa proper, army troops of the 77th Infantry Division invaded and captured the island of Ie Shima a few short miles off the coast of the Motobu Peninsula. Japanese resistance on Ie Shima was stiffer than expected, and it took the 77th Infantry nearly a week to secure the island. Sadly, one of the casualties of the fighting was the beloved war correspondent Ernie Pyle, killed by Japanese machine-gun fire on April 18. Except for the Motobu Peninsula and Ie Shima, the capture of the northern two thirds of Okinawa was swift and relatively cheap.

Hodge's XXIV Corps, which was attempting to move south during this same time, faced an altogether different situation. Between April 4 and 7, the 7th and 96th Infantry Divisions, advancing southward in line abreast, began to experience stiffening Japanese resistance as they approached Ushijima's carefully prepared underground defense area. On April 8, the U.S. advance hit the main Japanese defensive line, and all hell broke loose.

"Blowtorch and Corkscrew"

The army troops of Hodge's XXIV Corps received their belated April Fools' surprise when they moved into the rugged area containing Ushijima's main defensive positions just to the north of Shuri along the Kakazu Ridge. The swift advances of the previous week gave way to bitterly contested, agonizingly slow gains of only a few hundred yards. This nightmare warfare, reminiscent of the slaughter in the trenches of the First World War, characterized the three remaining months of the bitterly fought Okinawa campaign.

The 32nd Army's 62nd Infantry Division occupied, as we said, this part of Ushijima's underground defensive zone, and the unit's ten infantry battalions (eight of them 1,000-man units) had carefully prepared their fighting positions in the rugged, restricted terrain. Impervious to shellfire and bombardment, the enemy defensive

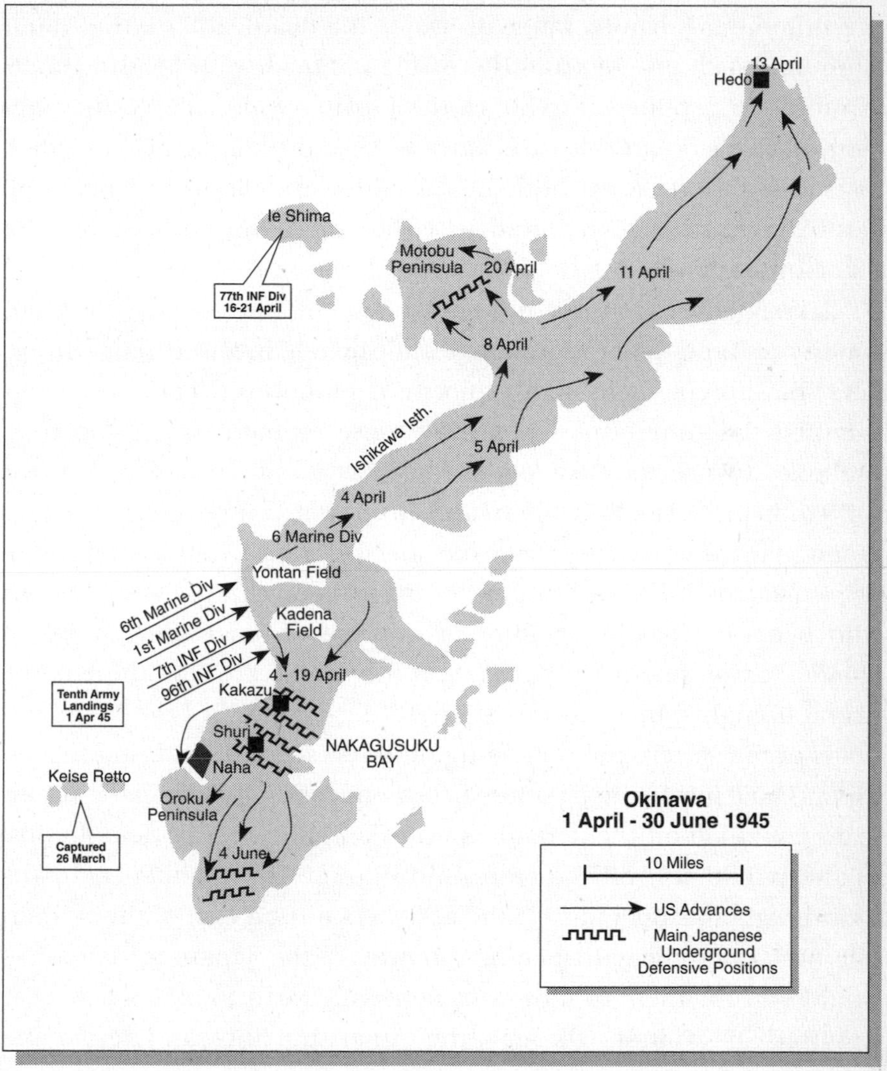
13 April
Hedo
Ie Shima
77th INF Div
16-21 April
Motobu
Peninsula
20 April
11 April
8 April
Ishikawa Isth.
5 April
4 April
6 Marine Div
Yontan Field
6th Marine Div
1st Marine Div
7th INF Div
96th INF Div
Kadena
Field
4 - 19 April
Kakazu
Tenth Army
Landings
1 Apr 45
Shuri
NAKAGUSUKU
BAY
Naha
Keise Retto
Oroku
Peninsula
Captured
26 March
4 June
Okinawa
1 April - 30 June 1945
10 Miles
US Advances
Main Japanese
Underground
Defensive Positions

Okinawa, April 1–June 30, 1945

positions were vulnerable only to close-in direct fire and physical assault. The "fire-swept zones" created by the interlocking fires of the numerous Japanese pillboxes exacted a deadly toll on the Americans, and such progress as was possible was made only by using tanks as mobile U.S. pillboxes to attack the Japanese ones. The tactics that evolved to carry out this cave warfare were brutal, dangerous, time-consuming, and costly, both in casualties and destroyed matériel. The Americans were required to either burn out or blast out the tenacious defenders.

Nicknamed "blowtorch and corkscrew" by Buckner's troops, the Americans' anti–pillbox-cave tactics ultimately involved flamethrowers ("blowtorches") or high-explosive demolitions ("corkscrews")— but first the Americans had to get close enough to the Japanese pillboxes to use their weapons. This was accomplished with great difficulty, primarily by artillery and firepower, which swept the protecting Japanese infantry from the surface, then by tanks and infantry, which rushed toward the positions to neutralize Japanese troops who had survived the shellfire or emerged from underground to challenge the American approach. If the Americans won these nasty, brutal firefights, they moved into the "dead zones" of the pillboxes' fields of fire, where the remaining defenders could not bring fire on them. Once inside the Japanese fire-swept zones, the attacking Americans could kill off the defenders with flamethrowers or demolitions, or they could seal off the cave (and entomb its inhabitants) by demolishing all its openings. If the attackers missed one of the numerous, well-camouflaged openings, however, the Japanese defenders would wait for them to move on, then sally forth to attack U.S. rear positions or infiltrate through the American lines and rejoin the Japanese defense. To counter the Americans' tactics, the enemy tried to destroy the U.S. tanks that protected the attacking troops, then counterattack aggressively.

Attack and Counterattack—The "Honorable Death" of the 32nd Army

Ushijima's defense in depth of the rugged southern third of Okinawa proved to be exceptionally effective since it forced the attacking Americans to battle for every inch of territory. Except for a wasteful general counterattack by the Japanese 62nd Division on the night of April 12, which seriously depleted the strength of that unit while inflicting no appreciable damage on the XXIV Corps, Ushijima's troops used pillbox and cave tactics throughout the month of April. The XXIV Corps, reinforced by the army's 27th Infantry Division on April 15, continued to struggle against the well-prepared Japanese positions for daily gains of only a few yards. Despite an all-out offensive by the three American divisions of XXIV Corps, on April 19, Ushijima's defensive positions continued to delay the American advance. Only when the Japanese commander, on April 24, withdrew the remnants of the 62nd Division southward to occupy new defensive positions near Shuri was Hodge able to make any appreciable advance. But this was short-lived, as Hodge's troops soon ran into Ushijima's next underground defensive zone. To stiffen his defenses, Ushijima moved his remaining two major combat units, the 24th Infantry Division and the 44th Independent Mixed Brigade, into the Shuri defense zone.

Buckner reacted to the increasingly strong Japanese resistance by reorganizing his southward-facing line. He moved Geiger's III Amphib Corps from northern Okinawa and split the southern front between Geiger's and Hodge's corps. Replacing the worn-out 27th and 96th Infantry Divisions with marine units and the relatively fresh 77th Infantry Division, Buckner had the Tenth Army take direct control of the now two-corps assault. Even when attacking the Japanese positions with this renewed combat power, the Americans made agonizingly slow progress. Ushijima's tactics were gaining the empire valuable time. On May 4, however, the 32nd Army made a move that instantly accomplished what all the efforts of Buckner's army had failed to achieve: they emerged into the open.

The Japanese general counterattack of May 4 probably did more to deplete the 32nd Army's dwindling combat power than any other action of the Okinawa campaign, and spelled disaster for Ushijima's defense-in-depth strategy. The decision was hotly debated by Cho, Ushijima's chief of staff, who wished to crush the American invaders in a single, decisive battle, and Senior Operations Officer Yahara, architect of the 32nd Army's brilliant defense, in depth. Yahara was convinced that moving out into the open to challenge the Americans, with their vastly superior firepower, would be disastrous. But it was Cho, whose ideas reflected the Japanese army's light infantry traditions of bold attack and close-in maneuver, who prevailed. Without comment, Ushijima approved Cho's proposal to launch a general counterattack on May 4. It would, he assumed, be an "honorable death attack" for his troops, in compliance with the rigorous demands of the warrior code of Bushido.

Timed to coincide with a massive kamikaze onslaught—the fifth of the Okinawa campaign—against offshore Allied naval vessels, Ushijima's great counterattack employed all the 32nd Army's available combat power, including its few remaining tanks in the 27th Tank Regiment and two amphibious landing forces from the Shipping Engineer Regiments, which were to attack shore installations deep in the American rear. After a thirty-minute preparatory artillery bombardment that began at 0450 hours on May 4, Ushijima's attacking units moved out. Despite the early optimism of 32nd Army headquarters in the command cave under Shuri Castle, realization of the ultimate futility of the counterattack set in by midday. Reports of Japanese advances and the rumbling of the Japanese artillery barrage gave way to news of the destruction of the attacking units, overwhelmed by the American counterbarrage. The amphibious efforts on both coasts were easily defeated by rear-area U.S. troops, and the 27th Tank Regiment was able to salvage only six operational tanks by May 5. Only individual units, using infiltration tactics to slip through the American lines and seize key terrain in the U.S. rear area met with any success. The mass frontal assaults failed, and U.S. attacks over the next two days erased even the few successful efforts to seize positions within and behind the American lines. At 1800 hours on May 5, Ushijima ordered the offensive halted and recalled the remnants of his attacking units. The counterattack had taken a heavy toll on Ushijima's remaining forces—he lost over 7,000 men— and his subordinate units, already suffering from the effects of the American campaign, were further depleted: of their original strength, the 62nd Division retained only one fourth, the 24th Division three fifths, and the 44th Brigade four fifths. Ushijima's supporting artillery retained only about half of its firepower. The surviving six tanks of the 27th Tank Regiment had to be relegated to earth-covered bunkers for the remainder of the campaign. For the Japanese, the May 4 counterattack was a catastrophe.

Yet weeks of difficult fighting still remained. The strong underground defensive positions of the Shuri area had to be reduced, one pillbox at a time, using the costly and tedious blowtorch-and-corkscrew tactics. Ushijima's staff may have been disheartened by their failure, but the 32nd Army troops manning the countless underground pillboxes and caves continued to fight to the bitter end, most preferring an honorable death to ignoble surrender and disgrace.

Between May 6 and 21, the key positions in the Shuri defensive area were finally captured, and Ushijima's strongest fortified area gradually came under Buckner's control. With the 6th Marine Division driving on Naha on the west (right) flank and the 7th Infantry Division outflanking the Shuri zone on the island's east coast, Ushijima realized that the battle for this portion of Okinawa was nearly over. At the end of May, the 32nd Army prepared to withdraw to its final defensive positions in the Kiyan Peninsula on the southernmost tip of the island.

Aided by torrential rains, which turned the Okinawan terrain into a sea of mud and caused cloud cover that prevented the ubiquitous American airpower from observing and interdicting its movements, the 32nd Army conducted a skillful withdrawal between May 29 and June 4. However, despite the lack of American pressure on the retreating units and the general absence of aerial attack during the Japanese withdrawal to the Kiyan Peninsula, the 32nd Army lost about 40 percent of its strength, mainly to rearguard actions, artillery interdictions, and the 62nd Division's sacrificial delaying attacks. By June 6, Buckner's forces had closed up.

The Bitter End

Ushijima's defensive positions on the southernmost tip of the island were not as extensive as those around the Shuri area farther north, but they were nevertheless tenaciously defended by the remaining Japanese troops. By June 6, when Buckner's two corps moved into position around the remnants of the 32nd Army, occupying the commanding heights of the Yaeju-Dake escarpment, the 1st and 6th Marine Divisions were still clearing the remaining Japanese naval-base forces from the vicinity of Naha airfield on the Oroku Peninsula. This operation, which included a marine amphibious landing on the north shore of the peninsula, was conducted between June 4 and 13, and resulted in the surrender of 159 men out of an original force of 9,900—the largest surrender of Japanese defenders on Okinawa (many of these, however, were Okinawan Home Guard personnel, old men and boys impressed into service).

After securing the Oroku Peninsula, Buckner moved his four divisions against Ushijima's remaining forces on June 12. The army's 7th and 96th Infantry Divisions pressed in from the east and north while the 1st and 6th Marine Divisions attacked from the west. By June 14, Buckner's troops had broken into Ushijima's last major defensive positions on the Yaeju-Dake escarpment in the face of stiff resistance. But the Japanese units refused to be broken and fought on. Nearing the end of their strength now, the 32nd Army's subordinate units received one last influx of replacements when the remaining service and support troops were assigned to the 24th and 62nd Divisions and the 44th Brigade. Not trained combat troops, these support troops, nevertheless, fought stubbornly.

It was during this final, frenzied phase of the fighting that General Buckner, on June 18, went to a forward observation post of the 1st Marine Division to watch the progress of the 8th Marine Regiment's

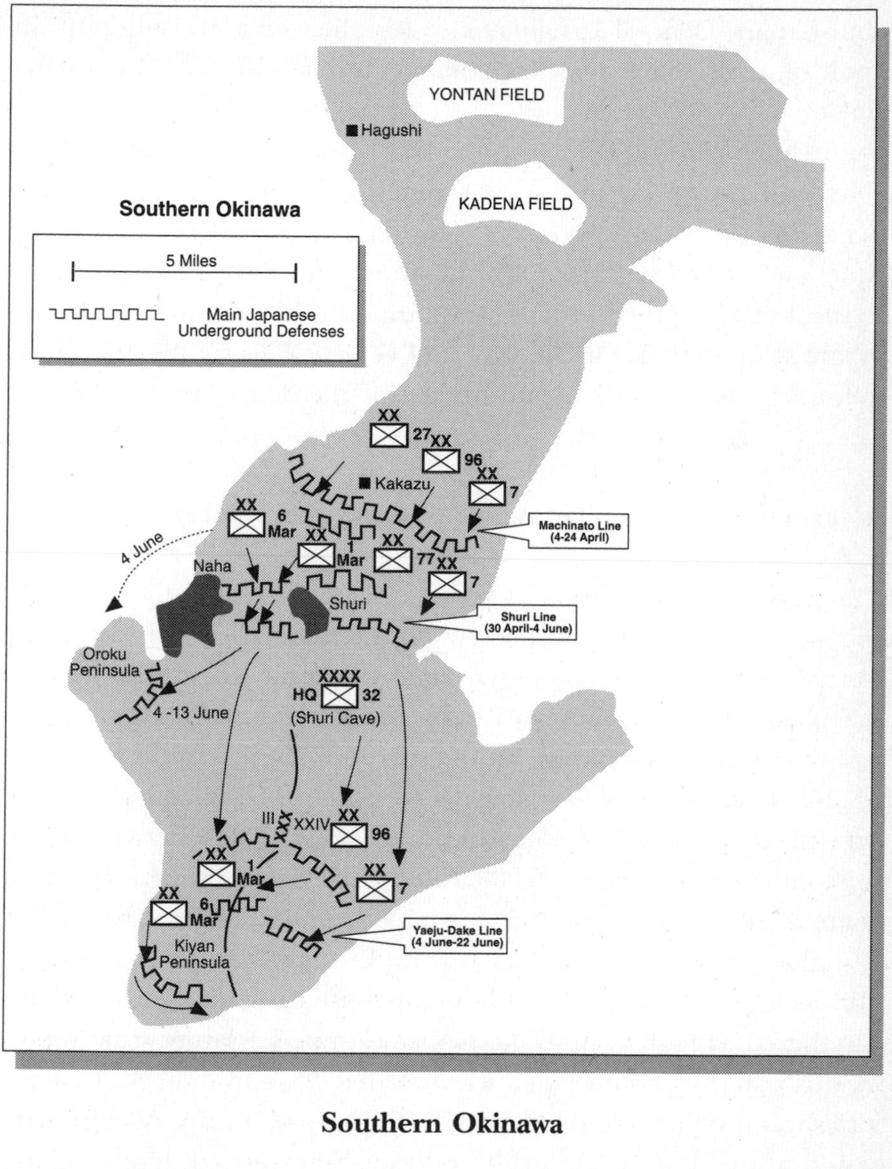
YONTAN FIELD
Hagushi
KADENA FIELD
Southern Okinawa
5 Miles
Main Japanese Underground Defenses
XX 27
XX 96
XX 7
Kakazu
XX 6 Mar
XX 1 Mar
XX 77
XX 7
Machinato Line (4-24 April)
4 June
Naha
Shuri
Shuri Line (30 April-4 June)
Oroku Peninsula
4 -13 June
XXXX HQ 32 (Shuri Cave)
III XXX XXIV
XX 96
XX 1 Mar
XX 7
XX 6 Mar
Yaeju-Dake Line (4 June-22 June)
Kiyan Peninsula

Southern Okinawa

tanks and infantry. He died there among the coral rocks when Japanese antitank rounds burst over his position. Three days later, his counterpart, General Ushijima, and his chief of staff, General Cho, knelt on a narrow ledge overlooking the sea and committed ritual suicide.

On June 22, the Tenth Army, now temporarily commanded by Geiger, declared organized resistance on Okinawa at an end and began mopping-up operations. During this week-long sweep, the Americans killed another 8,900 Japanese and took 3,800 prisoners. While this was proceeding, IGHQ announced on June 25 that all Japanese operations on Okinawa had ceased. This simple announcement also served as the death notice for the 32nd Army.

Aftermath—In the Shadow of a Mushroom Cloud

The appalling casualties on both sides of the Okinawa fighting were sobering to the American and Allied planners who were preparing for the inevitable invasion of the Japanese home islands. Besides the 6,319 troops the Tenth Army lost on the ground on Okinawa, nearly 5,000 Americans were killed on the surrounding seas, most as a result of the waves of kamikaze attacks—to which the Allies had devised no truly effective defense. In addition to the 12,000 Americans killed in combat, there were 66,000 other American casualties due to wounds, illness, injuries, and missing-in-actions. The total of Allied casualties on land, sea, and air for the Okinawa campaign was probably as high as 72,000. Meanwhile, Japanese casualties, mostly killed, numbered as high as 130,000. No one wanted a larger-scale repeat of this slaughter when Japan was invaded (one million Allied casualties was the operational estimate). The answer to this dilemma was tested at the Trinity Site in the remote New Mexico desert on July 16, 1945. The shadow cast by the burgeoning mushroom cloud rising over Alamagordo reached all the way to Okinawa.

Once the potential of the new atomic weapon was realized, President Truman had only one clear choice. If this new weapon could convince Japan to surrender without a costly invasion, untold millions of American as well as Japanese lives would be spared. The notion that there was some acceptable alternative is nonsense, created by a generation of revisionists who are unable to understand what it means to be in the midst of total war. And the Japanese, who have recounted every detail of Hiroshima and Nagasaki to their children, have neglected to point out that the two bombings were the direct result of their country's aggressive, expansionist war of empire. Given the terrible toll of Okinawa, no one can wonder why Truman authorized the use of the atomic weapons.

CHAPTER SIX

The Korean War

• 1950–1953 •

NAKTONG TO YALU:
THE BATTLE TO SAVE KOREA, 1950

"World War Two-and-a-Half"

When masses of North Korean troops, spearheaded by over 100 tanks, rolled south across the 38th parallel in a surprise, unprovoked invasion of South Korea at 4:00 A.M. on June 25, 1950, they began three long years of bloody fighting up and down the length of the Korean peninsula. Opposed to the North Koreans (and, after October 1950, Chinese "volunteers") were military forces from fifteen members of the five-year-old United Nations. Since the United States provided the bulk of the non-Korean UN forces, including the overall commander of UN troops, however, the conduct of the war took on a distinctly American character. One of the first modern wars of only limited objectives, the Korean "police action" sought primarily to restore the status quo on the Korean peninsula, not force the enemy to submit to unconditional surrender. This military endeavor seemed new and unfamiliar to a domestic population that was consumed in pursuing economic gain, enhancing prosperity, and getting on with the "good life." Fought to contain—not wipe out—the expansion in East Asia of what was then believed to be a worldwide, monolithic Communist bloc, the Korean War was not greeted with the total mobilization of civilian resources and national will that had taken place from 1941 to 1945, and was referred to derisively as World War Two-and-a-Half. But with a million casualties on the UN side and a million and a half on the Communist side during its three terrible years, the intensity and misery of the war in Korea was surely as real to the soldiers who were forced to fight it as a world war. When it finally sputtered to a halt in July 1953, both sides were left glaring at each other across the now heavily fortified 38th parallel—exactly where the war had begun three years before.

Osan, South Korea, July 5, 1950: HQ Task Force Smith: *U.S. Army lieutenant colonel Charles B. "Brad" Smith was only a few brief days removed from the undemanding duties his 1st Battalion, 21st Infantry Regiment had been performing in postwar Japan as part of the 24th Infantry Division, Eighth U.S. Army. As an occupying army, the understrength, inadequately trained Eighth Army soldiers had become more adept at fighting boredom, drunkenness, and venereal disease than real enemies, supported by real tanks and artillery. At 10:45 P.M. on June 30, however, Smith's world had been rudely interrupted when his battalion, along with supporting units, was placed on alert to move immediately to Korea "to support the ROKs" (Republic of Korea troops) who were steadily being driven south by the advancing North Koreans. Provided with very little useful information about the true tactical situation, Smith and his unit were ordered by the 24th Infantry Division commander, Major General William F. Dean, to move north of the south-central Korean town of Taejon and "stop the North Koreans as far north of Pusan as possible." By the morning of July 5, Smith's task force, consisting of about half of his 1st Battalion, 21st Infantry Regiment, A Battery, 52nd Artillery, and a few attached recoilless rifle and mortar sections from other units in the 21st, were dug in along a mile-wide, curving line in hilltop positions about three miles north of Osan (approximately sixty miles northwest of Taejon). The six 105mm howitzers of A Battery, emplaced about two kilometers behind the infantry positions as a precaution against enemy tanks, had been issued the complete inventory of high-explosive antitank (HEAT) artillery rounds the Eighth Army possessed prior to leaving Japan—all thirteen rounds of it. On the morning of July 5, they would need every round.*

At 7:00 A.M., Smith observed eight North Korean tanks approaching along the main road from the north. With no accompanying infantry, apparently operating well in front of the main body of North Korean troops, the Soviet-built T-34 tanks— World War II–vintage, but more powerful than anything the UN troops had ever deployed—clanked steadily toward the American positions. At about 2,000 meters, Smith ordered A Battery to begin firing. They might have saved their ammunition, since the standard high-explosive rounds burst among the tanks with no apparent effect. When the tanks were within 700 meters, Smith ordered his infantrymen manning the 75mm recoilless rifles and 2.36-inch bazookas to engage them. The 75s and bazookas could hardly miss at this distance, and as the tanks continued to close, the Americans fired on them at point-blank ranges. None of their fire had any effect.

Direct hits bounced off the T-34s' armor plate, and the tanks continued straight through Smith's infantry lines toward A Battery's howitzers.

One of A Battery's 105s, emplaced along the road to engage in direct fire on the tanks, opened up on the two lead T-34s with the HEAT antitank ammunition. Finally damaged, both tanks moved to the side of the road and stopped. Abandoned by their crews, they became the first UN war trophies of the conflict. But there was precious little time for rejoicing as the armored onslaught continued. The rest of the tank column, not even halting to assist their knocked-out comrades, rolled through the American positions and rumbled south toward Osan. Soon other North Korean tanks swept through, firing their main guns and machine guns to the left and right of the road to keep the Americans' heads down. The antitank howitzer, shortly after its success against the first two tanks, had been blasted by the follow-on T-34s, and all the remaining HEAT rounds had exploded.

Using 105mm high-explosive rounds and bazookas, A Battery was able to cripple two more of the North Korean tanks, but was unable to stem the tide of armor. By 9:00 A.M., thirty-three North Korean tanks had passed through Smith's position on their way to Osan. As yet no enemy infantry had appeared.

At about 10:00 A.M., however, Smith observed a long column of North Korean foot soldiers approaching in the far distance, steadily marching toward his position, and estimated that it stretched for at least six miles. Surely this must be the enemy's main body. The American commander allowed the column to close to within 1,000 meters of his hilltop positions before he gave the command to open fire with his mortars, 75s, and other direct-fire weapons. Despite the high volume of fire from Smith's men, the enemy, reacting almost immediately, set up a base of fire opposite Smith's positions while massing troops on both of the American commander's flanks. Since the earlier tank attack had knocked out radio and telephone communications with A Battery, no accurate indirect artillery fire could be placed on the enemy. Within two hours, enemy forces had occupied high ground overlooking each of Smith's flanks and were blasting his positions with machine-gun and small-arms fire, as well as pounding it with artillery and mortars. By 2:30 P.M., with his ammunition running out, no reserve to maneuver against the encircling enemy, and no assistance expected from any quarter, Smith made the decision to withdraw the task force to the rear— before his unit was encircled and cut off, he hoped.

The withdrawal of Task Force Smith, disrupted by unceasing enemy fire and under heavy pressure from thousands of North Koreans, had virtually no chance of proceeding in any orderly manner. Once the soldiers left the "safety" of their foxholes and defensive positions on the hills, the infantry companies rapidly disintegrated into small groups seeking the safety of the rear. Smith gathered around him what men he could, then picked up the remnants of A Battery as he passed the artillery positions along the road to the rear. The gunners had just completed disabling their howitzers by removing sights and breechblocks, and they quickly joined Smith. Finding their task-force vehicles where they had left them in Osan the night before, Smith and the remnants of his force climbed onto the trucks and motored south to Ansong, then Ch'onan, and finally Taejon. Of the infantry and artillerymen who had begun the fight that morning, about half were present with their commander twenty-four hours later. Although more survivors would wander in over the next few days, 153 officers and men never made it back. The saga of Task Force Smith served as a rude welcome to the UN forces, but it particularly shocked and startled the Americans. It was apparently going to take much more than the sight of U.S. troops to cause the North

Koreans to retreat, and the American soldiers and marines then deployed to aid South Korea would have to fight well if they expected to "win" this new kind of war.

With the bulk of U.S. resources in the Far East committed to rebuilding a devastated Japan, and with China now firmly in the enemy camp, the effort to maintain a large military presence in Korea to deter a Communist takeover had seemed superfluous. And with the advent of atomic weapons, U.S. planners thought that any new war would necessarily be a big war. To the U.S. joint chiefs of staff, Korea was more liability than asset. Why should the United States risk its prestige and resources defending such a wretched place? When Secretary of State, Dean Acheson, gave his famous speech to the National Press Club in Washington on January 12, 1950, in which he stated that Korea (and Taiwan for that matter) was outside the United States' security cordon in Asia, he was merely pointing out what everyone who followed such issues already knew. The North Koreans, and their Russian mentors, however, took him at his word. Plans for the invasion of the south—already being drawn up well before Acheson's speech—were finalized and readied for execution.

What the invasion planners and their bosses failed to realize, however, was that the United States does not always do exactly what its politicians and administration spokesmen say it will do. And when Truman and his advisers got around to analyzing the situation, it dawned on them that if they stood by and allowed South Korea to be overrun, the American position in Japan, a country that really mattered to U.S. interests, could be seriously threatened. Whether Korea was inside or outside the U.S. security cordon in Asia, its fall to Communist forces would breach that cordon just as surely as a Communist landing in Tokyo Bay. Having already "lost" China, the Truman administration could not afford to lose Japan. Therefore, when the North Koreans struck across the border into the south, they precipitated, much to their surprise and their Russian advisers' consternation, not just a war with South Korea, but a war with the United States. But given the sorry state of America's military forces in June 1950, the question quickly became, "Does it really matter?"

Weapons and Tactics

The weapons of the Korean War were essentially those of World War II, with the exception of jet aircraft. Indeed, both sides were being extensively armed with WW II–surplus weapons and often fired surplus ammunition. And if they weren't always the exact weapons that a GI carried on Okinawa or a Soviet soldier used at Stalingrad, they were similar or slightly upgraded versions of them. Like the larger war that had ended five years earlier, the Korean War was dominated, on the ground, by the tank, the artillery piece, and small arms.

The rugged terrain of Korea is not exactly classic "tank country," but it was the 150 World War II–surplus Russian tanks that spearheaded the North Korean attack on June 25, 1950, and that very nearly overran South Korea before the United States or the United Nations could patch together enough men and firepower to stop them. The tank used by the North Korean Peoples Army (NKPA) was the Russian-built T-34/85, the best medium tank to be mass-produced during World War II. Weighing just over thirty tons, the T-34/85 mounted an 85mm main gun that could defeat any armor sent against it. With about 50mm of frontal armor and 70mm of turret armor, the T-34s' four-man crew was relatively safe from the fire of the standard U.S. antitank weapons then available.

Artillery weapons were also World War II veterans, representing the full range of light, medium, and heavy guns used so effectively on European and Pacific battlefields. Despite the early NKPA advantage in numbers of weapons, the artillery advantage quickly shifted to the U.S./UN forces when U.S. support for the war swung into high gear. The U.S. "workhorse" artillery weapon of World War II became the workhorse of the Korean battlefield. The M101A1 105mm towed howitzer was the main U.S./UN artillery piece, providing the primary artillery close support on all battlefields. NKPA and Chinese artillery was standard Soviet-manufactured guns and howitzers of the Second World War—principally 76mm and 122mm guns, and 122mm and 152mm howitzers. After their initial advantage in numbers of weapons over the ROK forces' artillery was overcome, the NKPA was usually outgunned by its opponents. Primarily organized and employed as a light infantry force, the Chinese Peoples Liberation Army (PLA) was typically shorter on supporting artillery weapons and ammunition than its foes, although it usually stockpiled weapons and ammunition prior to each offensive. When these stocks were depleted, however, the UN control of the skies made resupply difficult and costly.

Each side employed "fire and maneuver" infantry tactics standard in World War II. Using tanks whenever their availability and the terrain permitted, both forces preferred to advance within the protection of an armored screen, often clambering onto the tanks for a free ride until enemy small-arms fire or artillery forced them to dismount. The favorite NKPA maneuver was a frontal assault to fix their foe in position while a strong flanking force maneuvered around the foe's exposed flanks, attempting to set up a blocking position in the enemy rear area. If successful—and it frequently was in the early days of the war—the flanked unit was forced to conduct a rapid retreat or risk being cut off completely. The PLA's favorite tactic was to infiltrate large numbers of troops through the usually porous U.S./UN lines, then execute a massed surprise attack against an unsuspecting unit. Preceded by an intense barrage, normally of short duration, the PLA attacks frequently overwhelmed the U.S./UN defenders by sheer numbers, if not superior firepower. Especially after the Chinese intervention, when the weight of numbers was consistently with the PLA/NKPA, the U.S./UN forces fell back on the tried-and-true U.S. tactic of using massive amounts of firepower, usually artillery, to make up for the extreme difference in troop strength. Digging in on entrenched, fortified hilltop positions or, when necessary, falling back in the face of overwhelming numbers, the U.S./UN forces plastered the hordes of PLA/NKPA troops with artillery projectiles, supplemented by close air support. As in World War I, artillery became the greatest killer on the battlefields of Korea.

The Battle to Save Korea—Naktong to the Yalu

June–November 1950

"Manzai!"

At 4:00 A.M. on Sunday, June 25, 1950, the first assaults of a general attack along the 38th parallel began on the Onjin Peninsula in western Korea and the Uijongbu corridor in central Korea, north of Seoul. Catching the South Korean forces completely by surprise, the North Koreans quickly overran their defenses, achieving nearly complete success at virtually every point. Only the ROK 6th Division at Chunchon, on the eastern side of the peninsula, held off the NKPA attacks for any length of time. This ROK unit, unlike virtually all of the others, was at 100-percent strength when the attack began. Refusing to join in the wholesale issue of weekend passes to their troops, a common practice along the 38th parallel, the 6th Division was able to properly man its defensive pillboxes and fighting positions as soon as the NKPA attack was discovered. The ROK 6th held off the assaults of the NKPA 2nd Division (the unit had no tanks to support it) for three days, until the NKPA 7th Division, along with some supporting T-34 tanks, was moved in to bolster the 2nd. In a scene that was repeated time and again during the NKPA offensive, the South's weak artillery and puny antitank weapons were unable to stop the North's tanks. Lacking their own tanks, the ROK was helpless.

At all other places along the border, the NKPA rapidly advanced along its four primary axes against disorganized and ineffective resistance. The farthest west, and one of the first to get under way, was the NKPA 6th Division's assault against the weak ROK 17th Infantry

Regiment. The 17th Infantry on the Onjin Peninsula, completely cut off by water and the North Korean border from South Korea, had to be evacuated by boat, leaving behind almost all of its weapons and equipment. On the far-eastern coast of the peninsula, along the narrow belt of traffickable terrain, the NKPA 5th Division pressed forward against disintegrating resistance. Skillfully utilizing amphibious operations to flank the ROK positions, the NKPA swiftly occupied the ground between the rugged Taebaek Mountain range, running along the spine of the Korean peninsula, and the coastal area. About sixty miles farther inland, the NKPA 2nd Division was blocked temporarily by the ROK 6th, then broke free with the aid of tanks and the NKPA 7th Division.

The main attack, however, was in the west, along the "classic" invasion route down the Korean peninsula. Here, the NKPA 3rd and 4th Divisions, spearheaded by the 105th Tank Brigade, raced southward down the Uijongbu corridor meeting only light resistance. Its sights fixed on Seoul, this North Korean attacking column was helped by a supporting attack on Kaesong, just to the west of the main axis of advance. Amazingly, a large force of North Koreans assisted in capturing Kaesong simply by riding in on a train to the town's main depot and calmly detraining in the midst of the defender's area. It seems that the night before, the NKPA had replaced the few miles of track that were removed to separate the North and South Korean halves of the train line when the country was partitioned. This vignette reveals just how successful the NKPA attacks were at this juncture. Throughout the battle area and into the far reaches of South Korea, the North Korean invasion was aided by sabotage and guerrilla warfare conducted by line-crossers, infiltrators, and North Korean agents already in the South. Shouts of *Manzai!* (Korean for "Hurrah!") echoed all along the 38th parallel.

The invasion was extremely successful all across the broad front, but clearly the greatest danger was posed by the main attack toward Seoul. The ROK 7th Division, defending an area much too large for its size and capabilities, was immediately pushed back toward Uijongbu, the last defensible position north of Seoul. Relentlessly, the NKPA 3rd and 4th Divisions, each of them with over forty tanks leading the way, pressed on toward the South Korean capital. By June 28, Seoul was on the verge of falling. With no means of pushing the enemy back, the South Koreans prepared to withdraw southward across the Han River and reestablish a defensive line they hoped could be strengthened enough to delay the NKPA advance. These hopes were dashed, however, when panicky troops guarding the bridges over the Han blew them up before the ROK units could safely withdraw. This precipitous action was a disaster for the cohesion of the ROK defense, trapping about 44,000 troops on the enemy side of the river. In the ensuing scramble to get across and south of the river, virtually all the ROK artillery, vehicles, and crew-served weapons were abandoned on the north bank. Now nearly disarmed, the ROK units south of the Han were in dire straits. They continued to make efforts to fight back, but without substantial assistance, the country would be overrun in a matter of days.

U.S. Intervention—Leading United Nations Forces

Upon learning of the unprovoked North Korean invasion, President Harry S. Truman instructed his ambassador to the United Nations to inform the UN secretary general and request an emergency meeting of the Security Council on the following day. Meanwhile Truman instructed the joint chiefs of staff to relay orders to General of the Army Douglas MacArthur that he was authorized to provide arms, ammunition, and equipment to the ROK forces. MacArthur was also instructed to evacuate American dependents and to provide the commander in chief with his assessment on how best the United States could help the South Korean war effort. The U.S. Seventh Fleet was ordered to steam at full speed from the waters around the Philippines and Okinawa to Japan.

The UN Security Council quickly produced a series of resolutions whose effect was to legitimize the world's response to what was officially labeled an "unprovoked act of aggression" by North Korea. With the Soviet ambassador to the UN absent—the Russians had boycotted the organization to protest the UN's failure to recognize

Red China—the Security Council resolutions passed unanimously and without fear of a Permanent Five member veto (Stalin considered this blunder his diplomats' biggest since Foreign Minister Molotov talked the dictator into agreeing to the Nazi-Soviet Nonaggression Pact of 1939). Although the Soviet ambassador to the UN, Yakov Malik, scurried back to Flushing Meadows when the Russians realized what their boycott was doing to their ability to influence the UN's actions, it was too late. North Korea was officially denounced as an aggressor, it was called upon to withdraw immediately back to the 38th parallel, and when this was not done, member nations were called upon to "furnish such assistance . . . as may be necessary to repel the armed attack and to restore international peace and security in the area."

This was exactly what the Americans wanted. Not only was the United States (and, of course, other member nations) asked to become actively involved in turning back the Communist attack, the UN had decreed the U.S. and its allies the official "good guys" in this fight. Truman wasted no time—indeed, he had little time to waste. MacArthur had informed his commander in chief that in his opinion, the South Koreans would be quickly beaten if U.S. forces were not soon committed. Truman had already, on June 26, authorized his Far East commander to employ U.S. air and naval strength against North Korean targets south of the 38th parallel. The following day, he expanded the target area to include all of North Korea. Additionally, he gave MacArthur permission to use American ground troops to defend Pusan, the remaining major port in South Korea.

After a dangerous, but ultimately fateful visit to Korea to observe the fighting and assess the ability of the ROK forces to repel the invasion, MacArthur asked Truman for permission to deploy a regimental combat team and eventually build this force up to a strength of two full divisions. One day after the fall of Seoul, Truman gave his permission. MacArthur was authorized by the president of the United States to use all forces then available to him to repel the invasion. Lieutenant Colonel Brad Smith's odyssey was about to begin.

Retreat to the Naktong River

General MacArthur had four divisions and a separate regimental combat team available to him in his occupation forces in Japan and Okinawa. The 1st Cavalry Division (dismounted), the 7th Infantry Division, the 24th Infantry Division, and the 25th Infantry Division—all in deplorable condition and none ready for immediate combat—were fulfilling occupation duties in various locations in Japan or the Ryukyu Islands. Because it was stationed in the southern region of Japan, closest to Korea, the 24th Infantry Division of Major General William F. Dean was selected to deploy first. Leadoff unit was Task Force Smith.

Smith's forlorn action of July 5 in front of Osan was a tragic beginning to direct U.S. involvement on the ground in Korea, but unfortunately, it was to prove typical of the early U.S. efforts. In exchange for the loss of almost all his equipment and 150 men, Smith exacted about 130 enemy casualties and destroyed just four of thirty-three North Korean tanks. The few hours' delay the North Korean advance suffered at the hands of Smith's force was hardly worth the sacrifice of the American unit and its equipment.

At the end of the 24th Division's first week of combat in Korea, three more units the same size or larger than Task Force Smith had been attacked, flanked, and pushed back by the NKPA advance. On July 13, the 24th Division was pushed back nearly sixty miles to Taejon, where it occupied positions along the major obstacle of the Kum River. While MacArthur and Eighth Army commander Lieutenant General Walton H. Walker scrambled to get the 1st Cavalry and 25th Infantry Divisions on their way to Korea, the 24th was losing the battle to defend Taejon and the Kum River line. The two additional U.S. divisions reached Korea on July 18, but the fourth division, the 7th Infantry, left in Japan, had to be gutted of personnel and equipment to bring the 1st Cavalry and 25th Infantry to something resembling combat strength. Two days after these two units closed on the Korean peninsula, the 24th was forced to evacuate Taejon after two

NKPA divisions crossed the Kum River, surrounding the division.

In the confusion of withdrawing from Taejon, General Dean became separated from the division and was eventually captured by the North Koreans. He remained in captivity for three years and, upon his release, was awarded the Medal of Honor for his tank-hunting actions. Dean's division, meanwhile, continued its fighting withdrawal from Taejon southeastward toward the Naktong River, which borders the Pusan area.

The NKPA main advance continued along the Taejon–Taegu–Pusan road, now pitted against the newly committed forces of Major General Hobart Gay's 1st Cavalry Division. But other NKPA divisions on the north and directly west of Pusan continued to press the U.S. or ROK forces that attempted to stop them. The most serious threat outside the main advance along the Taejon–Pusan road developed when an NKPA division that had been operating in southwestern Korea was directed to advance east toward Pusan, parallel to Korea's southern coastline. As it began its advance at the end of July, virtually no opposition was in its way. When General Walker realized the seriousness of the situation, however, he threw the 24th Infantry Division in front of it, then bolstered that tired unit with forces from the 25th Division. Together they managed to stop the North Koreans—but only just.

While his units were trying to stop the NKPA advance, Walker raced from headquarters to headquarters trying to make his subordinate commanders and their staffs realize the absolute necessity of holding fast wherever possible and, above all, maintaining contact with the enemy. Walker was only too aware of the tendency of his inexperienced U.S. troops to evacuate their defensive positions before the NKPA had placed much real pressure on them—indeed, some were leaving before the NKPA even showed up. Many left without permission from their commanders, giving rise to the derisive term *bugging out*. The oft-used and successful North Korean tactic of outflanking or encircling enemy units, however, fed the fears of the inexperienced troops, causing them to quickly abandon a position before they could be cut off. Walker was desperate to get his troops to stand fast. They were nearly back to the Naktong River line, the

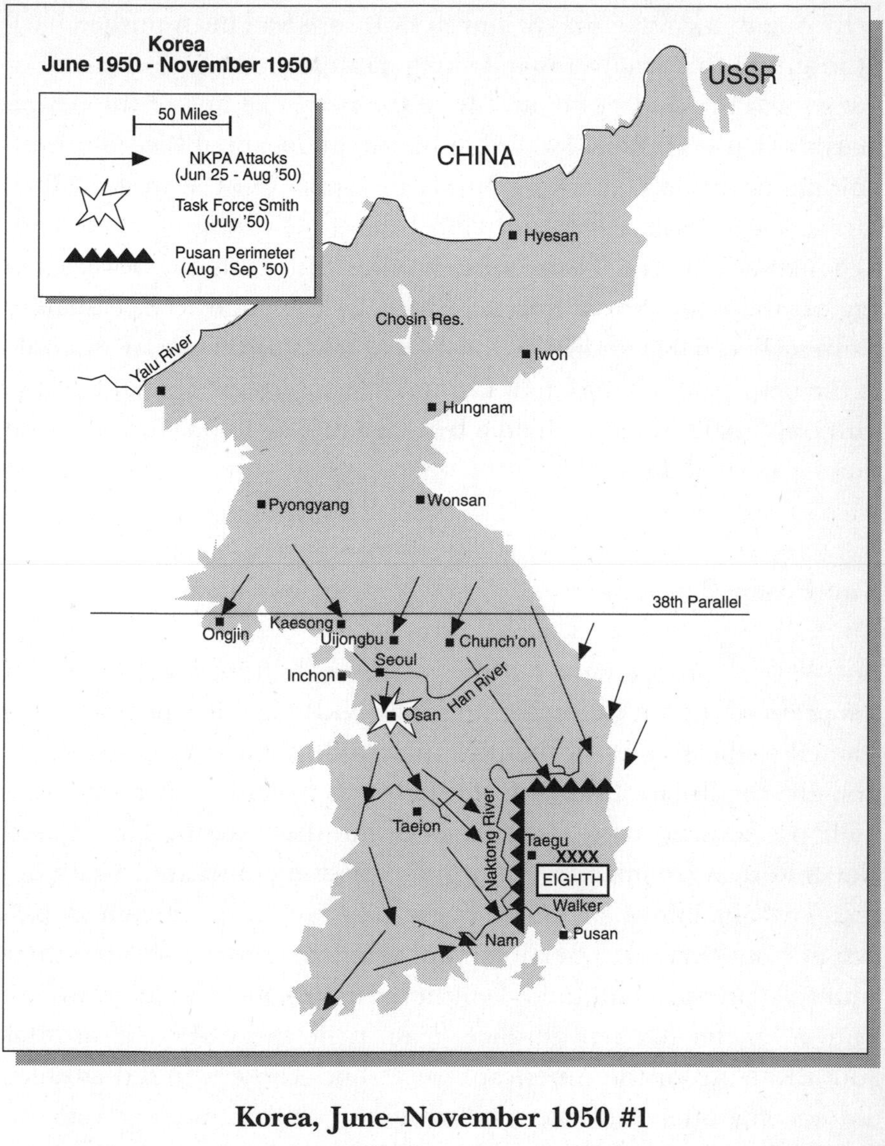
Korea
June 1950 - November 1950
50 Miles
NKPA Attacks
(Jun 25 - Aug '50)
Task Force Smith
(July '50)
Pusan Perimeter
(Aug - Sep '50)
USSR
CHINA
Hyesan
Chosin Res.
Iwon
Yalu River
Hungnam
Pyongyang
Wonsan
38th Parallel
Ongjin
Kaesong
Uijongbu
Chunch'on
Seoul
Inchon
Han River
Osan
Naktong River
Taejon
Taegu
XXXX
EIGHTH
Walker
Pusan
Nam

Korea, June–November 1950 #1

last defensible position protecting the last unoccupied area of South Korea—Pusan.

By August 1, Walker's U.S. and ROK troops had been pushed back into an approximately 140-mile-long perimeter around the city of Taegu and the port of Pusan. Along the northern line of the perimeter, the battered ROK 1st, 3rd, 6th, 8th, and Capital Divisions were holding against six attacking NKPA divisions. On the western line, the U.S. 1st Cavalry, 24th and 25th Infantry Divisions, and the 29th Regimental Combat Team were holding the Naktong River area against the main North Korean effort. By this time, U.S. casualties had reached 6,000 and ROK forces had lost 70,000. As an example of the desperate situation now facing Walker's troops, the 1st Cavalry, with only 7,000 riflemen, held a frontage of over 100,000 yards—ten times a normal division front.

The Pusan Perimeter

But Walker's troops were not the only ones suffering the effects of the previous month's campaigning. The NKPA had lost nearly 60,000 trained soldiers, most of them irreplaceable combat veterans. Additionally, the 105th Tank Brigade had lost a significant number of their precious hoard of T-34 tanks in the drive south. This caused North Korean commanders to begin impressing untrained South Korean civilians into their ranks. These men were not, of course, particularly motivated to serve in an army that was invading their country, and most had to be kept in the ranks, literally, at gunpoint. The ones who did not advance against the guns of their brother South Koreans or the Americans were shot. Those who did advance did so only after the most rudimentary combat training, with no possible time to acquire fighting skills. Many entered combat without weapons, and were instructed to pick one up from a dead comrade or enemy soldier. This was also not particularly effective in raising morale. With the remainder of the troops left over from the beginning of the invasion supplemented by reluctant draftees, the NKPA managed to field fourteen divisions (thirteen infantry and one armored) against Walker's Pusan perimeter.

By now the U.S./UN air component had established air supremacy over South Korea (which it would continue to have for the duration). This greatly aided Walker while further complicating the
NKPA mission. The close air support provided by the Allied air
forces assisted mightily in repelling the continuing NKPA attacks all
along the perimeter, while long-range interdiction of NKPA lines of
communications prevented the movement of supplies, replacement
equipment, and personnel to the increasingly weary North Korean
forces.

Walker then had about 47,000 U.S. combat troops and 45,000
ROK soldiers defending the line of the Naktong and the perimeter,
and additional units were being rushed to his aid. The 29th Regimental Combat Team arrived from Okinawa, then the 5th Regimental Combat Team from Hawaii, followed by the 2nd Infantry Division,
and finally the first of the marine units, the 1st Provisional Marine
Brigade. All were rushed to shore up the defenses around the perimeter. After their initial combat experiences, the two regimental combat teams were incorporated into two of the infantry divisions (the
29th RCT became part of the 25th Infantry and the 5th RCT was
attached to the 24th Infantry). A welcome addition from the UN, a
British infantry brigade from Hong Kong, arrived during this time
as well. Later, this unit was combined with an Australian battalion to
form the British Commonwealth Brigade.

In addition to personnel increases, Walker's troops received
needed matériel, including M-26 Pershing tanks and the 3.5-inch
bazookas. The arrival of increasing numbers of these weapons meant
that the enemy's T-34 tank no longer had a free run of the battlefield. With its 90mm main gun, the M-26 was perfectly capable of
penetrating the armor of the T-34, and with the 3.5-inch bazooka,
the infantryman no longer had to watch his antitank rounds bounce
harmlessly off the Soviet tanks. By September, over 500 medium
tanks were in place within the Pusan perimeter. Well supplied with
ammunition through the Allies' control of the sea-lanes and the air-
ways, Walker's troops were becoming stronger with each passing day.

The NKPA unwittingly helped Walker by failing to concentrate their forces for a massive strike. Instead they wasted their strength in usually uncoordinated attacks all around the perimeter. This allowed the Eighth Army, which had the advantage of interior lines, to move its reserve forces from point to point around the perimeter to meet, and defeat, each enemy threat as it developed. Walker's Eighth Army exercised this maneuver over and over again as the NKPA continued to hammer away relentlessly at the U.S./UN line. The NKPA established several bridgeheads across the Naktong only to see them eliminated by Eighth Army counterattacks.

By September, a sort of equilibrium had been reached all around the perimeter. Walker now had 180,000 U.S./UN troops, probably more combat troops than the attacking NKPA. Certainly, the supply situation within the perimeter was better than it was for the North Koreans outside. The time was approaching when the U.S./UN forces would be strong enough to launch a major counterattack to regain the initiative and take back the ground lost since June 25. As Walker built up his forces, the overall UN commander, General MacArthur, was devising a bold plan that would, in nearly a single stroke, achieve the liberation of South Korea—and an irresistible promise of much more.

Inchon—The Indirect Approach

General Douglas MacArthur was seventy years old when, in September of 1950, he devised and launched his greatest military triumph in over fifty years of distinguished service to his country. The landing at Inchon, deep in the enemy's rear, was a brilliantly executed example of the operational art of war, changing the nature of the Korean War in one fell swoop. Yet it should be remembered that this operation was launched against the odds and in the face of powerful opposition from the services and the joint chiefs of staff, under deplorable conditions at the landing site, and in the teeth of criticism from his detractors.

The Yellow Sea port of Inchon lies twenty-five miles west of Seoul near the mouth of the Han River. Although the port has no great value for military purposes, its proximity to Seoul and to the major north-south lines of communications gave it one great advantage: any successful landing there could cut off the bulk of the North Korean forces in South Korea from access to the north. But an opposed amphibious landing at Inchon had to deal with the port's tidal ranges, which, at thirty-two feet, are among the world's worst, making it extremely risky to land, then support, a force from the sea. Treacherous currents, extensive, nearly impassable mudflats, and a daunting sea-wall only further complicate such an undertaking. Nevertheless, MacArthur's plan was to place a sizable amphibious force ashore at Inchon, move it inland the short distance to capture Seoul and cut the NKPA's north-south communications, then launch the remainder of the Eighth Army north from the Pusan perimeter. Walker's forces would be a "hammer," smashing the NKPA against the amphibious force's "anvil."

MacArthur created and activated the X Corps, under his chief of staff, Major General Edward M. Almond, as his strike force. The corps consisted of the 1st Marine Division (a patchwork outfit created from the 1st Marine Provisional Brigade along with about six battalions of marines taken from the United States or the Mediterranean area) and his final infantry division in Japan, the 7th. After being cannibalized of much of its equipment and stripped of over half of its personnel to bring the 1st Cavalry and 25th Infantry Divisions up to strength in mid-July, the 7th had to be completely rebuilt before it could join MacArthur's strike force. Much of the 7th's replacement personnel were South Koreans, assigned to the division as part of the Korean Augmentation to U.S. Army (KATUSA) program. About 8,600 KATUSAs were assigned to the 7th Infantry Division, most just in time to embark on the ships taking them to the Inchon operation.

The navy began landing Almond's troops at 6:33 A.M. on September 15, 1950, after subjecting the intended landing areas and surrounding vicinity to a naval barrage for most of the two preceding days. By 8:00 A.M., the island of Wolmi-do, the principal port linked to Inchon by a long, narrow causeway, was reported to have been secured by marine commanders. But even with this early success, the remainder of the landing force had to wait twelve agonizing hours for the next high tide before the main landings could be completed. That evening at 5:30 P.M., the rest of Almond's troops went ashore and moved to secure Inchon. Despite stiffening resistance, the X Corps captured the town and began maneuvering toward Seoul within a few days, capturing Kimpo airfield on the evening of September 17.

The X Corps' drive to take Seoul intensified when the 7th Infantry Division got ashore and began moving toward the city from the south while the marines attacked the capital from the north. Eventually, ROK units were brought in, and after several days of brutal combat in the streets of Seoul against a fanatic NKPA rear guard, U.S./UN forces captured the city on September 28. Meanwhile Walker's troops within the Pusan perimeter were conducting their breakout against the NKPA units surrounding them.

The Eighth Army at Pusan attempted its breakout on September 16, just one day after MacArthur's landing at Inchon. Not surprisingly, this was not enough time for the effect of the deep strike into the enemy's rear to make itself felt along the Pusan front, and additionally, those North Korean commanders who did find out about the landings kept the news secret from their troops. Nevertheless, the NKPA units surrounding Pusan, which were actually still attacking Walker's forces when the Eighth Army's own offensive kicked off, could not keep up the pressure against the U.S./UN lines while their rear areas collapsed. The NKPA positions lacked depth, were hampered by insufficient reserves with which to reinforce any of their limited battlefield successes, and were gradually becoming weaker and weaker as few supplies got through to them.

On September 20, Walker's offensive began to achieve breakthroughs along most of the Pusan perimeter's front as the effects of MacArthur's landings made themselves felt. Only in the extreme south of the NKPA line were the North Korean units able to hold firm against the U.S. 2nd and 25th Infantry Divisions, newly redesignated the IX U.S. Corps. Walker's main attack, delivered along the Taejon–Taegu–Pusan road where his units had retreated in the earlier fighting, was struck by the U.S./UN I Corps—the 1st Cavalry

American 37mm gun crew of the 23rd Infantry Regiment in action typical of the Meuse-Argonne fighting (National Archives Photo no. WC 620).

German troops advancing in open order late in the war. The Hutier or "storm troop" tactics, developed late in the Great War, featured surprise, infiltration, bypassing of strong points, maximum fire support, and maintaining momentum; they were the precursors of World War II's "blitzkrieg" (National Archives photo no. 111-SC-97179).

Shell dump of the 1st U.S. Infantry Division in Tartigny, France, 1918. Modern explosives, advances in weapons technology, and mass-transportation means such as extensive rail networks helped establish artillery as the greatest killer on the battlefields of the Great War (National Archives photo no. 111-SC-14694).

American troops move past abandoned trenches in the Kriemhilde Stellung defensive line, November 3, 1918 (National Archives photo no. 111-SC-31488).

Montfaucon, France, 1918. An American officer stands amid the rubble of the city of Mont-faucon, a key position during the Meuse-Argonne campaign (National Archives photo no. WC 697).

Bitter legacy of the Great War. Sitting at left (under the X) in this picture of a group of German soldiers of the Great War is Corporal Adolf Hitler. Hitler capitalized on the German people's post-World War I feelings of betrayal, disorientation, and bitterness to forge the Nazi Third Reich—and help start World War II (National Archives photo no. WC 500).

Russian infantry along the Don River, Autumn 1942. As a result of Stalin's purges of the late 1930s, Soviet leadership at the beginning of World War II was generally weak and incompetent, and the performance of the Red Army was poor. After being forged in the fires of battle at Moscow and Stalingrad, however, Soviet commanders emerged with a skill and confidence that turned the tide on the Eastern Front (National Archives photo no. 111-SC-181848).

Red Army T-34 tank with infantry, 1942-43. Surviving the initial shock of the German invasion, the Soviet Union began producing tough, reliable equipment that turned back the Nazis at Stalingrad and Kursk. The T-34 tank was the best mass-produced armored fighting vehicle of World War II (National Archives photo no. 111-SC-152499).

Soviet infantry and tank in winter garb advance against German positions, February 1943. Surrounded by hundreds of thousands of such Red Army troops, the German Sixth Army at Stalingrad was cut off and annihilated (National Archives photo no. 111-SC-152520).

General of the Army Dwight D. Eisenhower and his principal subordinates in Western Europe, 1945. These are the primary leaders of the U.S. forces who fought and won the battles of France and Germany on the Western Front of World War II. Front row *(left to right):* Lieutenant General William H. Simpson, Ninth Army commander; General George S. Patton, Jr., Third Army commander; General Carl A. Spaatz, U.S. Army Air Forces commander; Eisenhower; General Omar N. Bradley, 12th Army Group commander; General Courtney H. Hodges, First Army commander; Lieutenant General Leonard T. Gerow, Fifteenth Army commander (formerly V Corps commander). Back row *(left to right):* Brigadier General Ralph F. Stearley; Lieutenant General Hoyt S. Vandenberg; Lieutenant General Walter Bedell Smith, SHAEF chief of staff; Major General Otto P. Weyland; Brigadier General Richard E. Nugent (National Archives photo no. WC 751).

German assault trooper, Ardennes Offensive, December 1944. One of a group of photographs taken in the vicinity of St.-Vith-Malmédy during the opening days of the Battle of the Bulge. The unit had just overrun elements of the U.S. 14th Cavalry Group protecting the left flank of the 106th Infantry Division (National Archives photo no. WC 1070).

American infantry on the St.-Vith-Houffalize road, Ardennes Offensive, January 1945. The rapid reaction of Eisenhower and the Allied High Command to the German offensive facilitated the movement of reinforcements to the threatened Ardennes region and doomed the German assault to failure (National Archives photo no. WC 1079).

Troops of the U.S. 27th Infantry Division moving across a valley on Okinawa, May 24, 1945. The struggle for Okinawa was the greatest—as well as the final—land battle in the Pacific Theater of World War II. The extensive network of Japanese underground positions and the tenacious defense by the Japanese 32nd Army made the battle one the bloodiest of the Pacific war (National Archives photo no. 111-SC-270930).

Death of the 32nd Japanese Army. These markers identify the graves of Lieutenant General Ushijima Mitsuru, commander of the 32nd Army, and his chief of staff, Lieutenant General Cho Isamu. Ushijima and Cho committed seppuku, ritual suicide, near their final command post at the end of the battle of Okinawa (National Archives photo no. 111-SC-215549-1).

MacArthur at Inchon. General of the Army Douglas MacArthur observes the landings at Inchon from his command post aboard the USS *Rochester* (CA-124) on September 15, 1950. Brigadier General Courtney Whitney of MacArthur's staff looks on. The Inchon landing was MacArthur's most brilliant military maneuver and turned the tide against the North Korean troops surrounding the tiny Pusan perimeter (National Archives photo no. 80-G-423192).

MacArthur, commander in chief United Nations Forces Korea, Lieutenant General Matthew B. Ridgway *(left)*, Eighth Army commander, and Major General Frank W. Milburn *(right rear)*, I Corps commander, visit the front in February 1951 (National Archives photo no. 111-SC-363407).

U.S. infantryman in Korea. PFC George Chintala, 25th Infantry Division, on a Korean hill, 1951 (National Archives photo no. 111-SC-363444).

Soldiers of the 21st Infantry Regiment, 24th Infantry Division, set up a 75mm recoilless rifle and dig in fifteen miles north of Seoul. Men from the unit's 1st Battalion under Lieutenant Colonel Brad Smith formed Task Force Smith in July 1950. The failure of their efforts to stop the North Korean tanks and infantry at Osan underscored the overall weaknesses of the U.S. Army at the beginning of the Korean War (National Archives photo no. 111-SC-355509).

Cannoneers of A Battery, 52nd Field Artillery Battalion, 24th Infantry Division, camouflage their M101A1, 105mm howitzer, ten miles north of Seoul on the road to Uijong-bu. Earlier, in July 1950, gunners from this unit were part of Task Force Smith, attempting to block the North Korean invasion at Osan (National Archives photo no. 111-SC-355510).

The ruggedness of Korean terrain is evident in this photograph of soldiers of the 3rd Battalion, 19th Infantry Regiment, 24th Infantry Division, as they move through the mountains ten miles north of Seoul (National Archives photo no. WC 1431).

Yalu River. Corporal M. J. Gardner and PFC T. Robinson, soldiers of the 17th Regimental Combat Team, 7th Infantry Division, arrive at the village of Hyesan, Korea, on the edge of the Yalu River, November 1950 (National Archives photo no. 111-SC-363298).

Frozen Chosin. Aerial photograph of the Chosin Reservoir in the mountains of northern Korea, November 1, 1950 (National Archives photo no. 111-SC-363260).

Hell below zero. Exhausted marines take a short break during their "attack in the opposite direction" to escape the Chinese trap at the Chosin Reservoir, November-December 1950 (National Archives photo no. WC 1392).

French Indochina terrain, 1946-54. Ho Chi Minh and Vo Nguyen Giap's Viet Minh used the rugged terrain in Vietnam as a valuable ally against the French army and colonial forces. The frontier outpost village of Dien Bien Phu rests in a valley surrounded by similar terrain. Air transport became the only means of resupplying the French garrison (National Archives photo no. 111-SC-348118).

Arrival in the Persian Gulf. Tank crews of the "Tiger Brigade," 2nd U.S. Armored Division, receive their M1A1 tanks and other equipment at a port in Saudi Arabia during Operation Desert Shield, the buildup to the Gulf War (Photo courtesy Lieutenant Colonel Volney J. Warner).

End of the Highway of Death. Soldiers of the 2nd Armored Division inspect a knocked-out Iraqi tank near the police barracks atop the Al-Mutla Ridge outside Kuwait City, shortly after the end of the fighting there, February 27, 1991. The road cut at the right of the picture marks the western end of the infamous "Highway of Death"—the main road leading out of Kuwait City, which at the end of the war was strewn with destroyed or abandoned Iraqi military vehicles and stolen civilian automobiles. The Iraqi tank appears to be a Chinese Type 79, the export version of the Soviet T-55, upgunned with a 105mm main gun (photo courtesy Lieutenant Colonel Volney J. Warner).

Two Iraqi tanks destroyed on February 26, 1991, by M1A1 gunners from the 3rd Battalion, 67th Armor, firing from positions on the Al-Mutla Ridge. These two tanks (they appear to be T-55s) tried to escape the Highway of Death by turning north onto a side road. Each was knocked out by a single round from the M1A1s (photo courtesy Lieutenant Colonel Volney J. Warner).

A U.S. M1A1 tank moves past a destroyed and abandoned Iraqi tank in the Kuwaiti desert, February 1991 (photo courtesy Lieutenant Colonel Volney J. Warner).

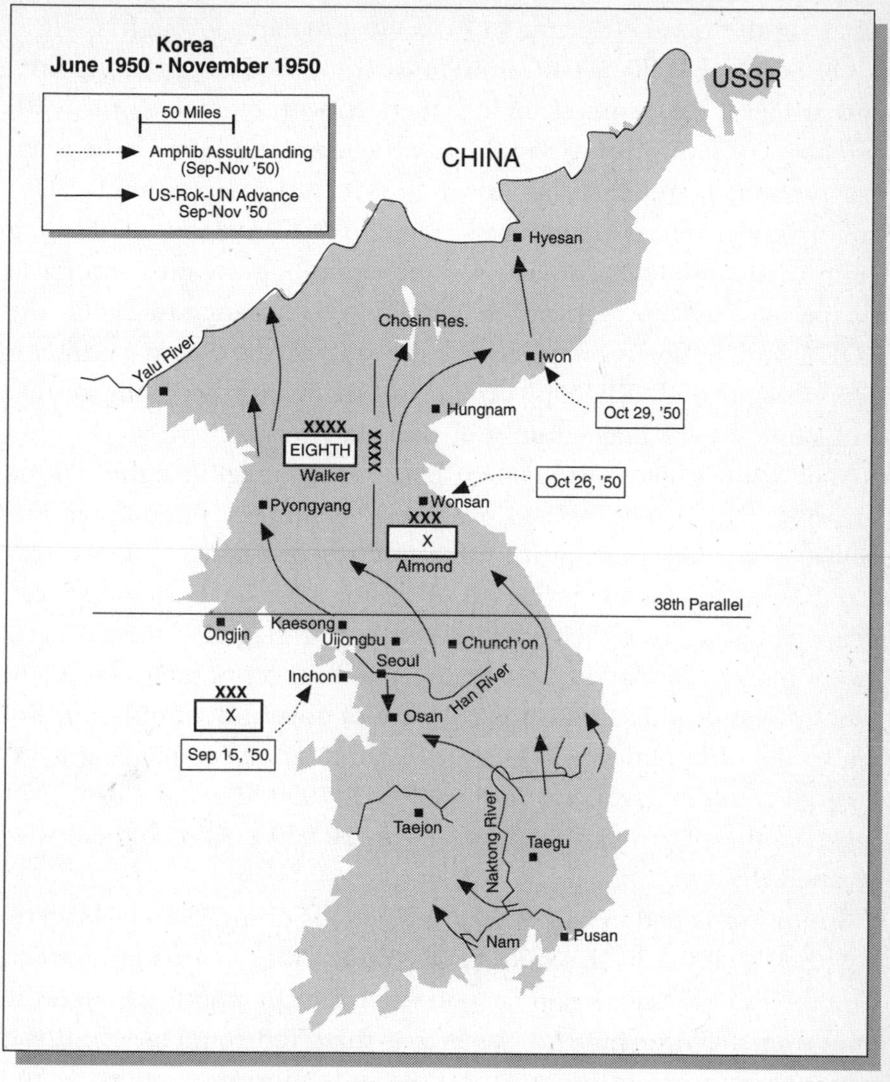
Korea
June 1950 - November 1950
50 Miles
Amphib Assult/Landing
(Sep-Nov '50)
US-Rok-UN Advance
Sep-Nov '50
USSR
CHINA
Hyesan
Chosin Res.
Iwon
Yalu River
Hungnam
Oct 29, '50
XXXX
EIGHTH
Walker
XXXX
Oct 26, '50
Wonsan
Pyongyang
XXX
X
Almond
38th Parallel
Ongjin
Kaesong
Uijongbu
Chunch'on
Seoul
Inchon
Han River
XXX
X
Osan
Sep 15, '50
Naktong River
Taejon
Taegu
Nam
Pusan

Korea, June–November 1950 #2

Division, 24th Infantry Division, 1st ROK Division, and the British 27 Brigade. By September 23, NKPA resistance had effectively collapsed all along the perimeter, and I Corps was breaking through.

On September 26, a 1st Cavalry unit composed of tanks, infantry, and artillery, Task Force Lynch, linked up with elements of the 7th Infantry Division outside Seoul, after racing the 100 miles between the perimeter and the Han River line in only eleven hours. This linkup effectively trapped most of eight NKPA divisions, forcing them to abandon virtually all of their equipment in their efforts to escape. As Task Force Lynch was making its advance to Seoul, the ROK I and II Corps on the northern side of the Pusan perimeter were forcing the NKPA units opposing them into headlong retreat and gaining back huge chunks of their territory.

MacArthur's bold envelopment had worked magnificently. To the surprise of his critics, he had executed his greatest operational maneuver in the face of daunting odds, and rescued the U.S./UN forces at Pusan as well as liberating all of South Korea at a single stroke. True to his histrionic character, MacArthur staged a formal ceremony in Seoul's National Assembly building on September 29, in which the old soldier returned the seat of government of South Korea to the old politician, Syngman Rhee, to an accompanying backdrop of rumbling artillery. On October 1, 1950, the U.S./UN forces reached the 38th parallel, chasing the 30,000 NKPA soldiers who escaped the trap.

South Korea had been saved by the actions of the U.S./UN forces, but the "victory" in this limited war didn't taste particularly sweet. The forces were once again back to their starting points (though the imposing NKPA of June 25 was now a shattered remnant), and two nations continued to occupy the Korean peninsula. Leaders on the south side of the 38th parallel began to consider that, perhaps, something more could be gained than merely saving South Korea.

To the Yalu—Across the 38th Parallel and Beyond

President Truman, General MacArthur, and the now victorious U.S./ UN forces were suddenly faced with a dilemma created by the unbelievable success of the Inchon landing and the Pusan breakout. Should they be satisfied with accomplishing their original mission of saving South Korea from North Korean aggression and reestablishing the status quo along the 38th parallel, or should they use the unexpected good fortune presented to them by the near-total collapse of the NKPA and move to unify all of the Korean peninsula under the ROK government? If the U.S./UN forces stopped at the 38th parallel, they would be leaving approximately six NKPA divisions (the 30,000 troops that had escaped north plus about 30,000 more still in training camps in North Korea). This would leave the South Koreans in not much better shape than they were prior to June 25. On the other hand, both China and the Soviet Union had warned the UN troops against invading North Korea, threatening to intervene (or cause trouble in Europe) if the 38th parallel were crossed.

By this point in the war, Eighth Army casualties had reached about 25,000 (including over 5,000 KIA). This figure, plus the larger number of casualties suffered by the ROK forces, constituted a substantial sacrifice for a so-called police action, and Truman found himself the target of severe criticism at home by a public and press accustomed to total victory and unconditional surrender. However, if the entire peninsula could be unified with only—one hoped—a small additional number of casualties, then the Truman administration could silence critics with a clear victory against the forces of international communism—one of the few places worldwide where the Free World had rolled back the Red Menace. MacArthur, now more than ever a military icon, counseled continued prosecution of the war with a drive to the Yalu. President Truman agreed, authorizing MacArthur on September 27 to allow his ROK units to cross the parallel, which they did on October 1. After the UN voted to allow the U.S./UN forces to cross the parallel several days later, U.S. units followed their ROK allies into North Korea on October 9.

By this time U.S./UN ground forces numbered about 200,000 troops out of a total force of nearly 315,000. Half the ground total were American, organized into five army divisions (1st Cavalry Division and the 2nd, 7th, 24th, and 25th Infantry Divisions) and the 1st Marine Division. MacArthur planned to conquer North Korea as far as the Manchurian border on the Yalu by pushing Walker's Eighth Army up the central and western portions of the peninsula while conducting an amphibious operation on the east side with Almond's X Corps—which was still kept independent of the Eighth Army. Despite shortages in minesweepers and amphibious shipping, preparations for landing the X Corps at Wonsan and Iwon went forward vigorously while Walker moved his U.S. and ROK units north of the parallel.

The North Korean capital of Pyongyang was the principal objective of Walker's main attack, with his I Corps leading the way. Having crossed the 38th parallel on October 9, the 1st Cavalry Division, supported by the ROK 1st, 7th, and 8th Divisions were halfway to their destination by October 14. The 24th Infantry Division cleared the area immediately to the west of the 1st Cavalry, reaching almost to Chinnampo on October 20. Pyongyang fell to the 1st Cavalry Division and the ROK 1st Division in fierce fighting during October 19–20, but Kim Il-sung and his Communist government had already fled northward. On that same day, the 187th Regimental Combat Team, an airborne outfit, was dropped north of the North Korean capital along the axes of retreat of the NKPA forces in an effort to trap the large numbers of enemy troops attempting to escape the advance of I Corps. Although the airborne operation failed to trap significant numbers of fleeing enemy troops, it moved the U.S./UN advancing front line rapidly northward.

Meanwhile the ROK forces in the center and eastern part of the peninsula were in close pursuit of the retreating NKPA units and rapidly moving closer to the Manchurian border. The ROK 3rd and Capital Divisions captured the port city of Wonsan on October 11 (the X Corps was still embarking for its amphibious operation), then pushed on to take Hungnam on October 17. The ROK advance continued unchecked, and on October 26 elements of the ROK 6th Division reached the Yalu River near the center of the U.S./UN line. Farther east, the ROK 3rd and Capital Divisions took the port of Iwon on the same day.

X Corps' amphibious operation finally got under way on October 19 when the 1st Marine Division arrived off the coast of Wonsan. It was delayed in landing, however, because the harbor was extensively mined. The U.S. Navy, which had mothballed or deactivated virtually all of its demining capability, was forced to patch together a minesweeping flotilla, which then took until October 25 to clear Wonsan Harbor (losing several boats to Russian mines in the process). After steaming back and forth across the mouth of the harbor for several days while the navy cleared the mines (the marines called this Operation Yo-Yo), the 1st Marine Division conducted an administrative landing on October 26. The remainder of X Corps, primarily the 7th Infantry Division, landed at Iwon on November 9. The extensive delay of the X Corps landings on the east coast effectively eliminated its participation in a westward movement to assist in the capture of Pyongyang. MacArthur, therefore, changed its axis of advance to a more northerly direction. This change of mission put the marines and, a short time later, the soldiers of the 7th Infantry on a march to clear a rugged area between the coast and the Yalu River. This area, which contained the Chosin and Fusen reservoirs, was also soon found to contain something else: about 300,000 Chinese troops.

The Chinese Intervention

ROK units pushing on toward the Yalu in the latter part of October had already been attacked and, in several cases, severely mauled by Chinese units (euphemistically referred to as "volunteers") of the PLA. It was not any great secret to the intelligence analysts of MacArthur's staff or Eighth Army that Chinese troops were assisting the remnants of the NKPA in areas of North Korea south of the Yalu River. But the strength of these PLA units was assessed at only several thousand (perhaps as many as 40,000 to 80,000), and neither Mac-Arthur nor any of his principal subordinate commanders was particularly worried about them.

After the mauling of the ROK units (and several U.S. units that were left unsupported by the destruction of the ROK units on their flanks) in late October and early November, the PLA went to ground and virtually disappeared—seemingly as quickly as they had appeared in the preceding few days. This mysterious occurrence failed to alarm MacArthur, and he ordered the advance toward the Yalu to resume.

Throughout most of November the U.S./UN advance continued to occupy the northern reaches of North Korea until, on November 24, only a small northwestern portion of the country was free of Allied forces. The U.S./UN line, from west to east, consisted of the Eighth Army's I Corps, then its IX Corps, and finally the ROK II Corps, occupying a wide zone reaching from the peninsula's central region to the rugged Taebaek range. Almond's X Corps, still operating independently of the Eighth Army, "occupied" a huge area comprising the entire northeastern region of North Korea. This expanded all the way to the Yalu River when elements of the 7th Infantry Division reached Hyesan on November 21. Except for some isolated patrol activity, there was, essentially, no contact between MacArthur's two major commands.

At this point, with the U.S./UN forces spread out over the entire range of territory in North Korea, at the end of a long and tenuous supply line, and just as the bitter Korean winter was setting in, the 300,000 Chinese troops launched massive attacks against the UN "invaders." Beginning on November 25 and continuing throughout the U.S./UN area for several days, the PLA launched a series of vicious, overwhelming attacks. By November 28, the UN forces began to disintegrate. The first phase of the Korean War ended in the miserable climate and brutal terrain of North Korea on November 25, 1950. Concerted and determined action by the U.S./UN forces since June had turned back the invasion and saved the young country of South Korea. The war, however, went on.

Korea
Nov 1950 - Apr 1951
50 Miles
Chinese Attack
Amphib Evacuations
US-ROK-UN Attacks
US-ROK-UN Line
(Apr 22, '51)
US-ROK-UN Line
(Jan 24, '51)
USSR
CHINA
Hyesan
Chosin Res.
Iwon
Yalu River
Hungnam
EVAC
Dec 15,'50
EVAC
Dec 15,'50
Pyongyang
Wonsan
April 22, '51
38th Parallel
Kaesong
Ongjin
Uijongbu
Chunch'on
Jan. 24, '51
Seoul
Inchon
Han River
Osan
XXXX
EIGHTH
Ridgway
Taejon
Naktong River
Taegu
Nam
Pusan

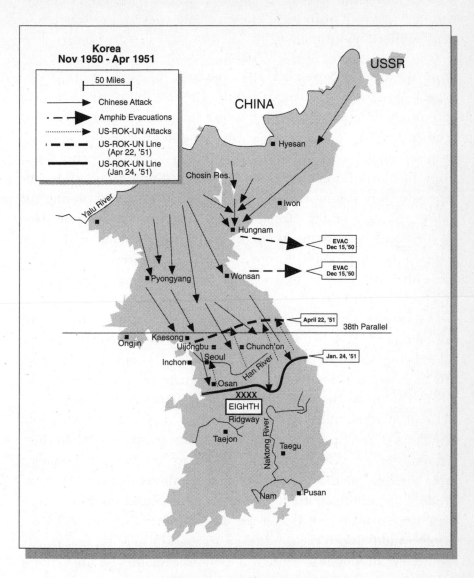

Korea, November 1950–April 1951

Aftermath

From the end of November 1950 onward, the very nature of the Korean War began to change, and the Chinese intervention made it an entirely different war from the one fought from June 25 to November 25. The first six months of fighting in what would eventually be three long years of conflict had undeniably saved South Korea from the North Korean invaders and a forced unification under the repressive Kim Il-sung regime. But the Allied dream of uniting the entire peninsula under a freely elected, democratic government led by the South was shattered by the active intervention of the PLA forces. From this point on, the U.S./UN forces were no longer at war with North Korea—they were at war with China, pretending to represent North Korea.

The massive Chinese intervention resulted in the complete withdrawal of all U.S./UN forces from North Korea and ended with the Allies being driven all the way back to the line Osan-Samchok, nearly fifty miles south of Seoul by the end of January 1951. There the U.S./UN forces, under the leadership of a new Eighth Army commander, General Matthew Ridgway (who would soon get MacArthur's job) reorganized, resupplied, and regained their confidence. When these renewed forces counterattacked on January 25, 1951, they inaugurated a seesaw method of warfare that continued, more or less unbroken, for months. First the Chinese would build up their forces, then launch a powerful offensive against the UN line. Ridgway's troops would absorb the attacks, give ground where necessary, and use massive firepower to cause tremendous casualties on the Chinese troops. When the enemy attack had lost all of its steam (resupply continued to be a major limiting factor for the PLA throughout the war), the UN forces would launch their own offensive. After months of this back-and-forth fighting, the front more or less stabilized around the 38th parallel, degenerating into a long period of stalemate, again reminiscent of the trench warfare of World War I. Finally, in July 1953, the belligerents signed an armistice at

Panmunjon, ending months of frustrating "peace" talks.

The Korean War settled little of the question of reunification of the Korean peninsula, but that had not been its original goal. It was fought because the Allied side was unwilling to allow communism to spread deeper into Asia, and because the United States intended to remain a world power. Had Truman chosen not to introduce American troops into a conflict between rival groups of Koreans, the United States would have immediately begun to relinquish its power to influence events and governments in Asia. Some have characterized the Korean War as "the first war the United States lost." Such characterizations are shallow and ignorant. Korea was a limited war fought for limited, political objectives. Truman set out to prevent a Communist takeover of South Korea, and he accomplished just that. And he avoided starting an atomic World War III in the process.

CHAPTER SEVEN

The First Indochina War

• 1946–1954 •

THE BATTLE OF DIEN BIEN PHU

Dreams of Empire—Dreams of Freedom

Japan's attempts to create a Greater East Asia Coprosperity Sphere in the middle years of the twentieth century ultimately led to its defeat and humiliation in World War II. But that country's shattered dreams of conquest left another legacy: the end of the European colonial empires in Asia. In the early years of this century, subjugated Asian peoples began to dream of shaking off the yoke of their Western colonizers and taking charge of their own destinies. Such dreams, however, remained unrealized in the face of the technological and military superiority of the European powers. But when the wave of Japanese conquest, beginning in China in 1937 and reaching its peak during the year after Pearl Harbor, brought the disruption of war to the nations of the central and western Pacific rim, the old order, already rotting from the inside, collapsed. After the Japanese defeat in 1945, the colonial powers tried to regain their former empires, but they found that nationalist revolutionaries, like Vietnam's Ho Chi Minh, were prepared to fight to prevent a return to the old ways. The sun was rapidly setting on the imperial powers in the East.

Drop Zone, Dien Bien Phu, 8:30 P.M., April 1, 1954: The men in the besieged
fortress complex of Dien Bien Phu heard the low drone of transport planes with both
relief and apprehension. Since mid-March, when the Viet Minh forces closed in on
the French and their colonial troops garrisoning the remote outpost, all supplies,
reinforcements, and equipment had to be air-dropped, a risky endeavor for the supply
planes, which had to evade intense antiaircraft fire from the surrounding hills, and
for the French paratroopers and Legionnaires on the ground, who had to brave a
hailstorm of enemy artillery and ground fire to retrieve the cargoes. By this time
restricted to a drop zone barely 500 yards long and only as wide as an airstrip, the
French pilots had to fly low and slowly, always on the same course, making multiple
passes over the tiny DZ. On this particular night, the transports were bringing in
men from the 4th Company, 2nd Battalion, 1st Parachute Chasseurs (II/1 RCP),
accompanied by a battalion command element and a gun crew from the 35th Airborne Artillery. Reinforcements were constantly needed to replenish the losses suffered
in the daily Viet Minh assaults and shelling. While the transports laboriously dropped
the troops a few at a time, other planes circled out of antiaircraft range waiting to
unload their desperately needed cargoes of ammunition and rations on the tiny DZ.

An inferno of antiaircraft fire erupted from the surrounding hills and engulfed
the transports, whose pilots were straining to keep on course above the explosions of
incoming artillery and the hot blasts of French cannon returning the fire. With
supreme difficulty, the planes dropped the bulk of 4th Company and accompanying
staff and artillery crew, one-half "stick" per plane during each pass. Seven men were
lost during the drop, five of them hit while they were suspended in their parachutes.
Since the transports had taken so long to drop the 4th Company and they still had
to unload the vital resupply of ammunition (French guns had expended 4,500
rounds that day alone), the aircraft carrying the remainder of the battalion aborted
their mission and returned to Hanoi. At this rate of reinforcement, French commanders would be unable even to make up for their daily losses

---

Begun as a plan to lure the elusive Viet Minh into a large, Western-
style, pitched battle where French firepower could destroy the guerrillas almost at will, the battle of Dien Bien Phu ended in a defeat
so thorough that it forced the French to abandon their Indochinese
empire. When the Viet Minh finally concentrated their forces, and
stood and fought, French leaders, who had been wishing for just this
circumstance, were crushingly humiliated.

Fighting Japanese and Frenchman

The greatest blow to French efforts to retain Vietnam as a colony was the Japanese takeover of Indochina in 1940. Although their new Japanese masters allowed Vichy French colonial officials to remain in their posts and continue to administer the region, the myth of European invincibility had been forever shattered. Just as the Japanese victory in the Russo-Japanese War of 1904–05 destroyed the image of Russian superiority, so did their seizure of Indochina from France, already weakened by the Nazi blitzkrieg in Western Europe, destroy the image of French superiority in Vietnam.

While many Asian nationalists welcomed the Japanese triumphs over their former colonial masters, Ho Chi Minh was reluctant to side with Japan, supposedly remarking that seeking Japanese assistance to rid Vietnam of the French was like "throwing a tiger out the front door while letting a wolf slip in the back door." Ho saw to it that the guerrilla movements within Vietnam were coordinated against both French and Japanese forces.

During the next four years, revolutionary cells were created all across the northern half of Vietnam while insurgent actions were carried out against French and Japanese occupiers. Ho, moving his headquarters into southern China in 1941, remained there for most of the war, only returning to Vietnam in the fall of 1944 when a Japanese offensive into that region of China threatened his operation. When he moved his headquarters back to Vietnam, 200 soldiers, who called themselves a Propaganda Detachment of the Liberation Army, and were under the command of Vo Nguyen Giap, accompanied him. This unit is considered the founding organization of the North Vietnamese Army (called the People's Army of Vietnam—PAVN).

By the time the Japanese seized control of Vietnam in March 1945 (after the collapse of the Vichy government), the Viet Minh forces numbered about 6,000 combat-experienced guerrillas armed with U.S. or Chinese weapons (or with weapons captured from the Japanese or French). By the end of that summer, this number had grown to more than 60,000, although many were peasant militia units, unsuitable for prolonged action against a disciplined foe.

The Japanese defeat successfully concluded the Vietnamese guerrilla campaign against the occupying Japanese troops. Still recovering from World War II, France was not yet ready to reoccupy its former colonies. Ho's forces, however, were perfectly positioned to exploit the Japanese defeat. By this time Ho was the best-known Vietnamese nationalist figure, and he and the Viet Minh took control of the country; on September 2, 1945, Ho announced the formation of the independent Democratic Republic of Vietnam.

France, of course, firmly rejected the Viet Minh's attempts to establish an independent Vietnam, but lacked the force in that part of the globe to back it up. All through the winter of 1945–46, French leaders set about strengthening their forces in the far south of Vietnam and in Laos in preparation for an effort to oust Ho and the Viet Minh. In anticipation of this, Ho purged the Viet Minh of "counterrevolutionary elements"—that is, political unreliables, non-Communists, and religious groups—executing, imprisoning, or driving off thousands of people during 1946 and 1947. Despite the Viet Minh's growing power, Ho and his subordinates realized they could not hope to stand up to the French once sufficient military forces arrived in Indochina. They did, therefore, what Communists always do when they find themselves in a weak position: they negotiated.

Ho met with the French in the winter of 1945–46 and continued to meet with them, attend joint conferences, and agree to frequent cease-fires and truces throughout the next year. By the fall of 1946, however, the French had tired of endless talks, and felt that their increased military strength gave them the edge over Ho's guerrilla fighters. French representatives made demands that Ho and the Viet Minh could not accept. The talks broke down at the end of November and open fighting followed within a few days. On the night of December 19, 1946, Viet Minh units struck several French positions inside Hanoi, and the First Indochina War began.

Weapons and Tactics

Except for air support, both sides used similar weapons, although in the early years, the Viet Minh had to rely on whatever they could beg, borrow, steal, or somehow fabricate themselves. In December 1946, the Vietnamese insurgents were armed with a motley collection of ancient or obsolete small arms and leftovers from the Japanese occupation. But the victory of Mao's Communists in China opened the way for a flood of up-to-date Chinese (and captured U.S.) weapons and ammunition. By the time the Dien Bien Phu campaign began in November 1953, Ho's forces had sufficient stocks of small arms, crew-served weapons, and artillery pieces to prevent overall French superiority in firepower from proving decisive.

The tactics employed in Indochina depended upon the relative strengths of the combatants during any particular phase of the fighting. Ho and Giap's forces resorted to classic guerrilla warfare when the strength of their French opponents made the risk of conventional tactics too costly—carrying out hit-and-run assaults on French outposts and relieving columns, or more sustained attacks on isolated strategic hamlets or other fortified areas. French countertactics were very similar to those later used by American forces during the Second Indochina War (1960–75)—including air strikes, punitive attacks on Viet Minh–controlled villages and regions, and frequent patrolling. When the combatants' relative strengths were more equal, PAVN reverted to conventional tactics such as fire-and-maneuver warfare supported by mortars and artillery. Classic siege warfare took place during the final sixty days of Dien Bien Phu, the Viet Minh employing thousands of rounds of artillery to neutralize French firepower while sappers tunneled to within a few yards of French strong points. Infantry assaults under cover of a massive barrage led to each position's capture.

The Battle of Dien Bien Phu

March 13–May 7, 1954

Navarre's Plan

The plan of French Indochina commander, General Henri Navarre, to lure large Viet Minh forces into a major battle around Dien Bien Phu seemed a good one at the time. Deceptively simple in conception, it rested on the premise that the French were superior in overall firepower—principally artillery and airpower—and this advantage could be used decisively if only the Viet Minh concentrated their elusive forces for a long enough period of time. But in war, as Clausewitz so wisely noted, it is difficult to execute even the simplest of plans.

Navarre had already realized that the kind of war his forces were waging when he took command in May 1953 could never end in a decisive French victory. What was needed, he believed, was a lengthy series of rapid, powerful blows, delivered by a strong, mobile force, backed up by a steady stream of reinforcements—and large amounts of U.S. aid. Political and military leaders in Paris, however, had already turned down this proposal as politically unfeasible. The best Navarre might expect was ten more battalions of reinforcements and perhaps some American aid. Another, less costly, strategy would have to be devised.

Behind Navarre's plan to turn Dien Bien Phu into a "meat grinder" for Ho and Giap's Viet Minh PAVN forces is the idea that a *base aéroterrestre* (fortified airhead) could cause the "rear" areas of the Vietnamese guerrillas to expend considerable combat power attacking French positions. The earlier French success in the siege of the fortified airhead of Na San supported this idea. During this six-month-long operation, the French fought off several Viet Minh assaults, in which Giap's forces used highly costly human-wave frontal attacks in attempts to overrun the French positions. Although the French later evacuated Na San when it ceased to be useful (Giap stopped wasting his soldiers in futile mass assaults), the memory of the French "body count" victory there was powerful. The larger size of the Dien Bien Phu position, it was thought, would even allow the French to use mobile forces, as well as tanks, against the enemy.

"Chief Village of the Province"—Dien Bien Phu

Lying in the largest valley in the northern mountain area of Vietnam, Dien Bien Phu roughly means "chief village of the province," or "seat of the border-county prefecture." Split by the Nam Yum River, the valley of Dien Bien Phu is approximately ten miles long and three miles wide. Appearing on maps and aerial photos as a smooth, broad plain, the valley floor contains some hillocks, but nothing approaching the peaks of the surrounding mountains, some as high as 3,000 feet; seen from the valley, these give the impression of dominating high ground in every direction. One observer wordlessly described the terrain by turning his hand palm up (to represent the village), his fingers and thumb rising straight up (to represent the enclosing mountains). He then proceeded to clench his fist—ominously.

Part of Navarre's attraction to Dien Bien Phu was its location—close to the Laotian border, about 150 miles west of Hanoi, only 40 miles south of the Chinese border, and on one of the major land routes into Laos from Vietnam. (At the time, Viet Minh guerrillas also threatened Laos.) French planners, grossly underestimating the Viet Minh's capabilities in moving personnel, equipment, and supplies by hand through rough terrain, assumed that air movement and air resupply would give their forces in this remote section of the country a significant advantage over their "primitive" foe. The fact that the valley is often fogbound and receives over sixty inches of rain during the monsoon season does not seem to have caused them much concern. But if meteorological vagaries, rough terrain and geographical remoteness, and a fiercely determined enemy prevent planes from delivering critical supplies and reinforcements, superior airpower ceases to be an advantage.

Operation CASTOR

The occupation of Dien Bien Phu, Operation CASTOR, began on the morning of November 20, 1953, when two battalions of French paratroopers descended about three miles apart in two drop zones. The 2nd Battalion, 1st Paratroop Chasseur Regiment, met little opposition, but the 6th Colonial Paratroop Battalion got into a firefight with PAVN troops just northwest of the village. Later that afternoon the 1st Colonial Paratroop Battalion landed, along with two batteries of 75mm howitzers, a mortar company, and a surgical unit. By 4:00 P.M. the French had the valley all to themselves as the PAVN forces (minus nearly 100 dead) withdrew.

Over the next few days French aircraft brought in more troops, more supplies, and construction equipment to rebuild the deteriorating fortifications left over from a previous French occupation. Concentrating on two former airfields, the French forces planned to prepare a series of fortified strong points as their base of operations. The larger landing strip, 16,000 yards long, was to the north, along the left bank of the Nam Yum River, while the smaller strip was about five miles to the south on the river's right bank. Two provincial roads ran along the banks of the river, then headed north, south, and northeast out of the valley.

The fortified strong points consisted of eight major bastions, each one surrounded by trenches, outposts, barbed wire, minefields, and bombproof shelters. The main complex of bastions, to the north, comprised seven strong points: Gabrielle, situated by itself at the far northern end of the complex; Béatrice, also somewhat isolated on the far northeastern section on the east bank of the river; Huguette-Françoise, Anne-Marie, and Claudine, protecting the main landing

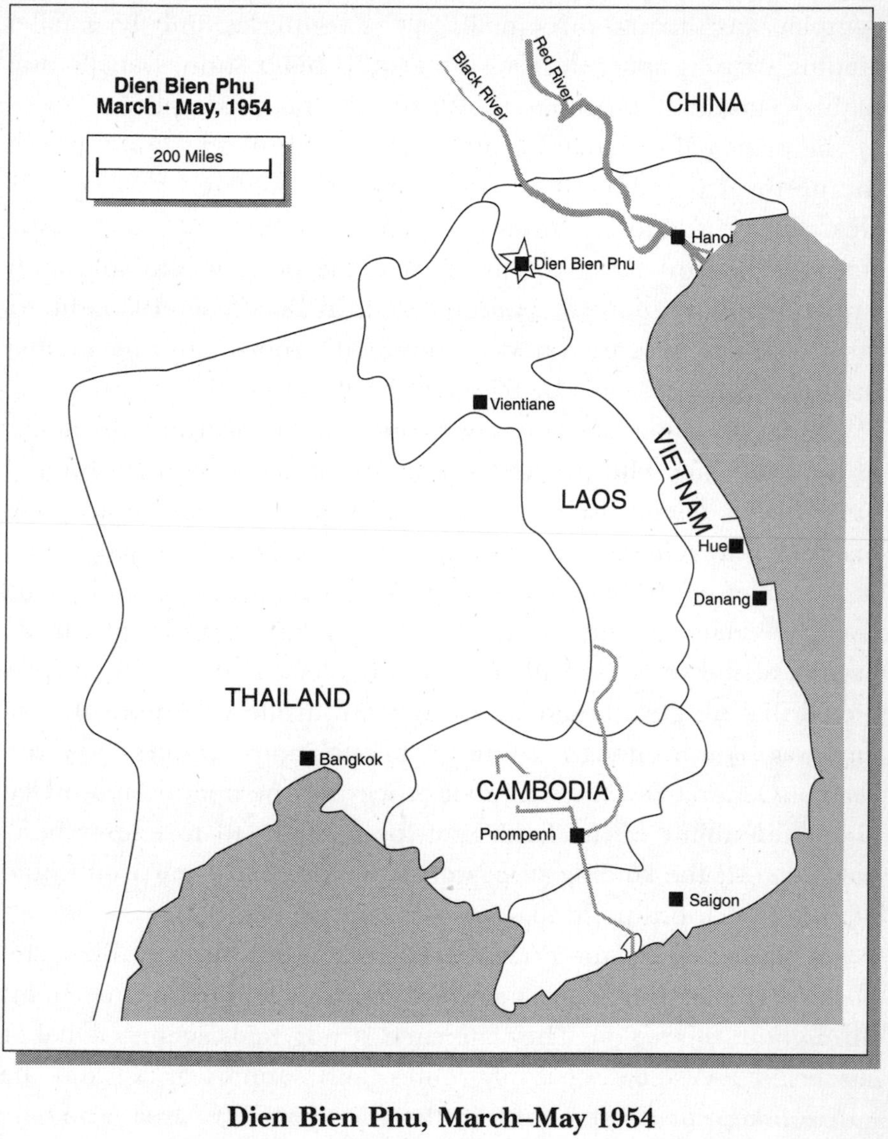
Dien Bien Phu
March - May, 1954
200 Miles
Black River
Red River
CHINA
Hanoi
Dien Bien Phu
Vientiane
VIETNAM
LAOS
Hue
Danang
THAILAND
Bangkok
CAMBODIA
Pnompenh
Saigon

Dien Bien Phu, March–May 1954

strip; and Eliane and Dominique on the east bank of the river, nearer the landing strip, but still separated from it. A supporting complex was situated three miles to the south, around the smaller landing strip. If attacked from the south, this bastion, Isabelle, was highly vulnerable to being cut off from the main complex.

The principal command center was located underground, just to the north of Claudine; the field hospital was situated here as well. Near this central location was a mobile strike force of tanks, howitzers, and infantry. Over the next weeks the position was constantly strengthened, reinforced, and improved. In December 1953, the total strength of the garrison was about 5,000 troops, but this number had more than doubled by the end of February 1954.

The French Command was not of one mind concerning the ability of the Dien Bien Phu position to accomplish its mission (or even of its ability to defend itself against PAVN forces). While Navarre and his chief staff officers were confident that the "bristling hedgehog" of Dien Bien Phu could defeat any PAVN force, they also felt it could decisively damage the overall Viet Minh effort. Colonel Piroth, French artilleryman and deputy commander for the garrison, predicted that his guns would sweep away any artillery weapons the enemy was foolish enough to fire on his positions. Others, however, such as General Fay, the senior air officer for the operation, worried about the ability of the landing strips to hold up to enemy bombardment. If the landing strips were interdicted, the garrison would be in a precarious position.

For three months the French actively utilized the Dien Bien Phu position as a forward base from which to attack and harass the enemy throughout the region. They launched strong raids against actual or suspected PAVN bases, supply routes, and support areas, and the garrison kept up active patrols in the Dien Bien Phu area. The base was used to assist the evacuation of the garrison at Lai Chau (another isolated position farther north), and attempts were made to infiltrate guerrillas behind PAVN lines. Most of these efforts, however, proved only marginally effective, and the use of the base for offensive purposes was generally a failure. By the end of January 1954, the bulk of these offensive operations were abandoned and French efforts shifted from taking the war to the Viet Minh to building up their own defenses at Dien Bien Phu. More troops and artillery were added to the garrison (twelve additional battalions of infantry arrived) and ten M24 Chaffee tanks were flown in and assembled. By the time the actual battle began in the middle of March, the total number of French and colonial troops was 10,800. This represented about 4,350 French regular troops and Legionnaires, 2,850 French colonial troops from Africa and North Africa, and 3,600 Vietnamese regular and auxiliary soldiers.

If the French at Dien Bien Phu had so far proven unsuccessful in taking the war to the enemy's rear areas, they at least hoped for a significant body-count victory by destroying large numbers of attacking PAVN soldiers. Giap, however, saw things slightly differently.

Closing the Trap

The commander of the Viet Minh PAVN forces, acutely aware of the losses he had sustained during the massed human-wave attacks so fervently urged on him by his Chinese advisers, was not about to comply with French expectations. In *Hell in a Very Small Place*, Bernard B. Fall quotes Giap as saying, "We came to the conclusion that we could not secure success if we struck swiftly. In consequence, we resolutely chose the other tactics: To strike surely and advance surely . . . we had solved the problems of closing in, of positioning our artillery, and of getting our supplies through."

Instead of precipitately launching another massed attack and suffering massive casualties, Giap, over a three-month period, methodically assembled elements of four infantry divisions and an independent infantry regiment plus a heavy-weapons division. By early March 1954, he had ringed the French positions in the valley with 50,000 soldiers, supported by about half that number of supply troops. Most important of all, the PAVN forces assembled an astonishing array of artillery, mortars, and antiaircraft weapons.

By disassembling the larger artillery pieces and mortars, Giap's PAVN troops were able to move the bulky weapons over the forbidding terrain and reassemble them in the hills around Dien Bien Phu. When the PAVN units began their all-out battle to seize the position, they had emplaced the fieldpieces of the artillery battalions, which supported the infantry divisions, plus the guns of the 351st Heavy Division, which included twenty-four U.S. 105mm howitzers (half the total number in their possession), fifteen U.S. 75mm pack howitzers, twenty Chinese-Soviet 120mm mortars, forty Chinese-Soviet 82mm mortars, and twelve to sixteen Soviet Katyusha rocket launchers. Some giant Soviet 160mm mortars may also have been present. When one adds the number of guns lugged into the area over the weeks of the battle to those already present with the 351st and the divisional artillery, PAVN forces had over 200 guns larger than 57mm. All forty-eight U.S. 105mm howitzers received from China may eventually have been brought to Dien Bien Phu and used against the garrison. French forces had about sixty artillery pieces and mortars of 57mm or larger on March 13, 1954, but rarely had as many as forty at any one time once the Viet Minh bombardments began.

Protecting the gun emplacements (which were cleverly camouflaged from aerial observation) was an equally impressive array of antiaircraft artillery weapons, including twenty 37mm guns and fifty .50-caliber machine guns. Captured PAVN logistics summaries revealed that by the opening of the battle, the Viet Minh had amassed 40,000 rounds of ammunition of 75mm or larger (including 15,000 105mm) as well as 44,000 rounds of 37mm and smaller. By the end of the battle, French artillerymen estimated that Dien Bien Phu had been hit by at least 30,000 105mm rounds and probably over 100,000 rounds of other calibers.

At 5:00 P.M. on the evening of March 13, 1954, Giap sprang the trap, launching the initial barrage on the surprised garrison.

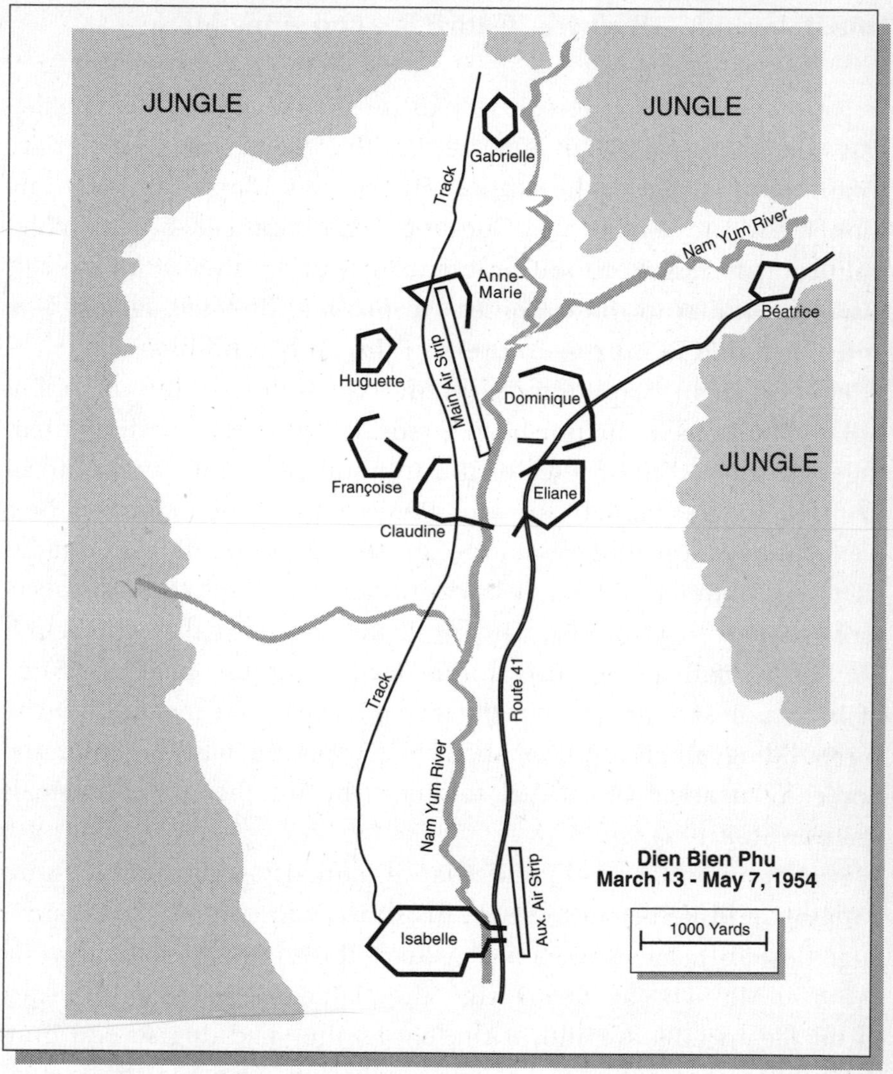
JUNGLE
JUNGLE
JUNGLE
Gabrielle
Track
Nam Yum River
Anne-
Marie
Béatrice
Huguette
Main Air Strip
Dominique
Françoise
Eliane
Claudine
Track
Route 41
Nam Yum River
Dien Bien Phu
March 13 - May 7, 1954
Aux. Air Strip
Isabelle
1000 Yards

Dien Bien Phu, March 13–May 7, 1954

Initial Assaults—Béatrice, Gabrielle, and Anne-Marie

Despite his claims to the contrary in his memoirs, Giap actually began the battle for Dien Bien Phu with one of the human-wave infantry frontal assaults he supposedly rejected. Giap's Chinese Communist adviser, General Wei Guoqing (who eventually became chief political commissar of the Chinese army), urged the use of massive assaults—similar to those Chinese troops had directed against U.S. and UN forces in Korea—to overrun the French positions.

The targets of Giap's attacks on March 13–15 were the somewhat isolated bastions in the northern sector. Following a thundering barrage that turned the center of the tranquil valley into a volcano of fire and smoke, massed waves of PAVN infantrymen stormed Béatrice. Despite appalling casualties, the strong point fell by midnight. Nearly without letup the attacks continued, shifting to the northernmost outpost of Gabrielle, which fell the very next day. On March 15, PAVN infantry swept over Anne-Marie, tenuously held by a force of Indochinese, who gave up the struggle early and melted into the surrounding jungle. Strewn about the captured bastions were the bodies of nearly 3,000 PAVN soldiers (the number of wounded is unknown).

Such a price was too high if Giap intended to capture the entire garrison, and he began to revise his strategy to conform to what he later described in his memoirs. A lull fell over the battlefield while the Viet Minh began to do what they later developed into an art form: digging. By the end of the battle, they had dug several hundred miles of trenches and tunnels, completely ringing the French positions, and gradually constricting them like a python suffocating its prey. While the digging proceeded, the shelling continued to pound the French positions, especially the critically important landing strips.

After the utter failure of French counterbattery fire to silence the PAVN artillery and mortar fire, the French garrison suffered a highly symbolic casualty. Colonel Piroth, the deputy garrison commander who was responsible for French artillery operations—and who had so recently boasted that his guns would wipe out the PAVN—pulled the pin on a hand grenade, clutched it to his chest, and committed suicide.

On March 30, Giap was ready to strike again.

The Second Phase—Battle for the Five Hills

During the lull in the fighting, which lasted about two weeks, French commanders attempted to fly in reinforcements and critically needed supplies, but were severely hampered in their efforts by artillery interdiction on the landing strips, which effectively kept the strips out of action. Airdrops of large quantities of supplies were somewhat effective, but could not keep up with the demand. Already disaster was approaching.

The next phase of the battle, lasting from March 30 to April 4, principally involved attacks against the bastions Huguette, Eliane, and Dominique—the so-called Battle of the Five Hills (Dominique 1 and 2, and Eliane 1, 2, and 4). Giap's troops, jumping off from hidden trenches within a few hundred feet of the French positions, assaulted Dominique and captured three of the fortified positions in the bastion. Counterattacks by Legionnaires failed to retake the lost positions, and the PAVN troops prepared to extend their gains to other positions within the complex. Eliane, sharing Dominique's exposed position on the east bank of the river, was also vigorously attacked and partially overrun.

Meanwhile the Viet Minh assaulted the outer defenses of Huguette on April 1, and part of the airstrip was in their hands by the end of April 2. With all available counterattack forces attempting to regain Dominique and Eliane, little outside assistance was available for the Huguette defenders. Nonetheless, PAVN gains were kept to the outerworks of Huguette and part of the airstrip.

On April 2, the PAVN 304th Division attacked isolated Isabelle in force. Fierce hand-to-hand combat ensued, and the French garrison of 1,600 was seriously threatened for some time. For the moment, however, Isabelle held, as did Huguette and parts of the Five Hills. By the time this phase of the fighting died down on April 4, PAVN forces held two strong points in Dominique, one in Eliane, and part of the airstrip. The total infantry strength of the garrison had been reduced to 4,500 effectives, despite reinforcement attempts by airdrops (including the jump of the 2nd Battalion, 1st Paratroop Chasseurs, on the night of April 1). Over the next few weeks the French High Command made repeated efforts to build up the garrison's strength through airdrops, with somewhat mixed results. On the night of April 11, for example, 850 Foreign Legion infantry volunteers were dropped over the Dien Bien Phu DZ. About 340 of these landed within Viet Minh lines and were killed or captured. These difficulties were compounded by the early onset of the worst monsoons in years.

Inching Closer—Attrition Warfare

The rains made life within the French garrison, already miserable, an agony. In addition to interfering with the airdrops and reducing the flow of supplies, the nearly constant rainfall turned the French strong points into sodden mud holes. Water seeped into everything, and no bunker was protection against it. At first, the French thought the wet weather would be a hindrance to their attackers, but soon realized quite the contrary was happening. The trench lines were creeping closer.

Isabelle was completely surrounded during the latter half of April and, since its tiny airstrip was useless, received only intermittent airdrop resupply. At about this same time renewed PAVN assaults against the northern sector resulted in the loss of three critical strong points in Huguette and more of the landing strip. The French garrison lost over 500 badly needed troops in this fight. Their situation was rapidly growing desperate.

In the second half of April, Navarre agreed to initiate Operation CONDOR, a last-ditch attempt to rescue the garrison by sending in a relief column. Originally meant to annihilate repulsed PAVN troops, recoiling from their battering by the Dien Bien Phu garrison, the plan had to be quickly changed to a desperate rescue mission. Launched between April 14 and 27, Operation CONDOR failed to punch through to the besieged garrison in time. The North African and Laotian troops of the CONDOR force were too inexperienced in jungle warfare and their mission was launched too late for any chance of success. By this time, anyway, Giap's units were positioned for the final assault.

Final Assault and End—May 1 to May 8

Giap felt pressured to bring the battle to a close during the latter part of April and the beginning of May. The Geneva Peace Conference was about to begin, and like the Chinese and North Koreans during the latter stages of the Korean War, he and Ho wanted substantive gains and unchallengeable victories to take to the conference table. Giap had been continually building up his forces in the area over the last few weeks while inching ever closer to the remaining French strong points. By May 1, he was ready to attack.

Reverting again to human-wave-like frontal assaults, PAVN units were more successful in avoiding massive casualties, since their jumping-off points were now only a few yards from the French trenches. Forgoing any preparatory barrage, Viet Minh troops threw themselves out of their trenches and tunnels and onto the French defenders. Counterattacking with fixed bayonets, French soldiers were able to recapture some of the lost positions, only to lose them again in the next PAVN attack. Trench by trench, bunker by bunker, Huguette and Claudine were overrun, and Eliane was in danger of falling. On the morning of May 7, the last strong points were overpowered and the French commander, Colonel Castries, ordered the fighting to stop at 5:30 P.M.

At now cut-off Isabelle, three miles to the south, the 1,600-man garrison still held out, but was close to falling. Castries gave Isabelle's commander, Colonel Lalande, permission to attempt a breakout, but this proved futile. After a 10:00 P.M. sortie by two companies failed,

Lalande surrendered Isabelle's garrison at 1:30 A.M. on May 8. The battle was over.

Aftermath

Shortly after the French tricolor was torn down and the Viet Minh's red flag with its single gold star rose over Dien Bien Phu on May 8, 1954, nearly 6,500 French officers and soldiers marched into captivity. Many of them, weakened by the siege, wounds, and disease, would not survive the brutal march or their months in confinement. Behind them, they left 2,200 dead comrades, and another 10,000 wounded and missing. Counting CONDOR casualties and prisoners of war, the French probably lost about 20,000 troops during the Dien Bien Phu campaign. Giap lost more, probably about 8,000 killed, with an additional 15,000 wounded. Given the primitive state of PAVN field medical care, it seems likely that a significant number of the wounded eventually died. In all, the better part of 50,000 men perished or became casualties in the valley of Dien Bien Phu.

The reasons for the French loss are several, but two stand out most clearly: their underestimation of the Viet Minh's capabilities, and the surprising ability of Giap's rather primitive army to solve major logistics problems. Navarre never imagined that the Viet Minh were capable of massing most of four full divisions of infantry plus heavy weapons in the remote river valley on Vietnam's western border, let alone of sustaining such a force for a prolonged siege. Primarily for that reason, the French forces allocated to the Dien Bien Phu campaign were never large enough to accomplish the mission Navarre planned. Neither did Navarre expect Giap to abandon frontal-assault tactics. The French commander, who privately admitted his suspicion that Dien Bien Phu might eventually fall, assumed the garrison would inflict huge numbers of casualties on the Viet Minh, even if it was, in the end, overrun. Such a "victory," if it could be achieved, would clearly have been Pyrrhic.

Giap's solving of the logistics problem is remarkable, given the fact that his army relied almost exclusively on human transport. While

French forces, backed by unchallenged airpower and modern tools of war, were unable to adequately supply a garrison of 10,000 (usually less than that during the siege), PAVN forces maintained a field force of 50,000 fighting men, 20,000 to 30,000 supply troops and porters, and 200 artillery pieces over jungle trails and remote mountain wilderness.

The Viet Minh victory at Dien Bien Phu ended the last hope of French empire in Indochina. Discouraged by the conflict and tired of sending young Frenchmen to faraway places to be slaughtered by people who only seemed to be defending their own territory, the French public forced its politicians' hands. As Ho, speaking to France, had prophesied: "You can kill ten of my men for every one I kill of yours, but even at those odds, you will lose and I will win." If only the United States had paid attention to his words.

CHAPTER EIGHT

The Yom Kippur War

• OCTOBER 1973 •

BATTLES OF THE SINAI
AND GOLAN HEIGHTS

A War of Atonement

The Arab-Israeli War that raged from October 6–25, 1973, was different from the previous conflicts between these intractable Middle Eastern enemies. This time, a surprise attack by Arab forces marked the war's beginning. Striking during the Jewish holiday of Yom Kippur, the Day of Atonement, allied Arab units, principally Egyptian and Syrian, caught the Israelis in a rare state of unpreparedness. Uncharacteristically reluctant to heed the available intelligence that was predicting the upcoming attack, the Israeli Defense Force had to scramble to recall soldiers from leave and to move rapidly to mobilize reservists. In an unusual show of unity and coordination among the fractious Arab nations, Egypt and Syria carefully timed their assaults to obtain the maximum impact. Israeli forces had come to regard complete dominance over Arab armies as a matter of course and were, therefore, surprised when the Arabs, especially Egyptian forces in the Sinai, proved tough and competent fighters. In the end, however, Israel rallied to again defeat its Arab enemies.

Suez Canal, 2:30 P.M., October 6, 1973: *Under cover of an artillery barrage of 2,000 Egyptian cannon—firing over 100,000 rounds within the first hour alone—1,000 rubber assault boats ferried 8,000 Egyptian commandos across the 100-yard-wide Suez Canal. After rising ropes and bamboo scaling ladders to scramble up the eighty-foot earthen berm the Israelis had constructed to restrict the landing of mechanized forces, Egyptian commandos fanned out to predetermined positions (some as far as ten miles inside the Israeli lines), armed with swarms of wire-guided antitank missiles to intercept the inevitable Israeli armored counterattack.*

Hot on their heels were Egyptian engineers, assembling Soviet pontoon assault bridges at a rate of nearly fifteen feet per minute at ten locations in preparation for crossing the main force. Other engineers, now executing in real combat an exercise they had rehearsed in secret training camps over 300 times over the past three years, used high-pressure water hoses to blast seventy-seven gaps in the Israeli sand berms, moving 640,000 tons of sand in the process. As soon as the pontoon bridges spanned the canal, the main assault force crossed and then hurried through lanes in the Israeli minefields that had been blown open by specially trained gun crews using 50mm mortars (after firing 6,000 rounds per crew—eighty-seven times the annual rate for normal gunnery practice!).

Protected by hundreds of Egyptian aircraft, which swooped over the assault bridgeheads and managed, along with dozens of batteries of surface-to-air missiles (SAMs), to keep the Israeli air force away from the crossing points, five entire Egyptian infantry divisions—over 40,000 troops—made the transfer to the east bank within the first ten hours of the operation. Soon after the infantry divisions crossed, their supporting armored formations of 800 tanks arrived. By daylight on October 7, the follow-on mechanized divisions of the main attacking Egyptian Second and Third Armies were ready to strike out of the two bridgeheads into the Israeli-occupied Sinai.

Proceeding like clockwork, this "Great Crossing" of the Suez Canal deserves a place among the many fine military actions of the century, and it is doubtful that any of the world's "major" armies could have executed it better. Seeing the Suez operation proceeding rapidly and successfully on its southwestern flank while simultaneously receiving determined Syrian attacks on the all-important Golan Heights in the northeast, Israel must have wondered at this dramatic transformation of their usually bickering Arab enemies. Had the Egyptian and Syrian field commanders been able to sustain the attack, the outcome of this war might have been altogether different. But after a promising start, characterized by several Israeli errors in judgment, the Egyptian-Syrian offensive bogged down, allowing Israel to gain the initiative. By the middle of October, the tide of war had shifted to Israel.

The years leading up to the Yom Kippur War saw the Arab armies continually built up by their Soviet sponsors and regular cross-border raids and small-to-large-scale engagements between Israel and its Arab neighbors. More and more the scene of a superpower confrontation between the United States and the Soviet Union, the Middle East between 1968 and 1973 was splitting up into Soviet client states like Egypt, Syria, and Iraq, on the one hand, and U.S.-backed Israel, on the other. The survival of the state of Israel became a crucial part of U.S. foreign policy during this time, a goal that went hand in hand with efforts to contain Soviet expansion.

Weapons and Tactics

By 1973, Israeli forces were principally equipped with American-made major weapons systems and aircraft while Arab forces possessed Soviet weapons and planes—although the Israelis, of necessity, possessed weapons from other sources as well. Since the main theater of battle was again the desert, the principal weapon was the main battle tank—although in this instance it was seriously challenged by infantry employing wire-guided missiles.

On the Arab side, the standard tank was the Soviet T-54/55, supplemented by smaller numbers of the T-62. Mounting a 100mm main gun, the T-54/55 provided adequate service, although its target acquisition over long distances was poor. Egypt had about 1,500 of these tanks and Syria probably about 1,000. Both sides had several hundred T-62 tanks, which, with its improved fire control and 115mm smoothbore main gun, was a formidable weapon. The Arab armies also had lesser quantities of older tanks, such as the WWII-vintage T-34/85. Israeli armored formations used a variety of tanks, but the best were the British Centurions and the U.S. M48s and M60s. Other tanks in the Israeli inventory included "super" Shermans (WWII-vintage M4s up-gunned with a 105mm main gun) and captured Soviet models, modified for Israeli use.

The second part of the triad of modern combined arms warfare is artillery. The Soviets had lavishly provided their Arab clients with artillery pieces, and these saw extensive use. Models represented all types then available in the Soviet system, principally the 85mm, 100mm, and 122mm gun-howitzer, including self-propelled versions of the latter. Also valuable in this desert war were the Soviet 130mm guns, capable of hurling a projectile nearly twenty miles. Israeli artillery was seriously outnumbered during the war, and a shortage of guns was a definite handicap at its beginning. Principal Israeli artillery pieces included the U.S. M109 (155mm) howitzer and the long-range U.S. M107 (175mm) gun.

The third part of the triad, infantry, nearly proved to be the downfall of Israeli forces in the Sinai when, early on, Israeli-tank counterattacks unprotected by infantry, were stopped by Egyptian forces employing wire-guided antitank missiles. The Soviets provided the Egyptians and Syrians with huge numbers of Sagger and other models of these tank killers, and the initial Arab assault forces employed them with great skill (in fact, the Egyptian Sagger teams were forbidden to take leave for months before the outbreak of the war lest their skills deteriorate). Israel also possessed U.S. and German versions of these antitank missiles (Dragon, TOW, and Cobra), but not in the numbers held by its enemy. Both sides' infantry soldiers were armed with the complete range of modern infantry small-arms and crew-served weapons, Soviet on one side, American (and, increasingly, Israeli) on the other. Soviet infantry weapons included the ubiquitous AK-47 assault rifle, 82mm and 120mm mortars, and 7.62mm to 14.5mm machine guns. Israeli infantry used M16 rifles, Uzi submachine guns, 81mm-to-4.2-inch mortars, and 7.62mm, .30-caliber, and .50-caliber machine guns.

Once their reservists brought the combat formations up to strength, the Israelis had an advantage in tactical mobility of infantry due to the large number of armored personnel carriers in their force structure (about 6,000 in October 1973). Arab forces had the advantage in antiaircraft artillery weapons and surface-to-air missile systems, and (probably remembering the lesson delivered by Israeli pilots on June 5, 1967) used hundreds of these weapons to protect their ground forces and critical installations. Gun systems included the excellent Soviet radar-directed models, and SAM systems were of all types, including the handheld SA-7. At the beginning of the war, Israel possessed about 450 combat aircraft to Egypt's 500 and Syria's 300. The Israeli air force, which failed to destroy the Arab air forces on the ground as they had done in 1967, was not as decisive as it had been in the earlier war. Nevertheless, for a loss of 100 of its own aircraft, Israel destroyed about 370 of the Arab planes (two thirds of these Egyptian).

The belligerents in this particular Arab-Israeli encounter employed somewhat different tactics from earlier conflicts, at least in the initial phases. After the Egyptians' brilliant crossing of the canal, the first Israeli counterattacks used the "armored charge" tactics that had been so effective in earlier wars. This time, however, the presence in considerable numbers of wire-guided missiles made such tactics a disaster. Recovering quickly, however, the Israelis reverted to more traditional combined arms tactics (although delivered in the now characteristically bold and daring Israeli style). Longtime disciples of Liddell Hart's "indirect approach," Israeli battlefield commanders always attempt to attack the enemy's weak points and, with Liddell Hart's "expanding torrent" as a guide, exploit any success with imaginative and vigorous action. For their part, the Arab armies attempted to put the Soviet military doctrine of their Russian advisers into practice. At first, in crossing the canal and establishing strong bridgeheads in the Sinai, they seemed to achieve stunning success, but Egyptian commanders failed to exploit their early victories. Much the same was true on the Syrian front, although the specialized terrain of the Golan Heights provided additional obstacles and leadership challenges. The Israelis, shaken at first, and suffering some dramatic setbacks, quickly adjusted their tactics. The Arabs, though finally seeming to have found an organization and a doctrine that fit their particular military situation, saw victory quickly slip from their grasp.

The Battles of the Sinai and Golan Heights

October 6–25, 1973

Deception and Intelligence

Plenty of evidence was available to Israeli intelligence by October 1973 that the Arab nations, principally Egypt, were planning a massive strike. Possessing the best intelligence network in the Middle East—arguably the best in the world—Israeli political and military leaders were briefed on several ominous developments in Egypt and Syria. Military activity on the Egyptian side of the Suez Canal, and within Syria directly below the Golan Heights, had been occurring for weeks when, suddenly, the families of Russian advisers were evacuated from the two countries. For several days Israeli soldiers occupying the fortifications on the east bank of the Suez Canal reported unusual activity on the Egyptian side and, by October 5, had informed their higher headquarters that at least five Egyptian infantry divisions supported by large numbers of tanks were massed behind the 160-foot-high sand berms on the canal's west bank. They also observed 200 batteries of Egyptian artillery and large quantities of bridging equipment. Some kind of large-scale attack was clearly imminent.

The Egyptians had, in fact, attempted to screen the deployments and preparations, hiding troop movements in the cloaks of scheduled training exercises practicing the intricate Suez Canal crossing maneuver in sealed camps in the Nile Delta, and camouflaging the demining of assault lanes in the canal as defensive mine-laying operations. The date for the attack was scheduled to coincide with Ramadan, the Muslim holy days. Combined with a government-controlled press that actively participated in a public disinformation campaign, the deception plan seems to have reinforced the idea of higher levels of Israel's government that a major attack was *not* imminent.

Special international and domestic political issues also influenced the Israeli government to avoid premature mobilization. Because of superpower competition in the region, Israel was compelled to appear to be always acting in its own defense. Too early mobilization of its reserves could be interpreted as "aggressive" or "provocative" actions by Arab states, their Soviet sponsor, and sympathizers in the UN. Domestically, a too early mobilization of large numbers of reservists could have had devastating consequences on the fragile Israeli economy. At any rate, the Jewish religious holiday of Yom Kippur had arrived, and officials did not want to disturb the civilian population or cancel military leaves and passes. Despite desperate attempts by some intelligence officials and a few military officers to provide warnings of the attack, the necessary steps to mobilize were not taken. Prime Minister Golda Meir, Defense Minister Moshe Dayan, and other government officials did, however, become sufficiently alarmed to schedule an emergency cabinet to discuss the situation at 2:00 P.M. on October 6, 1973. At that very moment 2,000 Egyptian cannon were firing the opening barrage of the Yom Kippur War.

Attack in the Sinai—The Great Crossing

Even before the main attacks of the war began on the afternoon of October 6, commando attacks had been carried out against Israeli oil pipelines. Intended to prevent the Israeli defenders from turning the Suez Canal into a "fire lake" of burning oil, these Egyptian operations blocked the pipes without the defenders even realizing it.

The crossing itself was initiated by a massive barrage (probably 1 million rounds of artillery and rockets were fired during the operation), followed closely by the attacks of several hundred aircraft. While the engineers assembled the pontoon bridges and washed away gaps in the sand mountains with water cannon, the Egyptian commandos bypassed the Israeli strong points along the canal and moved into positions in a three-to-ten-mile strip of territory behind the fortified line to intercept the arrival of armored reinforcements. The Israeli defensive line was to be taken by the follow-on forces.

Called the "Bar-Lev Line" after a former Israeli chief of staff, the extended defensive position consisted of sixteen fortified strong points garrisoned by about 500 reservists and supported by 100 tanks (300 tanks when reinforced on full-alert status). Backed up by two more lines of defensive positions (prepared but not manned), the Bar-Lev Line extended about 100 miles along the east bank of the Suez Canal. Supporting it was one division-sized unit of three brigades, the 265th Ugda, commanded by Major General Mandler. Because of the Yom Kippur holiday, among other things, the positions in the line were undermanned—a few were unmanned—when the attack began. Although they were bypassed in the initial assault, the Egyptian commandos later captured all but one of the Bar-Lev strong points (a few were evacuated under fire by daring Israeli relief raids). One strong point in the far north of the line held out until the end of the war.

Mandler's reserve armored units, in accordance with contingency plans, were quickly launched on counterattacks to take up prepared positions along the supporting lines, relieve the fortified strong points, and repel the Egyptian incursions. But these tank units, lacking much of their supporting infantry and thrown at the Egyptian forces in a piecemeal fashion, were repulsed with heavy losses. Using the armored charge tactics that had been so effective against Arab forces in 1967, Mandler's unsupported tank brigades lost about 200 of their 300 tanks by the end of the first day's fighting (one brigade lost 75 of 100 tanks). Most of the losses were to the swarms of wire-guided antitank missiles with which the Egyptian assault troops had been liberally armed.

By the end of the first full day's fighting on the Sinai front, the Egyptians had moved five infantry divisions and their supporting armored vehicles across the canal, defeated several Israeli armored counterattacks, and were consolidating their two major bridgeheads

MEDITERRANEAN SEA
Port Said
Yom Kippur War
October 1973
25 Miles
Suez Canal
Bar-Lev Line
Egyptian Attack
Furthest Egyptian Advance
Israeli Counterattacks
Furthest Israeli Advance
Bar-Lev Line Fortified Strong Points
XXXX
SECOND
Egyptian
Suez Canal
Southern
Command
Gonen/Bar-Lev
Ismailiya
GREAT
BITTER
LAKE
Giddi
Pass
2
XXXX
3
Mitla
Pass
XXX
THIRD
Egyptian

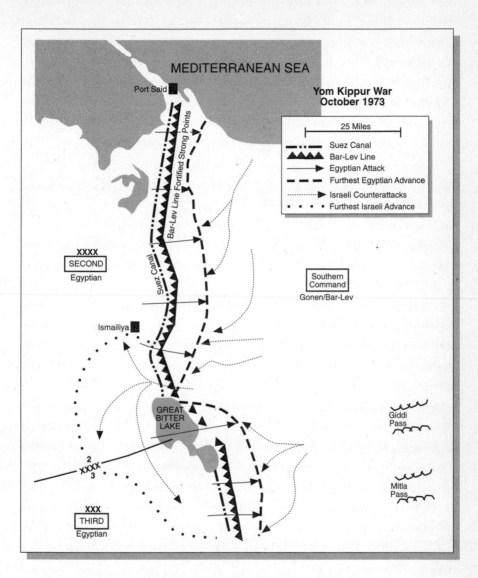

Yom Kippur War, October 1973

in preparation for crossing the armored and mechanized divisions. On October 7, the Egyptian force on the east bank numbered at least 40,000 troops (some sources claim 80,000), backed up by the first of about 800 tanks. Significantly, however, in terms of the battle's outcome, the Egyptian heliborne commandos sent to seize the strategically important desert passes at Mitla and Giddi were defeated. Israel, therefore, still held the keys to reinforcing their hard-pressed units in the Sinai and reversing the battle's tide.

Recovery and Counterattack

Used to reacting rapidly to Arab threats, the Israeli High Command began mobilizing reservists and reorganizing the Sinai front as soon as they realized the scope and nature of the attack. The day after the Egyptian assault, reservists started to arrive in their units. Given the suddenness of the attack and the simultaneous Syrian offensive against the Golan Heights, this particular mobilization was conducted with singular desperation. As they arrived at their mobilization points, reservists were frequently formed into makehift units (instead of joining their designated combat units), and in many cases, individuals were formed into hastily gathered tank and artillery crews and dispatched immediately to the front. Stories of reservists driving their own automobiles to the Golan front and reporting directly to their units under fire were common. Despite the late start, Israel's reservists confounded their Arab enemies by mobilizing with unbelievable rapidity and, in a matter of days, most were in combat. Arab planners had estimated that the mobilization would take a week.

The first reservists arrived in the Sinai on October 7 to find the front (referred to as the Southern Front; the Northern Front was against Syria on the Golan Heights) in the throes of hasty reorganization. Under the overall command of General Shmuel Gonen, the Southern Front became a three-division operation. In the north was General Adan's 162nd Armored Ugda, probably composed of three armored brigades, a paratrooper brigade, and an infantry brigade.

Recalled to active duty to command the center division was General Arik Sharon, whose 143rd Armored Ugda also contained three armored brigades, a brigade of paratroopers, and an infantry brigade. Mandler's battered Ugda took over the southernmost portion of the front.

Gonen ordered Adan to conduct a sweeping, southward-moving counterattack on October 7 and 8 in an attempt to roll up the Egyptian line from the north, while Mandler held firm in the south. Sharon was to launch a supporting attack when ordered. Adan's counterattack, however, ran into serious problems, despite what seemed to be easy initial going. Executing his southward sweep too far to the east to roll up the Egyptian line, Adan merely drove his tanks in front of enemy positions. Since many of his tank units were still unsupported by sufficient numbers of infantry, the Egyptian wire-guided antitank missiles once again inflicted serious casualties. One entire tank battalion of the 190th Armored Brigade was wiped out in this attack, and the battalion commander was captured.

Misinterpreting Adan's easy progress in the early stages as battle-field success, Gonen ordered Sharon's units to begin their attack, then, recognizing the true situation, countermanded his order. Sharon, a brilliant commander but a difficult subordinate, clashed with Gonen (whom he outranked), leading to Gonen's request that Sharon be relieved of command. This confrontation led to the recall from retirement and appointment of Chaim Bar-Lev as Southern Front commander, with Gonen as his subordinate. Bar-Lev also requested that Sharon be relieved, but Dayan let the volatile but talented commander stay on. This bickering was distracting to the Israeli command, but the Egyptian commanders were incapable of capitalizing on it.

Momentum Shifts—Sinai Counteroffensive

After establishing their two bridgeheads on the east bank of the Suez Canal and successfully thwarting the initial Israeli counterattacks to dislodge them, the Egyptian Second and Third Armies were presented with an opportunity to launch their main armored forces and seize the key Sinai passes at Giddi and Mitla. Perhaps they were stunned by the success of their canal crossing, but whatever the reason, the Egyptian commanders were slow to begin the next, crucial phase of the Sinai offensive, and spent the next few critical days consolidating their bridgeheads and moving armored units across the canal. In doing so, they ignored the tactical doctrine of their Soviet mentors, which called for an immediate and vigorous advance in order to exploit their recent success. This mistake was heightened by a particularly aggressive "defense" mounted by Sharon's Ugda. Forgoing the passive defense ordered by the Southern Front commander, who wished to buy time in order to build up Israeli forces, Sharon's armored units struck at the Egyptian positions, penetrating them in several places and extracting survivors who still held out in some of the Bar-Lev Line strong points.

The Egyptian effort to break out of the bridgeheads and capture the passes was launched on October 14 by five armored and mechanized columns over a ninety-mile front. Using over 1,000 (possibly as many as 1,500) tanks, Egyptian forces attempted to engage the Israelis all along the broad front while simultaneously moving to outflank the main defensive positions. Occurring as much as a week after it should have, the attack was a complete disaster. Facing well-prepared and reinforced Israeli units, including tanks dug into hull-down positions, the Egyptian tanks and armored vehicles proved to be little more than targets for Israeli gunnery practice. Moving out into the open desert and away from their blanket of antiaircraft protection, the Egyptian tanks also exposed themselves to decimation by Israeli aircraft, a vulnerability the Israelis were quick to exploit. By the end of October 14, the Egyptians had lost nearly 500 tanks and armored vehicles against an Israeli loss of about 40. Heralded as the greatest tank engagement since the 1943 battle of Kursk, the massive armored battle was a decisive Israeli win. The best chance for Arab victory had been wasted.

With Egyptian forces now completely on the eastern bank of the Suez Canal (only about one armored brigade was left on the west bank), the conditions were perfect for one of those daring, war-winning maneuvers that have characterized Israeli warfare style for forty-five years, and Arik Sharon was the perfect commander to execute it. The Israeli plan was to split the Egyptian Second and Third Armies in two while simultaneously sending Sharon's Ugda to the west bank of the canal to cut both armies off from their bases. Punching a corridor between the Egyptian Second and Third Armies near a strong point misnamed the Chinese Farm (it had been, in fact, a Japanese experimental station) at 5:00 P.M. on October 15, Sharon's infantry forces began crossing the canal at an unguarded point at the north end of the Great Bitter Lake. Despite hard fighting around the Chinese Farm and suggestions that the forces across the canal be withdrawn, the Israeli counteroffensive pressed on, eventually strengthening the narrow corridor and getting armored forces across to reinforce the west bank. On October 17, a major pontoon bridge was thrown across the canal and a large Egyptian attack to destroy the corridor was repulsed with heavy losses (the Egyptians lost eighty-six of the ninety-six tanks and all their support vehicles). By the end of October 18, large Israeli armored forces were established on the west bank, the corridor was secured, and a steady flow of traffic into and out of the west-bank pocket was assured. By leaving a recently formed reserve Ugda along with some of the veteran armored forces on the east bank to prevent the Egyptians from moving any farther east, the bulk of the Southern Front forces was transferred to the west bank of the canal. Another week of vicious fighting followed, but this bold Israeli counteroffensive had trapped the main Egyptian forces, effectively ending the Sinai campaign.

The Yom Kippur War, however, was being fought on two fronts. While these desert battles in the Sinai raged, desperate fighting was also occurring on the Syrian front.

Attack in the north—The Battle for the Golan Heights

The Syrian assault on the Israeli-occupied Golan Heights was timed to coincide with the Egyptian attack across the Suez Canal: at 2:00 P.M. on October 6. The Syrian plan was simple enough, calling for general attacks by the three infantry divisions and their tanks sitting opposite the Israeli positions; the goal was to open gaps in the Israeli lines that could then be exploited by the two armored divisions located to the rear of the infantry units. Once Syrian units overran the Golan Heights, their forces planned to push on to capture Tiberias, then cut off the whole north of Israel.

In their first-line assault units, the Syrians had about 700 tanks. The Israeli units manning the "Purple Line" defensive positions on the Golan Heights were elements of the 7th Armored Brigade (situated on the northern end of the line, from Mount Hermon south to Al Kuneitra), the 188th Armored Brigade (occupying twenty-five miles of more open country from Kuneitra south to the Jordanian border), and an infantry brigade. With fewer than 200 tanks, the Syrians outnumbered the Israelis three to one in armor.

With the fire of 1,300 artillery pieces supported by air units, the Syrian infantry divisions began their assault on the Purple Line. Initially, the Syrian assault units' inability to deal rapidly with the antitank ditch the Israeli defenders had constructed along the entire length of the Purple Line delayed their advance. Syrian forces planned to cross the ditch at multiple locations using mobile armored assault bridges, but Israeli artillery destroyed many of these before they could be brought up and emplaced. As a result, the advance moved more slowly than planned, which gave the Israelis time to mobilize. Nevertheless, with the weight of numbers on their side, the Syrian forces were able to push back the defenders.

In the north, the Israeli 7th Armored Brigade had reasonably good luck in preventing a major breakthrough, although Syrian paratroopers in helicopters captured the key position anchoring the northern end of the Purple Line, Mount Hermon, on the first day. After an initial Israeli counterattack was smashed later that day, the Israeli 1st Infantry Brigade retook the position during a night assault. Although some penetrations had been made by midnight on October 7, the line in the north was holding fairly well. During the first two days of the war, the 7th Brigade destroyed about 200 Syrian tanks and another 260 mobile bridges and armored personnel carriers. In the southern part of the front, however, the situation was critical.

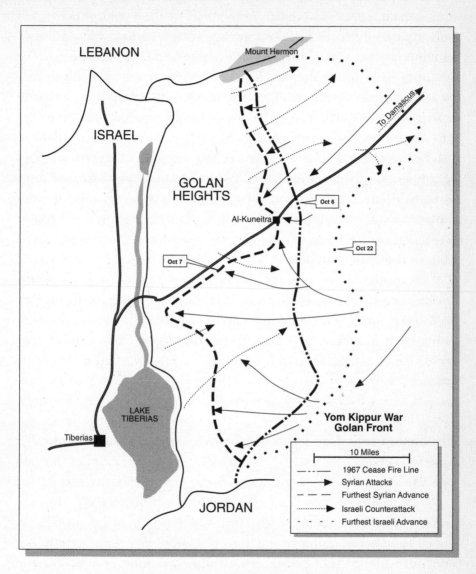

Yom Kippur War, Golan Front

The 188th Armored Brigade, defending the more open country south of Kuneitra, was essentially overrun by the Syrian 9th and 5th Infantry Divisions and their supporting armor. Syrian units advanced as many as ten miles into the Israeli lines and threatened to take positions from which they could launch their armored divisions in a decisive thrust into Israel. But just in time to prevent a complete collapse of the Golan Front, Israeli armored reserve formations began appearing in front of the Syrian units. These formations, patched together with arriving reservists by frantic officers at the foot of the Golan plateau and then thrown into combat as soon as they assembled enough tanks and crews to form a fighting unit, blunted the Syrian attack and saved the front from disintegration. Of major assistance to the effort on the ground was the commitment of the bulk of the Israeli combat air assets to this Northern Front. Lacking the overpowering antiaircraft assets of the Egyptians, the Syrians could not prevent Israel's airpower from devastating its ground effort. Short on SAMs and forced to recall much of its air defense assets from the front to protect domestic targets from a massive Israeli air campaign, Syria left its units extremely vulnerable to air attack.

Northern Front Counteroffensive—Victory on the Golan

By October 9, the Syrian advance on the Golan Heights had stalled for good under increasing Israeli air attacks and sharp counterattacks on the ground. The 7th Armored Brigade in the north, reduced to only seven operational tanks by October 9, had nonetheless held off superior numbers of Syrian attackers long enough for the reconstituted 188th Armored Brigade to arrive and prevent further Syrian incursions. To the south of Kuneitra, the 19th, 20th, and 79th Armored Brigades were poised to join an Israeli counteroffensive on the same day. With the initial Syrian attack stopped (the Syrians had probably lost 600 tanks by October 9) and the Egyptians taking their time preparing for their breakout from the Suez bridgeheads, the Israeli High Command decided to deliver a knockout blow against

Syria before turning their efforts on the Egyptians. October 10 was set as the date for the northern counteroffensive.

The Israeli northern offensive was a two-pronged attack launched over concentrated areas to the north and south of Kuneitra. On the north end of the line, the 188th Armored Brigade and a strengthened 7th Armored Brigade carried out the principal assault, while the 19th, 20th, and 79th Armored Brigades attacked in the far south, and two additional brigades fought nearer the center. Striking a mostly played-out Syrian force, the Israelis made good progress and, by October 13, had punched a huge salient in the Syrian front lines, reaching halfway to Damascus. But here the Israeli attack lost its momentum. A massive influx of Soviet equipment and ammunition, begun about the same time as the counteroffensive, was by now pouring into Syria and stiffening the Syrian defenses. Assisting the Syrians in slowing the Israeli advance were counterattacks launched between October 13 to 18 by allied Arab units, including the Iraqi 3rd Armored Division and the Jordanian 40th Tank Brigade. The Israeli forces were able to defeat each of these counterattacks and inflict heavy losses on the Arab units in the process, but the fighting succeeded in wearing down the Israeli attackers and contributed to their decision to give up on further advances on the Northern Front. The opposing forces eventually settled into a stalemate along the limit of advance the Israelis reached on October 18. By this time, with the critical Golan area relatively secure, the Israeli main effort had already shifted back to the Sinai to complete the destruction of the Egyptian forces.

Aftermath

As the Israeli forces, once again, demonstrated superiority over their enemies, absorbing the severest blow the Arabs had yet delivered, then counterattacking to defeat Egypt and Syria decisively, the superpowers stepped in to limit the conflict. Working through the UN and applying pressure to their respective client states in the region, the United States and the Soviet Union brokered a cease-fire for

October 22. The Israelis, understandably reluctant to cut off their successful counteroffensives before achieving all their objectives, continued their attacks for another three days, finally stopping the fighting, and the war, on October 25.

The cost on both sides was substantial, and once more, the Arabs lost more men and matériel than the Israelis. The Egyptians and Syrians together probably lost about 19,000 killed, 51,000 wounded, and close to 10,000 captured (although at the conclusion of the fighting the entire Egyptian Third Army was surrounded by the Israelis). But Israeli casualties had not been light. The IDF lost over 600 officers (including General Mandler) and 6,900 troops. Additionally, about 370 Israeli soldiers had been captured on the Northern and Southern Fronts. Equipment losses were extremely high. The Arab forces lost approximately 1,300 tanks and 370 combat aircraft, while Israeli losses included 840 tanks and about 100 combat aircraft. In terms of territory, the Israelis had pushed the Syrians back completely from the Golan Heights and occupied an additional 160 square miles of Syrian land, while, on the Southern Front, Israeli forces on the west bank of the Suez Canal held 600 square miles of Egypt.

Despite the one-sidedness of the outcome, the Israeli victory was tarnished by the surprisingly effective performance of the Arab forces, especially the Egyptians. The Great Crossing was a superb tactical achievement and the individual Egyptian soldier fought tenaciously. The relatively strong showing of the Arab forces was one of the major factors in both sides agreeing to serious peace negotiations (which eventually led to the U.S.-sponsored Camp David Accords). Closer relations between the United States and Egypt have developed since the end of the war, and this has assisted in maintaining peace in the region. Despite smoldering conflict, all-out war between Israel and the Arab states has been avoided.

CHAPTER NINE

The Gulf War

• 1991 •

THE 100-HOUR
AIRLAND BATTLE

Hail Mary! The U.S. Military's Greatest 100 Hours

After forty days and nights of incessant pounding in the most one-sided air campaign of modern warfare, the ground forces of the U.S.-led Allied Coalition began the most impressive 100 hours of ground combat in American military history. At 0400 hours, February 24, 1991, U.S. and Allied forces roared out of Saudi Arabia to liberate Kuwait and destroy Saddam Hussein's massive military machine. One hundred hours later, at a cost of few Allied casualties, they had thrown Saddam's forces out of Kuwait, the stunned survivors eagerly surrendering to American and Allied troops or fleeing for their lives toward the interior of Iraq. It had been, as one journalist described it, "a third world country fighting World War II against a global superpower waging World War III."

Somewhere in the Kuwaiti Desert, February 26, 1991:   U.S. Army Major Jim Warner, operations officer of the 3rd Battalion, 67th Armored Regiment, an element of the Tiger Brigade of the 2nd U.S. Armored Division, thought the advance across the vast Kuwaiti desert in his M1A1 Abrams tank was going well. Assigned to give some added M1A1 "punch" to the 2nd U.S. Marine Division (which had only one

M1 battalion and one battalion of aging M60s), Warner's battalion was about twenty-five kilometers southwest of Kuwait City, part of the general Allied advance. The left-flank battalion of the Tiger Brigade's "two up, one back" formation, its mission was to reach a key crossroads on the main route out of Kuwait City—soon to be known as the "Highway of Death"—in time to block the retreat of Iraqi units to Basrah. Limited only by the relative slowness of its supporting vehicles (trucks and thin-skinned, non-fighting vehicles) the unit was, nevertheless, clipping along the mostly flat terrain at fifteen to twenty kilometers per hour. Suddenly, directly in front of it and masked from long-range observation by the slight variations in the desert terrain, the characteristic bunkers, fighting positions, and dug-in, hull-down T-55 Soviet tanks of an Iraqi fortified position loomed up in the shimmering waves of heat. With the lead tanks and Bradleys already entering the horseshoe-shaped fortified position's "fire pocket," Warner's battalion commander, Lieutenant Colonel Doug Tystad, had just a split second to decide how to handle a life-or-death situation. Wishing to minimize the unit's exposure in the "kill zone" and exploit the superior U.S. weapons and fire-control systems, he chose to execute a rapid frontal assault with long-range fire, and simply roll straight through the Iraqi positions.

Two tank companies and one mechanized infantry company sliced through the Iraqi defenses, flowing around the bunkers and dug-in tanks like "water through the weak points of an earthen dam," in Liddell Hart's well-known image, and pinning the Iraqis inside with overwhelming firepower. This completed, however, the American battalion was scattered, its neat traveling formation disrupted by its hasty maneuver.

Warner's tank and accompanying Bradley fighting vehicle had knifed through a soft spot between the Iraqi position's center and left flank and was now on the opposite side when Warner spotted an intact Iraqi T-55 about 300 meters away, dug in and supported by several infantry bunkers. He rejected his first inclination to let the battalion's reserve forces take care of the Iraqis in a classic mopping-up operation for fear of exposing the battalion's soft-skinned support trucks and logistics vehicles to attack. Instead he decided to take care of the position himself—and quickly.

After ordering his gunner to lay the Abrams's main gun on the Iraqi tank, Warner realized that if he fired on the enemy tank, he risked inflicting friendly casualties on his own unit's B Company, just then situated directly opposite the Iraqi strong point. Although the M1A1 could hardly miss the T-55 at such a short range, the Abrams's 120mm main gun often put its high-velocity, armor-piercing, antitank round right through the Soviet armor. Even a direct hit, then, could end up striking friendly forces.

Warner, therefore, told his driver to step on it, and his Abrams and accompanying Bradley, machine guns blazing, roared across the 300 meters separating them from the enemy position. Pulling up suddenly just a couple of dozen meters away from the "buttoned up" T-55, he barked at his loader to cover the infantry bunkers with the tank's machine gun while his gunner kept the main gun laid on the enemy tank. Grabbing some incendiary thermite grenades, Warner leaped out of his M1A1 and ran the short distance between the U.S. and Iraqi tanks, silently hoping he didn't step on any of the antipersonnel mines the Iraqis had buried throughout the area. If the Iraqi tank crew or supporting infantry opened fire, his only weapon—a .45 pistol—would be useless. Fortunately, his luck held, and the enemy small-arms fire from the bunkers was ineffective. Scrambling onto the rear deck of the T-55, Warner quickly pulled aside the enemy tank's engine access panel, pulled the pin on a thermite grenade, and placed it directly on the tank's engine. While the incendiary grenade burned through the T-55's engine, he raced back to his own tank. Once again, the Iraqis, either still in shock from the speed of the American attack or fearful of drawing a torrent of U.S. fire, held their fire—some of them even tentatively displaying white flags.

As Warner reentered his Abrams, the engine of the T-55 blew up, sending a shower of burning fuel and exploding fragments into the air and throughout the Iraqi tank. A fraction of a second later the tank "cooked-off," its ammunition and internal components burning and exploding. As if in response, more white flags appeared from the Iraqi infantry bunkers and trenches. Too busy to linger over the proffered surrenders, Warner and his crew quickly gathered up the prisoners, disarmed them, and ordered them to move south toward the Coalition POW cages. Within minutes, the men rejoined the battalion's advance. After the war, Major Jim Warner was awarded a Silver Star.

The striking battlefield triumph of the American-led Allied Coalition in the Persian Gulf War of 1991 has been simultaneously labeled the "final victory of the Cold War" and the "first victory of the New World Order." There is truth to both of these labels. The Iraqi forces of Saddam Hussein, although primarily armed, trained, and supplied by the Soviet Union, had received arms and other forms of assistance from both East and West, and had therefore profited from the superpower confrontation of the Cold War years. But the West's victory in the Cold War and subsequent thawing of relations with a rapidly imploding Soviet Union had removed the linchpin of Soviet support from Iraq, leaving it vulnerable to concerted action by a United States unrestrained by fears of Soviet retaliation or UN Security Council veto. A Soviet Union sidelined by economic collapse and desperately needing Western aid was forced to leave Iraq on its own to suffer the consequences of its ill-advised invasion of Kuwait. In this sense, then, the U.S.-led Coalition's desert victory in 1991 can truly be characterized as the final victory of the Cold War.

It can, with equal validity, be characterized as the initial success of the so-called new world order. No longer threatened by superpower confrontation, the post–Cold War world assumes that containment and bipolarity have been replaced by regional conflicts and multipolarity. Instead of determining how each regional problem affects the U.S. strategic position vis-à-vis the Soviet Union, the new world order seeks global stability and the resolution of localized conflicts through regional, rather than global, coalitions. Using its heightened prestige as the "winner" of the Cold War, the United States, along with the United Nations, created an anti-Iraq coalition to resolve a regional conflict, then led it to victory. In this sense, the Gulf War triumph can be seen as a victory of this new world order.

Weapons and Tactics

The weapons employed by both sides ran the full gamut of high-tech, low-tech, and no-tech instruments of death. Although the threat of chemical and biological warfare constantly loomed over the combatants, the actual fighting was conducted with conventional, but often highly advanced, means. During the 100 hours of the ground war, the master of the battlefield remained the main battle tank, supported by its retinue of armored fighting vehicles and artillery weapons. While unchallenged Coalition airpower seemed to use the vulnerable Iraqi tanks for live-fire target practice, the Iraqi tank's American opponent, the Abrams tank, swept its opposition aside with surprisingly little effort.

The M1A1 Abrams tank is a nearly seventy-ton armored monster carrying a crew of four and capable of cross-country speeds of over thirty miles per hour. Mounting a 120mm smoothbore main cannon, it also has a .50-caliber machine gun and two 7.62mm machine guns. About 2,300 M1A1 tanks were shipped to the Gulf region and 1,800 entered combat. The tank's long-range engagement ability—it can effectively kill enemy tanks over 1,000 meters outside the enemy's maximum engagement distance—exceptional thermal sighting system, laser ranging, and unmatched capacity to shoot accurately while on the move made it the dominant armored fighting vehicle in the desert war. Of the eighteen Abramses that sustained significant combat damage during the war, nine were victims of "friendly fire" and the rest suffered mostly repairable mine damage. It is significant that no enemy-tank main-gun hits knocked out any M1A1 tanks. Teamed with the M2 Bradley infantry fighting vehicle, which mounts a 25mm chain gun and a TOW antitank missile, the Abrams-Bradley combination proved to be unstoppable. The shortcomings of the Abrams-Bradley team were in two areas: the Abrams's extremely high rate of fuel consumption required a large logistical "tail" to maintain a continual advance; and the tanks' higher speed was often too much for the slower support vehicles (including critical combat support such as field artillery).

The Abrams's opposite number was most often the obsolete Soviet T-55 (including the Chinese version, the Type 79) or T-62 tanks, although the more modern T-72 was available in Republican Guard and a few other armored units. Smaller than the Abrams, the Soviet tanks were deficient in virtually every area, most notably acquiring and engaging targets at longer ranges. With the U.S. tanks' superior thermal sights giving them the ability to fire on Iraqi tanks at least 1,000 meters beyond the maximum engagement range of the Soviet vehicles, the Iraqis were reduced to trying futilely to return fire at barely discernible U.S. muzzle flashes. Despite the T-72's larger main gun (125mm vs. the U.S. 120mm), the tank-to-tank clashes were as one-sided as the rest of the war. Even when the Iraqi tanks were placed in dug-in positions, U.S. tank fire frequently knocked them out, blasting right through the protective earthen berm before continuing on to penetrate their armor.

Artillery remains a critical fire support element for ensuring the battlefield success of modern armies. This held true during the Gulf War, but was somewhat overshadowed by the Coalition's free and nearly unrestricted use of airpower. The ability of Allied fixed-wing and helicopter air assets to range to and fro over a nearly flat, treeless expanse of battlefield, provided maneuver unit commanders with almost instant access to this deadly, tank-killing and bunker-busting form of fire support. Air support, limited only by weather and visibility, compensated for the supporting artillery's lack of speed. Iraqi artillery, much more numerous than the Coalition's at the beginning of the war (over 3,000 pieces), was mainly composed of standard Soviet guns of 100mm, 122mm, 130mm, and 152mm. Additionally, the Iraqis had obtained some excellent French and Austrian artillery.

The U.S.-led Coalition's mastery of the air was the single most decisive factor in the war, and paved the way for the Allied armies'

stunning victory on the ground. Allied airpower achieved unprecedented dominance in the forty days prior to the ground campaign
and was never seriously challenged by Iraq's large but ineffective air
force. U.S. and Coalition air assets began the fighting war with a
textbook example of how to establish air superiority on the modern
battlefield. First, they blinded the Iraqi air defenses and cowed the
Iraqi air force into hiding (or by destroying those Iraqi planes they
could find). Next, they destroyed the "brain" of Saddam's military
forces by targeting centralized command and control centers. They
then immobilized the Iraqi forces and sealed off the Kuwaiti Theater
of Operations by attacking roads, bridges, routes of advance, and
choke points all over central and southern Iraq. Blind, immobilized,
and lacking effective centralized control, the Iraqi army was open to
unceasing air attack by Coalition air combat units. Although the
ground war was essential to ejecting the Iraqi forces from Kuwait,
the air campaign that preceded it set up Saddam's army for the
knockout blow. Any examination of the phenomenal success of the
ground war must recognize the absolutely crucial role played by
the opening air campaign. Even though air forces cannot complete
the enemy's destruction by occupying the ground, they make such
occupation possible.

The overwhelmingly decisive war-fighting tactics of the ground
phase of the Gulf War were based on the Coalition's application of
the U.S. military's primary war-fighting doctrine—AirLand Battle.
Emphasizing maneuver warfare, over costlier, bloodier attrition warfare, and the close cooperation of ground and air support elements,
AirLand Battle doctrine was developed in the late 1970s and early
1980s to fight a strong Soviet attack into Western Europe. According
to the U.S. Army's "bible" for this doctrine, FM 100-5 *Operations,*
AirLand Battle is "based on securing or retaining the initiative and
exercising it aggressively to accomplish the mission." To defeat the
enemy, the manual asserts, forces must "throw the enemy off balance with a powerful blow from an unexpected direction, follow up
rapidly to prevent his recovery and continue operations aggressively." Instead of a slow, deliberate advance, which might give the
enemy a chance to recover, forces should execute combat operations

that the foe perceives as "rapid, unpredictable, violent, and disorienting."

The four basic tenets of this style of war fighting in 1991 were initiative, agility, depth, and synchronization. Subordinate commanders must understand the higher commander's intent, then execute the operation with imagination and an offensive spirit, which forces the enemy to react constantly to their actions. Friendly forces must react faster than enemy forces to the continually changing battlefield situation, concentrating strength against the enemy's weaknesses. Commanders at all levels must look beyond the immediate situation in time, space, and resources to extend their own force's influence into future operations. Above all, the forces, matériel, and activities must be arranged and coordinated in such a manner as to produce the maximum possible effect on the enemy at the decisive time and place.

To oppose this dynamic, aggressive method of prosecuting war, the Iraqis chose to fight a static, nearly immobile war of attrition, which turned out to be unimaginative, tentative, and futile. Seeming to be safely entrenched behind an extensive system of impressive-looking fortifications, the large and (on paper at least) well-supported Iraqi forces were content to yield the initiative to their Coalition opponents. Saddam Hussein apparently expected his dug-in troops to inflict an increasingly large number of casualties on the U.S.-led forces, which would surely find it difficult to force their way through the interlocking system of bunkers, trenches, antitank ditches, and supporting strong points. If the battle developed into a replay of the grinding, bloody attrition warfare of the eight-year-long Iran-Iraq War, Saddam confidently expected the United States and its Coalition partners eventually to give up in the face of ever-increasing domestic opposition. Packing his units into the relatively small environs of Kuwait, Saddam achieved a high density of troops and equipment that appeared formidable. Outside observers predicted massive casualties for Coalition forces that attempted to breach the strong Iraqi defenses. What Saddam had apparently not considered was that his opponent had no intention of fighting this kind of war. Had he listened to joint chiefs of staff chairman Colin

Powell's press conference before the ground war began, he might have gotten a clue as to the fate awaiting his army when Powell remarked, "We're going to cut it off, then we're going to kill it."

The 100-Hour Ground War

February 24–28, 1991

The Plan

General Colin Powell's succinct summary of the Coalition's intentions is a simple, straightforward example of "commander's intent" for this particular AirLand Battle, and the campaign plan devised by the staff of the "warfighting CINC" (commander in chief), Central Command's General H. Norman Schwarzkopf, was its operational embodiment. The Coalition intended to complete the battlefield isolation of the Iraqi forces in the Kuwaiti Theater of Operations (KTO), first prosecuted by an intensive air campaign, by rapidly moving a large force of ground troops into southern Iraq and northwestern Kuwait. This force would seal off the KTO from further reinforcements of Iraqi troops and equipment while simultaneously preventing those Iraqi forces already there from escaping to central Iraq. While CENTCOM's XVIII Airborne Corps executed this wide west-to-east sweep, the powerful armored-mechanized forces of VII Corps would conduct a similar sweeping maneuver, just to the inside of the XVIII Corps' arc, with the purpose of smashing and destroying the principal Iraqi armored operational reserve forces (primarily, the Republican Guard divisions), which were backing up the fortified, dug-in Iraqi army in Kuwait. Meanwhile the I Marine Expeditionary Force (I MEF) and Allied Arab Coalition forces (aided by the deceptive threat of an amphibious assault against Kuwait City or other likely areas in the Iraqi rear) would fix the main Iraqi forces in the KTO in place by a more direct assault against the Kuwait–Saudi Arabia border area.

Under this operational plan, consistent with the tenets and principles of AirLand Battle, CENTCOM intended to eject the Iraqi forces occupying Kuwait by throwing approximately 200,000 Coalition troops into an unexpected, giant left hook against the weakest part of the Iraqi defenses, while the remainder of the nearly 600,000 Coalition ground and air combat forces executed a supporting attack to keep Iraqi attention focused on their futile static defensive fortifications in south and central Kuwait. It was this wide-sweeping maneuver, centerpiece of the CENTCOM plan, that Schwarzkopf christened his "Hail Mary" play in the postbattle briefing. But the Hail Mary pass play in football actually refers to a last-second "long bomb" thrown into the end zone in the desperate hope that someone on your own team will catch it, thereby snatching victory from the jaws of defeat. Despite Schwarzkopf's catchy title, the carefully planned, brilliantly executed CENTCOM maneuver was anything but desperate. As effected by the Coalition forces, this unexpected and powerful sweep around the flank of the Iraqi defenses was closer to the old Notre Dame "student body left" play, or even an "end run," if we insist on using football jargon. Whatever one calls it, however, the Coalition's successful battle strategy effectively routed the Iraqi forces, made irrelevant their intricate fixed fortifications, and prevented them from mounting any kind of cohesive defense.

Moving the equivalent of seventeen divisions hundreds of miles over a very primitive road network, the Coalition Allies worked twenty-four hours a day for nearly two weeks to position the massive strike force in advanced locations, preparatory to the beginning of the ground campaign. Possessing mastery of the air, the Allies were able to accomplish this prepositioning without being observed by the now blinded Iraqi forces. Reduced to gleaning whatever information they could from Cable News Network or other media broadcasts, the Iraqi armed forces remained generally ignorant of their impending disaster until it was too late to influence the outcome.

As the Allied buildup proceeded, Schwarzkopf bided his time, trying to calculate the precise moment to give the command for the ground war to begin. Along with his subordinate commanders and the CENTCOM staff, he considered the many variables: the estimated success of the continuing air campaign in "attriting" the Iraqi forces; the overall pace of the force deployment in putting the right amounts of combat power in just the right place; the level of stocks of logistical support and resupply to arm, fuel, and man the attack; the worst weather in the region in over a decade; and the political will and cohesion of the Coalition. Strike too soon, before the Iraqi forces were sufficiently attrited or before amassing sufficient combat power and logistical support, and the attack risked failure or unnecessarily heavy casualties. Delay the attack too long in an effort to effect a larger buildup of troops and supplies while the Iraqis received a more thorough working over, and risk the possibility of rifts developing in the Coalition. All the judgment, skill, and experience of the Coalition commanders and staff went into the decision. Finally, Schwarzkopf set the date of ground campaign (G-Day) for February 24, 1991.

Iraqi Force Strength and Deployment

Coalition intelligence immediately prior to the air campaign (January 15, 1991) indicated that approximately 545,000 Iraqi troops in forty-three divisions had arrived in the KTO since the August 1990 invasion. Of these, twenty-five divisions were assessed as being "committed" to active defensive positions, ten were in operational reserve, and the remaining eight were in strategic reserve. The best of the Iraqi divisions, the Republican Guard units, were primarily deployed in reserve positions in preparation for their use in strong, mobile counterattacks. Major Iraqi equipment was estimated to consist of 4,280 tanks, 3,100 artillery pieces, and 2,800 armored personnel carriers.

The well-prepared Iraqi positions were arranged in successive defensive belts, five to fifteen kilometers deep, characterized by alternating minefields and antitank fire trenches, and backed up by heavily manned and fortified brigade-sized strong points. Providing cover to each of the forward defensive belts were numerous platoon-, company-, and battalion-size strong points, typically triangularly shaped, earth-bermed fortifications up to 2,000 meters wide. To the rear of these formidable defensive belts, armored counterattack forces were stationed for use against any penetration of the defensive lines. By dawn of February 24, however, over 100,000 air combat missions had been flown against the Iraqi forces, causing significant attrition. Exactly how many Iraqi troops, tanks, artillery pieces, and personnel carriers remained intact by that time was, and remains, unknown. Battle Damage Assessment (BDA) of air attacks on ground targets (in areas still controlled by the enemy) is often imprecise, and exact knowledge of the effects of every long-distance air attack is impossible to acquire. Part science, part art, BDA usually depends upon poststrike photo analysis, pilot debriefs, and radio intercepts of targeted enemy units. Nevertheless, the commander who has over-all responsibility for the operation must take these estimates, apply them to the particular situation, then make the best decision. That is what Schwarzkopf did during the final week of February 1991.

At the kickoff of the ground offensive, Coalition intelligence estimated that at least 450,000 troops and significant numbers of still-operational equipment were prepared to meet the attack. Much of the air attrition had taken place in the forward Iraqi units (in accordance with the overall deception plan), however, and the stronger armored formations, such as the Republican Guard divisions, were relatively intact. The Iraqi command and control system, it was believed, was severely disrupted.

Coalition Force Strength and Deployment

Coalition ground forces, comprising nearly 600,000 troops, were arrayed along a 500-mile line stretching from the Persian Gulf to hundreds of miles west of the Kuwaiti–Saudi Arabian border. From right to left, these forces were arranged in five principal subgroupings: the Joint Forces Command–East (JFC-E); the I Marine Expeditionary Force (IMEF); the Joint Forces Command–North (JFC-N); and the two major forces of the Army Component, Central Command (AR-CENT), consisting of VII Corps and XVIII Airborne Corps. JFC-E, commanded by Saudi Lieutenant General Khalid bin-Sultan, consisted of units from the Gulf Cooperation Council (Saudi Arabia, Kuwait, Qatar, Oman, Bahrain, and United Arab Emirates). IMEF, commanded by U.S. Marine General Walter Boomer, consisted of the 1st and 2nd Marine Divisions, the 5th Marine Expeditionary Brigade, and the 1st Brigade, 2nd U.S. Armored Division. JFC-N, also commanded by General Khalid bin-Sultan, consisted of Egyptian, Syrian, Saudi, and Kuwaiti mechanized and armored forces, supported by Arab ranger and Special Forces units. The U.S. VII Corps, commanded by Lieutenant General Frederick Franks, contained the 1st Armored Division (with 3rd Brigade, 3rd Infantry Division attached), the 3rd Armored Division, 1st Infantry Division (with 2nd Armored Division Forward attached), the 1st Cavalry Division, 2nd Armored Cavalry Regiment (ACR), 11th Aviation Brigade, VII Corps artillery (containing four field artillery brigades), and tactical control of the 1st United Kingdom Armoured Division. Anchoring the Coalition line in the far west was the U.S. XVIII Airborne Corps, commanded by Lieutenant General Gary Luck. It contained the 82nd Airborne Division, the 101st Airborne Division (air assault), the 24th Infantry Division (with 197th Mechanized Infantry Brigade attached to make up for the 24th's National Guard combat brigade, which was not deployed), the 3rd Armored Cavalry Regiment, the 12th and 18th Aviation Brigades, XVIII Corps artillery (containing three field artillery brigades), and tactical control of the 6th French Light Armored Division. The U.S. 5th and 3rd Special Forces Groups, along with navy, air-force, and other army special operations units, provided theater support in a variety of special operations.

Heavily supported by continuing Coalition air and naval operations, the ground campaign of the Gulf War began at 0400 hours on February 24, 1991. Approximately 100 hours later, the mission of the Coalition to liberate Kuwait was completed.

G-Day, February 24, 1991

The opening phase of the ground war occurred in three areas along the Allied line. The first of the key attacks was launched by the XVIII Airborne Corps on the far west of the line, when LTG Luck ordered the French 6th Light Armored Division (with operational control of the 2nd Brigade, 82nd Airborne Division) to begin a ground attack into southern Iraq while the 101st Airborne Division simultaneously executed an air assault on the French unit's right flank. The mission of these units was to secure forward operating bases deep in the Iraqi rear area. On the Coalition's far right flank, JFC-E and IMEF began breaching the Iraqi obstacle line and defensive belts with a more direct assault against the enemy main line of resistance. While these two major attacks were either fixing the Iraqi main forces in place or beginning to establish bases in the Iraqi rear to cut off any retreat, VII Corps conducted a feint with the 1st Cavalry Division in preparation for launching the Coalition's main attack against the Iraqi armored reserves.

"The Cork in the Bottle."   Colonel Tom Hill, commander of the 1st Brigade, 101st Airborne Division, led his unit on what became, by the end of the first day of the ground war, the largest helicopter operation in history when his 2,200 troopers landed at Forward Operating Base (FOB) Cobra, ninety-three miles inside southern Iraq. Spearheading the airmobile operation which complemented the 6th French Light Armored Division's ground advance into Iraq farther west, Hill's brigade was to create FOB Cobra from scratch, support the division's efforts to push on to the Euphrates River fifty miles north, then prepare to continue the attack to the confluence of the Euphrates and Tigris rivers. If the 101st Airborne was successful in these maneuvers over the next few days, they would bottle up the Iraqi forces in KTO. Hill's brigade was slated to be the cork in the bottle.

Within three hours of first touching down at FOB Cobra, the 1st

Brigade, 101st Airborne, had brought in 2,200 combat troops, fifty TOW antitank missile sections mounted on HUMM-V utility vehicles, two field artillery batteries, a complete command and control lash-up, four aid stations, and other supporting units. This was accomplished using seventy of the new UH-60 Blackhawk helicopters, along with ten UH-1 Huey and thirty CH-47 Chinook helicopters, sturdy veterans of the Vietnam era. Hill's executive officer started a road march of the brigade's 700 supporting vehicles toward FOB Cobra at the same time as the helicopters began lifting off, arriving at 3:00 P.M. that same afternoon. During this first day, the 101st (using an additional 30 CH-47s) delivered 175,000 gallons of fuel by air and an additional 150,000 gallons of fuel by ground to the forward operating base. By noon of February 24, the base was supporting attack helicopter operations all along the Euphrates River.

With the success of XVIII Airborne Corps' westward sweep proceeding well beyond CENTCOM planners' expectations, Schwarzkopf moved up the attack time of the corps' heavy-combat division by five hours. Well ahead of schedule, MG Barry McCaffrey's 24th Mechanized Infantry Division, its right flank protected by the 3rd Armored Cavalry Regiment, roared out of assembly areas into the Iraqi desert, its three brigades moving abreast at over twenty miles per hour. Against light opposition, the 24th was seventy-five miles into southern Iraq by midnight on G-Day, linking up with Hill's brigade on Cobra at 3:00 A.M.

Getting the Main Attack Started.   The VII Corps, the most powerful combat force on the Coalition side, was charged with executing the main attack against the Iraqi armored reserve forces, principally the Republican Guard units, Iraq's strongest combat divisions. This operation was originally scheduled to begin this massive right wheel into Iraq behind Kuwait on G+1, February 25, but the success of Coalition attacks all along the line caused CENTCOM to move it up a full fifteen hours, directing that it begin on February 24. The corps commander, LTG Franks, planned to envelop the flanks of the opposing Iraqi positions by sending the 1st and 3rd Armored Divisions, led by the 2nd Armored Cavalry Regiment, through the Iraqi defen-

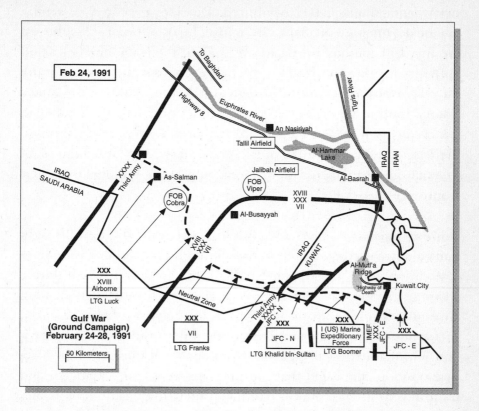

Gulf War (Ground Campaign), February 24, 1991

sive lines and around his west flank, while the 1st U.S. Infantry Division and the 1st UK Armoured Division executed a similar maneuver on his east flank. By midnight of February 24, the 1st Infantry Division had breached over half of the Iraqi minefields and defensive fortifications and was preparing to assist the passage of the 1st UK Armoured Division through its lines to continue the attack against Iraqi armored forces. On the VII Corps left, the 2nd ACR, followed closely by the 1st and 3rd Armored Divisions, was through the Iraqi lines, but all three units were ordered to halt for the night to await the east flank divisions' breaching of the minefields to their front.

Deliberate Attack in the East.   Meanwhile, IMEF, with JFC-E on its right flank along the coast, moved to breach the Iraqi main defensive lines established along the Kuwait–Saudi Arabia border. The 1st Marine Division on the east and the 2nd Marine Division farther west, cleared multiple lanes through the Iraqi defensive belts, captured thousands of prisoners, and was twenty miles inside Kuwait by day's end. Combat experience gained from attacking these strongly fortified positions indicated that the previous weeks' air campaign and more recent ground attacks had taken their toll on the morale and fighting spirit of the Iraqi defenders. Despite some dogged resistance to the marines' frontal assaults, the Iraqis quickly surrendered when the Coalition forces appeared behind their flanks or in their rear areas. By midnight on February 24, the marines had captured about 8,000 Iraqi POWs. The JFC-E, farthest east of all the Coalition forces, had seized all of its assigned objectives by the end of G-Day.

The first day of the Coalition ground attack had gone extremely well for the Allied forces. The giant wheel in the west was proceeding apace; VII Corps was poised to deliver the main attack and maneuver in its own right wheel inside the XVIII Airborne Corps' arc; and the direct assault against the main Iraqi defensive lines in Kuwait had ruptured the enemy lines, placing the Allied forces in a position to continue the attack to seize the key terrain directly west of Kuwait City. There was as yet no indication that the Iraqi forces were evacuating the KTO in a mass stampede; indeed, they seemed to be frozen in place. Large numbers of Iraqi soldiers were surrendering to Coalition troops, and "friendly" casualties had been minimal. The Allied prospects for continuing the attack on the following day seemed excellent.

G+1, February 25, 1991

The second twenty-four hours of the ground war proceeded much as the first, despite worsening weather conditions and subsequent poor visibility, and sharp Iraqi resistance in some places. This second day of all-out combat saw the destruction of a large share of Iraqi tactical forces in KTO.

Action Continues in the West. The XVIII Airborne Corps' wide sweep around the main Iraqi forces in order to sever the units' lifeline to Iraq proper continued with little organized Iraqi opposition. Using the same aircraft that had rapidly delivered the 1st Brigade, 101st Airborne, to FOB Cobra the morning before, the division's 3rd Brigade moved the 175 miles from assembly areas on the Saudi-Iraqi border to the south bank of the Euphrates River on February 25. This air assault operation became the deepest such undertaking in the history of helicopter-borne warfare. Establishing what was, in effect, a brigade-size ambush position just west of the town of An Nasiriyah, the 101st now sat astride Highway 8, principal supply route in the Euphrates River valley. There would be no escape for Iraqi units fleeing the KTO through this route. The next step in sealing off the KTO was planned for the following day when the division's 2nd Brigade would lift to a point ninety miles east of FOB Cobra in preparation for projecting Hill's 1st Brigade seventy-five miles beyond that point to the confluence of the Euphrates and Tigris rivers. This operation would close tight any remaining escape route.

The 24th Mechanized Infantry Division continued to push all three of its brigades northward, capturing a series of objectives against weak Iraqi resistance in the XVIII Corps' eastern sector. Throughout the night of February 25–26, the 24th established positions from which it could launch its eastward assault against the Republican Guard.

VII Corps' Main Attack Progresses. The powerful heavy divisions of the VII Corps burst out of the Iraqi defensive lines and continued to attack northeastward on February 25. The 1st Armored Division and its attached 3rd Brigade, 3rd Infantry Division commanded by Colonel Jim Riley, battered units of the opposing Iraqi 26th Infantry Division—a battering so severe that they defeated a brigade-size counterattack the next day by destroying fifty Iraqi tanks and armored vehicles in barely ten minutes of intense combat. On the 1st Armored's right flank, the 3rd Armored Division, led by the 2nd ACR, advanced north, then turned east to confront Iraqi armor and mechanized infantry, destroying the Iraqi 50th Armored Brigade. As the weather turned bad that night, the units established defensive positions from which to continue the advance the following morning. On the VII Corps right flank, the 1st Infantry Division created lanes in the Iraqi deliberate defenses, then destroyed two Iraqi brigades that were defending the area. Once this was completed, the 1st UK Armoured Division passed through the lanes created in the minefields and defenses, moved through the 1st Infantry Division's lines, then turned east and began what would be a two-day running battle with the Iraqi 52nd Armored Division.

IMEF Moves Deeper into Kuwait. On the eastern end of the Coalition line, the 1st and 2nd Marine Divisions, with the "Tiger" Brigade of the 2nd U.S. Armored Division attached, met its stiffest resistance of the 100-hour war as the units continued to plow through the carefully prepared Iraqi defenses inside Kuwait. Both divisions encountered brigade- and division-size counterattacks from desperate Iraqi units holding key positions south and west of Kuwait City. Weather conditions combined with the dense, black smoke caused by hundreds of oil-well fires reduced visibility to only a few yards in some places and added to the confusion and disorientation already present on the modern battlefield. By the end of G+1, IMEF had defeated the counterattacks and moved deeper into Kuwait proper.

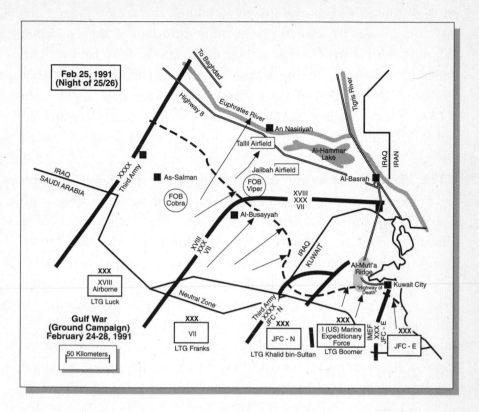

Gulf War (Ground Campaign), February 25, 1991

The 2nd Marine Division was in possession of key terrain west and south of Kuwait City and prepared to launch the army "Tiger" Brigade on a dash to seize the important position of the Al-Mutl'a Ridge, which controls access and egress to the Kuwaiti capital. The 1st Marine Division, having withstood an Iraqi counterattack that produced 100 destroyed Iraqi armored vehicles and 1,500 Iraqi POWs, ended February 25 by occupying the Ahmad al-Jabir airfield and establishing defensive positions only ten miles south of Kuwait City.

The results of the second day's fighting of the ground war continued to be encouraging for the Coalition. Despite some spirited counterattacks by individual Iraqi units, there was no evidence of a centrally controlled, cohesive defense on the Iraqi side. Allied intelligence analysts pronounced the Iraqi corps formations in the KTO as "combat ineffective," incapable of mounting anything other than local, ultimately futile, counterattacks. Completely outmaneuvered and outfought by Coalition forces, Saddam Hussein ordered his armies to evacuate the KTO and return to Iraq. Whether or not his blinded, decapitated forces could even receive this order, let alone comply with it, was problematic by midnight on February 25.

G+2, February 26, 1991

During the third day of the ground war, Coalition forces continued the destruction of Iraqi forces in the KTO, attacking Iraqi second-echelon tactical reserves in Kuwait and southern Iraq. As the fight against the Iraqi forces in the KTO went on, Allied units in the far west and north continued their efforts to seal off the battlefield. The panicked northward exodus of Saddam Hussein's occupation army began in earnest on February 26. With Coalition forces hundreds of miles inside southern Iraq and other Allied combat units continuing to push aggressively forward, mass surrenders of Iraqi army units increased. By midnight on February 26, approximately 30,000 Iraqi POWs had been collected. But some units, including Republican

Guard divisions, resisted the Allied advance from well-prepared positions.

XVIII Airborne Corps: Screen, Protect, Attack. Combat units of LTG Luck's XVIII Airborne Corps directed their main efforts into the attack toward Republican Guard forces to the northeast, while protecting the far flanks of the Coalition line from any interference from the north and west. The 6th French Light Armored Division established a security screen on the corps far left flank while the 101st Airborne Division held the Euphrates River valley lines of communication. The 101st prepared to push two of its brigades farther north and east when directed. McCaffrey's 24th Mechanized Division experienced its toughest combat of the campaign when its three brigades ran into dug-in units of the Republican Guard Nebuchadnezzar Division along with elements of the Iraqi 47th and 49th Infantry Divisions. Despite the favorable positions the rocky terrain afforded the Iraqis, the 24th (relying heavily on the superior thermal sights and greater acquisition range of its M1A1 tanks) blasted the units out of their positions in four hours of heavy engagement. By the end of the day, all three brigades of the 24th were occupying strong positions just south of the Iraqi airfields at Jalibah and Tallil. The XVIII Airborne Corps reported to CENTCOM that all assigned objectives had been achieved by midnight on February 26.

VII Corps: Right Turn. The corps began G+2 with a continuation of the armored divisions' attack to the north on the corps' far left flank. After the 1st and 3rd Armored had attacked and secured Objective Collins, east of Al-Busayyah (and after the 1st Armored secured the town), Franks turned VII Corps sharply right to move against the Republican Guard units north of Kuwait. Like a giant door swinging on its hinges, four VII Corps units, in line abreast, wheeled right to attack east. On the left flank, moving the farthest, was the 1st Armored Division. Next came the 3rd Armored Division, then, on the corps right flank, the 2nd ACR and 1st Infantry Division. The 1st UK Armoured Division, still chasing the 52nd Iraqi Armored Division, pushed its prey toward the corps right boundary, just to the rear of the 1st Infantry Division.

Later that day, the 3rd Armored Division attacked the Republican Guard Tawakalna Division, which was occupying defensive positions to the northeast of the VII Corps left flank. The 1st Armored Division joined in the assault on the Tawakalna Division later that night in a well-executed night attack. When fighting ceased the next day, dozens of Iraqi armored vehicles littered the area.

While leading the advance of the corps right-flank units, the 2nd ACR ran into stiff resistance in the vicinity of 73 Easting (a convenient map reference to the location of these Iraqi defensive positions). Beginning about 4:00 P.M. on February 26, 2nd ACR began destroying the dug-in Iraqi tanks and armored vehicles, capitalizing on superior thermal sights of the M1A1. Manned by elements of the Tawakalna Division and the 12th Armored Division, the Iraqi positions were strong, but ultimately proved vulnerable to 120mm main-gun fire from Abrams tanks. For about four hours the Americans stood off several thousand meters away and killed one Iraqi tank after another. The 2nd ACR estimated it knocked out about fifty Iraqi tanks and armored vehicles.

After receiving a drubbing from the 1st and 3rd Armored Divisions earlier in the day, then blasted by the 2nd ACR in the afternoon, the Republican Guard Tawakalna Division was finally rendered combat ineffective by a renewed attack by the 3rd Armored Division at the end of the day. In terrible weather, which cut visibility to as little as 100 meters, the 3rd Armored, supported by several multiple launch rocket systems and cannon artillery battalions, flung two of its brigades against the Tawakalna's 29th and 9th Brigades. To complete the unit's destruction, AH-64 Apaches later flew attack missions against the remnants of the division when the weather finally permitted the helicopters to fly.

Farther south, while 1st UK Armoured Division destroyed forty tanks and captured the Iraqi armored division commander, the 1st U.S. Cavalry Division was released back to the corps and moved north.

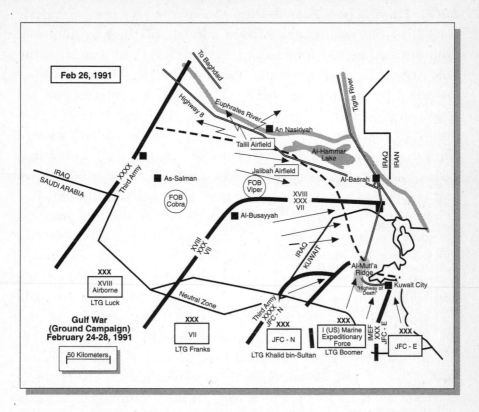

Gulf War (Ground Campaign), February 26, 1991

IMEF: "Tiger" Brigade Takes the High Ground. In an effort to quickly seize the key terrain of the Al-Mutl'a Ridge, the high ground that dominates all escape routes from Kuwait City, IMEF launched the U.S. Army "Tiger" Brigade out ahead of the 2nd Marine Division. Propelled by the superior speed of their M1A1 Abramses and M2 Bradleys, the "Tiger" Brigade (including Major Jim Warner's tank unit—3rd Battalion, 67th Armor) rolled up on the Al-Mutl'a Ridge from the west at about 3:30 P.M., February 26. Plugging up the pass through which streams of Iraqi soldiers with all manner of vehicles and equipment were escaping the trap of Kuwait City, the 3rd Battalion, 67th Armor seized the police barracks and fighting positions guarding the critical ground. In a sharp fight lasting from 3:00 P.M. to 11:00 P.M., the Americans destroyed the Iraqi mechanized forces, then rooted out stubborn defenders from trenches along the ridge and buildings in the barracks. Before midnight, the "Tiger" Brigade had cleared the area, blocked the Iraqis' final avenue of escape, and dug in on the highest ground in hundreds of miles.

The road leading out of Kuwait City, which now ended abruptly at the "Tiger" Brigade positions, came to be known as the Highway of Death, as news footage of blasted, twisted, burned-out vehicles (military and civilian) was broadcast to the world. But in reality, TV audiences saw more "dead" (deserted) vehicles than dead enemy soldiers. Most of the drivers and passengers had abandoned their "sitting duck" targets and fled into the desert when the attacking planes swooped down to blow them apart. Graves registration teams from C Company, 502nd Forward Support Battalion, found only 150 bodies along the road, among the thousands of abandoned vehicles, and in the surrounding area. Of these, more than 100 had been killed in the battle for Al-Mutl'a Ridge. Relatively few bodies were removed from vehicles. Most likely, the former occupants of the vehicles were among the 1,000 or more prisoners who surrendered after the pass fell to the Americans. In fact, even these scenes were somewhat deceptive, since many of the automobiles and other vehicles were still in perfectly good working condition when the American ground troops arrived. Many of them were even left with their motors running, and the engine noises and thermal signatures tended to confuse the Americans' target acquisition efforts throughout that first night. And despite the complete devastation attributed to the air attacks, Iraqi military traffic was still flowing briskly along the highway and through the pass, only finally stopping when the "Tiger" Brigade seized the pass and occupied the ridge. The Americans did, however, round up a large bag of prisoners from the surrounding desert (about 2,000 POWs) as well as collecting seven huge tractor-trailer loads of enemy weapons, ammunition, and other ordnance in the strip of highway leading to the pass. Warner estimated that many of the vehicles fleeing Kuwait City were members of the Palestine Liberation Organization. Invited to use Kuwait as a base for their terrorist organization by Saddam Hussein, they became stranded on the highway while trying to evacuate arms, ammunition, and other weapons to use later against Israel or elsewhere.

While the "Tiger" Brigade seized the important high ground west of Kuwait City (and held it for more than a day before the first marine units arrived), the 1st and 2nd Marine Divisions cleared defensive zones closer to the capital. The 2nd Marine Division destroyed the Iraqi rear guard near Al-Jahra, uncovering an extensive series of underground positions and bunkers, while the 1st Marine Division met heavy fighting clearing Kuwait airport. At the conclusion of the fight for the international airport early the next morning, the 1st Marine Division counted 250 destroyed Iraqi tanks and seventy other armored vehicles. By dawn of the following day, IMEF commander, General Boomer, informed CENTCOM that its primary objective—the Al-Mutl'a Ridge—and its other objectives had been achieved. All IMEF units now stood by on the outskirts of Kuwait City to await the arrival of the two Arab forces, JFC-E and JFC-N, which were to be the first Coalition units to enter the Kuwaiti capital. The "liberation" of Kuwait City by the pan-Arab forces was scheduled for the next day, February 27.

G+3, February 27, 1991

On the last full day of combat before the cease-fire, the remaining Iraqi divisions in the KTO disintegrated. By this time, all Iraqis who could manage to disengage from contact with the rapidly pursuing Coalition forces were making for Iraq proper as fast as they could. Many simply abandoned their equipment, fleeing on foot toward Al-Basrah, essentially their final refuge in southern Iraq. Coalition intelligence analysts estimate that as many as 80,000 Iraqi troops from numerous destroyed units escaped into Al-Basrah during this phase of the war, most of them coming from the estimated thirty-three Iraqi divisions rendered combat ineffective by midnight on February 27. With Kuwait City set for liberation and most Iraqi resistance crumbling in the eastern, central, and southern sectors of KTO, XVIII Airborne Corps and VII Corps concentrated their full attention on the remaining Republican Guard divisions.

XVIII Airborne Corps: Viper and Final Assault. While the 6th French Light Armored Division and elements of the 101st Airborne Division continued to screen and protect the corps' left flank and northern reaches, the 2nd Brigade, 101st Airborne Division, prepared to establish FOB Viper, about 100 miles east of FOB Cobra. Intended to provide a launching pad and support platform for a further airmobile move to the Al-Basra area, south of the confluence of the Euphrates and Tigris rivers, the 2nd Brigade's FOB Viper operation kicked off at 10:00 A.M.. General Luck gave the go-ahead to launch the 2nd Brigade, 101st Airborne, as soon as he received word that McCaffrey's heavy combat unit, the 24th Mechanized Infantry Division, had secured the Tallil and Jalibah airfields, located to the northeast and northwest of the 24th's area of operations. The 101st closed on FOB Viper by noon, and the base was by then already supporting attack helicopter operations against Iraqi units fleeing into the Euphrates River valley. Throughout the day, attack helicopters flew continuously, striking the masses of Iraqi vehicles streaming

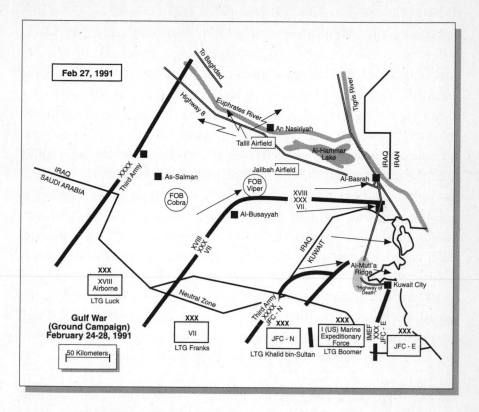

Gulf War (Ground Campaign), February 27, 1991

northward out of KTO. Cutting the Al-Basrah causeway and interdicting the area around the barrier of the Al-Hammar Lake, the
helicopter units, despite extremely limited visibility caused by black,
billowing smoke from the oil fires, destroyed hundreds of vehicles
and helped set up the remaining Iraqi Republican Guard unit between the rapidly closing ground forces of XVIII and VII Corps.

After securing the two airfields to the north, the 24th Mechanized
Infantry Division swung east to bring its full combat power to bear
on the remaining Republican Guard divisions. Moving so rapidly
over the past few days that it had outrun the tanker trucks carrying
its vital fuel supply, the 24th's support units had scrambled throughout the previous night to get the precious fuel up to the forward
combat units and prepare them to continue the attack on schedule.
Advancing eastward along the main transportation artery of Highway
8, the 24th anchored its right flank on the VII Corps directly to its
south. From the Euphrates River valley in the north to well inside
the Kuwaiti border on the south, the Americans now had a solid wall
of powerful, heavy-armored and mechanized infantry divisions moving relentlessly eastward against the Republican Guard forces.

VII Corps: The Final Envelopment.   Franks's corps continued to move
eastward against the last remaining major Iraqi forces in their zone—
including the Republican Guard al-Medinah, Hammurabi, and Tawakalna Divisions, heavily attrited by the previous days' fighting. With
the 1st Cavalry Division trying to reposition itself onto the VII Corps'
left (northern) flank, Franks now had (from north to south) the 1st
Armored Division, 3rd Armored Division, 1st Infantry Division, 2nd
ACR, and 1st UK Armoured Division in action for the final assault.
These units continued to advance against the disintegrating Iraqi
forces to their front on February 27, throughout the night and into
the next morning. With attack helicopters, close air support, and
long-range artillery fire disrupting the Iraqi rear elements, VII Corps
divisions pushed the Iraqi forward combat elements back into the
swirling, churning mass of support units in their rear areas. If the
1st Cavalry Division completed its movement to the corps left flank,
Franks intended to send it and the 1st Infantry Division on the right

flank on enveloping attacks around the flanks of the Iraqi forces to the corps front. This final double-envelopment maneuver would trap the remaining Iraqi forces in a steel vise between these two rapidly moving units and the other advancing VII Corps divisions. Unfortunately, 1st Cavalry was unable to get into position before the cease-fire took effect, and this maneuver could not be completed. By the morning of February 28, VII Corps had completed its attacks against the Republican Guard and other Iraqi mechanized units and had established blocking positions on the direct route from Kuwait to Al-Basrah. VII Corps fire-support units continued to pound the Iraqi positions until the general cease-fire at 8:00 A.M. on February 28.

IMEF, JFC-E, and JFC-N Liberate Kuwait City.   While General Boomer's IMEF forces consolidated their positions around Kuwait City and conducted final mopping-up operations of isolated Iraqi holdouts, lead Egyptian and Syrian pan-Arab forces of JFC-N passed through IMEF lines from the southwest en route to the Kuwaiti capital. JFC-E resumed its advance from south of Kuwait City, linking up there with JFC-N entering from the west. U.S. Army, Air Force, and Navy Special Operations Forces participated in the elimination of Iraqi holdouts in Kuwait City by assaulting and capturing the American embassy, Kuwaiti police headquarters, and other important government buildings.

G+4, February 28, 1991

Offensive operations continued all along the XVIII Airborne Corps and VII Corps front until the cease-fire. By that time the Coalition forces had achieved all the military objectives the Allied political leadership had set for them. Iraqi forces had either been ejected from Kuwait or were secured in Coalition POW cages; Kuwait City had been liberated; Republican Guard forces had been destroyed in place or else their remnants had fled back to Iraq proper; and Allied forces were in firm control of the lines of communication between KTO and southern Iraq. Coalition intelligence estimated that only five to seven of the forty-three Iraqi combat divisions present in the KTO at the beginning of the ground war were still capable of anything resembling offensive operations. Most were not even in a position to defend themselves, and mobs of leaderless Iraqis were attempting to surrender to single AH-64 Apache helicopters flying over them. News reports endlessly replayed the tapes of the pathetic image of helpless Iraqi soldiers kissing the hands of their American and Coalition captors. Over 85,000 Iraqis ended the war in Allied POW cages, 64,000 captured by U.S. units. Final estimates (the exact figure will never be known) indicate the following tally of Iraqi equipment destroyed: 3,847 tanks; 1,450 armored personnel carriers; and 2,917 artillery pieces.

Like the estimates of equipment destroyed, the exact numbers of Iraqi dead and wounded will never be known. In the years since the ground war, various political factions have attempted to use estimated numbers of Iraqi war dead for their political gain. Pacifist organizations in the United States and elsewhere in the world claim that 100,000 or more Iraqi soldiers and civilians were killed in the air campaign or the ground war, but such numbers have no factual basis. In early 1993, a former intelligence analyst, using much more precise and systematic means, estimated that the actual number of Iraqis killed during the war was very likely quite low—as few as 1,500. Despite Iraqi propaganda, the air attacks against Baghdad were conducted with a high degree of precision, and even the lethal environment of the ground war proved more deadly to vehicles and equipment than to Iraqi soldiers. Except for Republican Guard and a few other well-disciplined units, Iraqi soldiers tended to abandon their crew-served weapons and fighting vehicles when seriously attacked. Many simply melted away into the desert while the Allied forces blasted away at tanks, fighting vehicles, and other weapons. The United States went to great lengths to avoid setting a final number of Iraqis presumed to have been killed in the war, apparently wishing to avoid the Vietnam "body-count syndrome." Estimates by outside observers, therefore, ranged from 150,000 to 15,000 to 1,500—no one, not even Saddam Hussein, knows for certain. But the small number of Iraqi corpses found on the battlefield argues a lower figure. In the final analysis, the number of dead Iraqis has little effect on the outcome of the war: the defeat suffered by Iraqi forces was about as complete as possible.

The Coalition lost few soldiers. America lost 390 killed—most due to accidents, not combat—and 21, including two women, were taken prisoner. All Coalition prisoners were returned safely at the end of the war.

Aftermath

The February 28 cease-fire ended offensive operations, but, unfortunately, failed to stop the killing elsewhere in Saddam Hussein's troubled country. Encouraged by the statements of Coalition political leaders at the end of the ground war, Iraq's two largest ethnic groups—the Kurds in the north and Shi'ia Muslims in the south—revolted against Saddam's rule. Using the remnants of his military forces—including helicopters that Schwarzkopf had been deceived into allowing to fly after the cease-fire for what he thought would be "humanitarian" purposes—or Iraqi security forces that had been held back from the fighting against the Coalition, Saddam ruthlessly put down these challenges, again exterminating his opposition. The Kurdish population fled nearly en masse north into ethnic Kurdish regions of Turkey and Iran, where the Allies, principally the United States, were forced to provide humanitarian assistance. This aid mission, named Operation PROVIDE COMFORT, began shortly after the end of ground fighting in 1991. Three years later it continues.

Despite the the Coalition's overwhelming success, the Allied victory has been criticized for failing to remove Saddam Hussein from power. At the end of the ground campaign, U.S. and Coalition forces were unchallenged masters of the battlefield, able to project ground, air, and naval forces to any remote corner of the region. On February 28, XVIII Airborne Corps combat units sat astride the main route to Baghdad, with no organized Iraqi resistance between them and Saddam's capital. Seizing the city seemed to be as simple a matter as President Bush giving the word to go for it. But the American president did not issue the order. Toppling Saddam from power was never the stated goal of the Allied Coalition. This unprecedented partnership, linking Western nations with regional Arab allies, would probably never have formed if subjugation of Iraq as a nation had been its goal. The Allies set out, in accordance with United Nations' resolutions, to eject Iraqi forces from Kuwait and liberate the tiny nation, and that's exactly what they did. As much as U.S. political leadership may have hoped for Saddam Hussein's removal from power, it did not create the Gulf War Coalition or fight the most successful war in modern history to realize that hope. The Gulf Allies must instead satisfy themselves with their prodigious accomplishments on the battlefield in Kuwait and southern Iraq.

INDEX

Morelock, J. D., 1946-
The Army times book of great land battles : from the Civil War to the Gulf War / J.D. Morelock ; edited by Walter J. Boyne. --Berkley trade pbk. ed. --New York : Berkley Publishing Group, 1999, c1994.
xv, 331 p., [32] p. of plates : ill., maps.

Includes index.
951288 ISBN:0425165310 (pbk.)

(SEE NEXT CARD)